the
thirty-ninth victim
a memoir

BLUE FEATHER BOOKS, LTD.

For Erin

I give you my truth

I give you my love – unconditionally

For Tom

You gave me the strength

the

thirty-ninth victim

a memoir

A BLUE FEATHER BOOK

by

Arleen Williams

The Thirty-Ninth Victim

Cover design by NgocDzung Nguyen Smith & Jason Holt Smith

A Blue Feather Book
Published by Blue Feather Books, Ltd.
P.O. Box 5867
Atlanta, GA 31107-5967

www.bluefeatherbooks.com

ISBN: 0-9794120-4-8

First edition: April 2008

Printed in the United States of America and in the United Kingdom.

Acknowledgements

I would like to acknowledge a number of special people without whom this story may never have been told: Jack Remick, my mentor, who introduced me to the world of writing, challenged me through innumerable rewrites and offered a lifeline whenever I was about to give up; Robert Ray, who taught me to turn inward, to quiet the noise, and to find my voice each time I put pen to paper; my classmates in Jack and Bob's memoir writing program at the University of Washington, who endured many tears as I began to put memories into words; and the writers who show up at Louisa's Café every Tuesday and Friday to write, to share, and to offer their support.

Appreciation and gratitude also go to the many family members, friends, colleagues and mere acquaintances—far too numerous to mention by name without risk of omission—who generously offered their constant, loving encouragement. This has been a long and difficult journey. One I could never have survived alone.

My writing journey has been supported by faculty development grants from the Seattle Community College District and South Seattle Community College, for which I am very grateful.

I also want to thank my editor and cyber-friend, Jane Vollbrecht, for her gentle guidance and the detailed answers she gives to every sort of dumb question I key in her direction, without even a hint of laughter in her responses. And finally, a huge hug of gratitude to Caitlin d'Aguiar and Emily Reed of Blue Feather Books, who were willing to take a risk on an unpublished writer with a memoir told from a victim's perspective when so many others in the industry were only interested in a story about the killer.

Author's Note

This work is a memoir based on the personal recollections and perceptions of the author. All dialogue is reconstructed from memory. All quotations from written documents are reproduced exactly as they appear in the original copies, including spelling and typographical errors. Some names have been changed or omitted.

Chapter One: Chrysanthemums

Gary Ridgway murdered my baby sister. Now known as the Green River Killer, Ridgway murdered at least forty-eight women during the height of his killing spree from 1982 to 1984. He continued to kill through the 1990s. Today, no one, not even the killer himself, knows the gruesome total. My sister Maureen was the thirty-ninth victim of his slaughter.

My writing mentor insists that to write Maureen's story, I must understand Ridgway. I must see, feel, express this story from all points of view. I must be Gary Ridgway. But I can't do it. I don't want to do it. I can't write about Ridgway, or Ridgway's motives, or Ridgway's point of view about murder, because to do that, to be Ridgway, I have to try to understand why a man kills, what motivates a man to pay for sex, to promise to pay for sex, knowing that he'll never pay.

He won't have to pay. The girl will be dead.

On a Thursday in late September 1983, Ridgway left work at the Kenworth Truck Company in Renton, Washington, and cruised fourteen miles into Seattle with the intent to kill. Where did he find my sister? I don't know. No one knows, not even Ridgway. "I killed so many women," he has said, "I have a hard time keeping them straight."

They meant nothing to him. They were garbage to him. Maureen was garbage. Not human. Not a girl with family, dreams, potential. Ridgway knew nothing about, cared nothing about these girls, about Maureen.

Where did he kill Maureen? In the canopy on the back of his truck, the police now know. But where was the truck parked? The International District? Under an Interstate 90 overpass? Lower Beacon Hill? Near Seattle University?

All of these areas I knew well, both before and after the murder. As a student at Seattle University in the early 1970s, I worked at Todd Chemical Company on Rainier Avenue. I walked to and from my dorm room in Campion Tower, clutching a small can of mace in my pocket. Always aware of who was in front, beside, behind. Aware of doors, alleys, danger spots. I was a farm girl, just like Maureen, living in the big city for the first time.

Was I just born streetwise, and she wasn't? Was I born lucky, and she wasn't? How can I be Ridgway? How can I understand his motives, his desires, his needs? How can I imagine the thoughts that went through his mind as he cruised for prostitutes? He called it "patrolling." Later, he told the Green River Task Force that he was helping the police clean up the streets of Seattle by getting rid of prostitutes. As if they were rats.

The Task Force suspected Ridgway early on, while Maureen was still alive. They questioned him on May 4, 1983, four days after victim twenty-nine, Marie Malvar, disappeared, but they said that they had no hard evidence connecting Ridgway to her disappearance. I have to wonder: how hard did they look before writing him off as a suspect?

They had a chance when Marie Malvar vanished. Following her disappearance, two police detectives stood at Ridgway's door to question him about Marie. Then they left. Marie's body lay in the woods, only a few miles away. Ridgway took them to the spot in September 2003, twenty years later.

Victims thirty through forty-eight were still alive the day the police questioned Ridgway about Marie Malvar. Maureen was still alive. It nags me: how hard did they look?

How can I pretend to be the man who stood in his yard chatting with two cops, knowing that the body of his most recent victim was still warm in her shallow grave? A good old white boy passing the time. An average Joe. How can I be the man so devoid of human emotion that he passed a lie detector test with flying colors?

I can't. So I tell my story—mine, not his—and I tell Maureen's story, because she can no longer tell it.

* * *

Maureen was nineteen when Gary Ridgway murdered her. It was impossible to believe, even harder to accept, that my sister got lost in the world of prostitution. For twenty years, there was no proof that she had. But with Ridgway's confession, denial was no longer an option. Denial does not honor Maureen. The truth must be examined and understood. It must be accepted.

Maureen was missing for thirty-one months before her remains were discovered, less than ten miles from our family home on Tiger Mountain. On May 2, 1986, a worker at a nearby residence for juvenile delinquents came across some scattered bones in the woods. A skull, a jawbone, a tibia. Dental records proved the unfathomable.

My worst nightmares could not stand up to the horror of the reality that Ridgway had murdered my baby sister and left her body to decompose in the foothills of the Cascade mountain range. It's beautiful country, not far from Echo Glen Children's Center, where our mother worked as a night nurse. Mom could have known the young man who found her daughter's strewn remains. She could have been working in the infirmary the night Gary Ridgway dumped the body of her youngest child practically at her doorstep.

Even today, Mom relives her fear of working the graveyard shift: "Have I told you about the night it was snowing so hard my car couldn't get up the hill?"

I only smile, unwilling to cut her off by telling her that in the past few years, I've heard her memories so often they've become my own.

"I was on my way to work. You know I worked at Echo Glen, don't you?" She glances at me, and I nod my head. "That night, it was snowing so hard I couldn't get up that big hill, so I just stopped under the I-90 overpass."

I know my line here. "Did you have a blanket or anything in the car?"

"Always," she says. "But I didn't have to wait for long. When I didn't show up for my shift, the night watchman came looking for me. He drove out in that horrible snow and picked me up in his big truck."

I smile again as a distant terror washes over her face. "That was really nice of him."

"It just makes me sick to my stomach to think that horrible man was out there killing girls right there where I was parked." Tears fill her eyes. "He could have been out there with her."

My mother doesn't mention Maureen by name, but I know who she's talking about. And we sit together in silence, remembering.

I don't know if the night Mom's car refused to face the snowy hill actually coincides with the date of Maureen's death. Neither does my mother. Frankly, it doesn't matter. The fear, the pain, and the place associations are what matter to me. For my mother, the memory of her many years of dedicated service at Echo Glen will always be tainted by its proximity to her youngest daughter's long-lost remains.

Prior to the discovery of Maureen's body, I had loved nature. I was a hiker and a backpacker. I wandered the forests of the Pacific Northwest with the abandon of an inquisitive child, and I felt more spiritual peace in the woody, damp undergrowth than I ever felt in any church. Since the discovery of my sister's remains, I cannot even take a walk in a wooded city park without imagining bones in the undergrowth. It's a constant battle I fight with myself. I want to be in the woods. I want to feel that peace, that ease I felt before my youngest sister disappeared, but it has left me.

I finally drove to that spot in the woods only a short time ago. I wanted—no, I needed—to see the spot where my sister's spirit soared, where her spirit left her body, where nature reclaimed her physical remains. So I went to the spot where Ridgway dumped my sister's body in search of what? Her soul? My peace?

I'd thought of going since that day in 1986 when I first learned that Maureen's remains were found at the junction of Interstate 90 and Highway 18, but I hadn't known the exact location. I couldn't bring myself to learn it. Almost twenty years later, I sat in reporter-turned-professor Tomas Guillen's Seattle University office. I asked questions about the investigations that he and fellow reporter Carlton Smith had conducted back in the early eighties, when the bodies of the earliest victims were first being pulled from the Green River. Later, they co-authored a book about the murders.

Professor Guillen asked me if I'd visited the site. When I told him no, when I said that I wasn't even exactly sure where it was, there was an unspoken question in his eyes that I chose to ignore for another year or so. That didn't mean it wasn't a good question.

On a dry, sunny day in Seattle in the summer of 2005, I finally faced my fears, climbed into my car, and headed east on Interstate 90 headed towards Snoqualmie Pass. I'd done my research. I knew where I was headed.

Again, I tried to follow my writing mentor's advice: I tried to be Gary Ridgway, to imagine the thrill of the kill, the body of my sister hidden inside the camper on the back of his pickup truck. I tried to understand why anyone would do what he had done, but I couldn't. Instead, I lost myself in a cassette recording of Ernest Gaines's *A Gathering of Old Men*, and denied my fears. Unlike Ridgway, I felt sick to my stomach. Unlike Ridgway, I stopped when I reached Issaquah.

I was alone. My husband had offered, had insisted on going with me. A girlfriend had promised she'd sit in the car with *Harry*

Potter for as long as I needed. I thought about their offers for a long time, but I knew this was a journey I'd begun alone and needed to finish alone. So I said no to both of them and drove alone towards Issaquah, just Ernest Gaines on the tape player and me.

Downtown Seattle to Issaquah is only twenty minutes. It can be two or three times that during rush hour, of course, but I left Seattle in the early afternoon, and the road was clear. I felt compelled to stop at a grocery store off I-90 to buy some flowers. Maureen has no gravesite. I'd never taken her flowers.

As I looked over the wide assortment of bright, fragrant bouquets, I realized I didn't know my sister's favorite flower, or even her favorite color. As children, we gathered armfuls of the Shasta daisies and brightly colored foxgloves that grew wild every spring in any cleared spot of land, but I hadn't known Maureen as a young woman. What would she have chosen? My eyes moved from the cut flowers to the potted plants and lighted on a large pot of soft white chrysanthemums, and I was overwhelmed with memories.

I remember nothing of the memorial service itself, only that my mother had adorned the church and altar with dozens of virginal white, potted chrysanthemums. The service was held at Saint Joseph's Catholic Church in Issaquah in the summer of 1986, after the Green River Task Force released the skeletal remains of Maureen's body they had recovered from that spot in the wilderness. After dental records had been matched, after forensics had determined an approximate date of death, after cremation of what little remained of my baby sister. After the service, Mom planted the flowers in her garden, where she tended them for the duration of their natural life cycle. I left the store with a large pot of chrysanthemums, climbed back into my car while wiping tears from my eyes, and continued east on I-90.

On the car seat beside me lay page 105 of the *King County Prosecutor's Summary of Evidence*. It was a dense, gruesome document outlining Ridgway's unspeakable crimes, the evidence that would have been used had the case gone to trial. Because he confessed, he was never tried. He admitted his guilt, leading police to sets of remains, in exchange for his life. The death penalty was taken off the table. The document was released to the public on the Internet, just after Ridgway's confession to forty-eight counts of first-degree murder.

I knew I would never remember the details of Ridgway's description of the spot. I couldn't memorize the minutiae. My brain couldn't hold them. So I carried the page with me:

Nearly three years later, on May 2, 1986, an Echo Glen (juvenile detention center) employee was looking for an escapee when he came across some of Maureen's remains. They were found on the west side of Highway 18 at 105th, a short distance south of the intersection of Highway 18 and Interstate 90. A pull-out and utility shed were near the area. Tina Thompson's remains had been found two years earlier on the other side of Highway 18. The Task Force subsequently recovered Maureen's remains, which were spread out over some distance. Some bones were found near a barbed wire fence. (*Superior Court of Washington for King County, State of Washington vs. Gary Leon Ridgway, Prosecutor's Summary of the Evidence, p. 105*)

Some ten minutes later, I exited onto Highway 18. The spot I was looking for had to be just off the interstate, on the right side of the highway. I stopped at the first pull-out. There was no utility shed and no barbed wire fence, only a chained metal gate blocking access to a narrow, one-lane road into the wilderness. An old logging road, perhaps. The road went straight for a ways and then curved to the right.

I parked by the gate and got out, my notebook and pen in hand. My shield against pain. I felt the old, familiar cloak of distance and denial engulf me; I was a child again.

I didn't allow myself the luxury of emotion. I stayed near the car, not venturing past the gate or onto the dry, dusty trails heading off on opposite sides of the pull-out into the thick forest of cedar and fir.

There was minimal undergrowth near the highway, but I could see that it grew denser as I left the roadside. The loud roar of non-stop Thursday afternoon traffic filled my senses, huge semis barreling past me, shaking the earth under my feet. New traffic. Traffic that didn't exist when Ridgway chose this spot, twenty years before. The area was littered with garbage. A Miller Genuine Draft twelve-pack box, a crushed Franz Old-Fashioned Donut box, a discarded CD. I didn't venture deep enough into the woods to see the title.

It felt like I was in the right place, but a green Washington State road sign hanging across Highway 18 told me I was wrong. "SE 104th St.," it read. The *King County Prosecutor's Summary of Evidence* had said 105th. Damn.

I climbed back into my car and headed south on Highway 18 in search of 105th. A little over a quarter of a mile from the Interstate 90 intersection, I found another pull-out, but it was unmarked. I had no idea if it was 105th, but it felt wrong. It was too far from the I-90 intersection and too well used. Frustrated, I made a U-turn and headed back to 104th.

I pulled off the road to the east of Highway 18, just across the highway from where I'd stopped a few minutes before. On this side of the highway, 104th was a small, paved road that headed off into a rural residential area. I coasted to a stop and tried to figure out what to do next.

I was parked in a large, open area next to 104th. A smaller dirt road went off into the woods in a different direction. There were large piles dirt and gravel, zigzagged with the telltale tire marks of BMX bicycles and motorbikes. As I sat staring into space, a young man drove past on a dirt bike, and I jumped out of my car to stop him. "Is there a 105th around here somewhere?" I asked the dark glasses and helmet.

"Not that I know of." It turned out that he was a local firefighter, and he lived up the road, so I figured he knew what he was talking about. He asked me what I was looking for, so I showed him the *Summary of Evidence* and said I was doing some research. We talked a bit about the case, and then I thanked him for his help and watched the dust settle behind him as he sped up 104th.

I climbed back into the car and reread page 105 slowly, carefully: "...the west side of Highway 18 at 105th, a short distance south of the intersection of Highway 18 and Interstate 90." What was I missing? My eyes dropped to the bottom of the page. "Norm Maleng, Prosecuting Attorney." An address followed, and a phone number.

I dialed the number from my cell phone at exactly 4:27 p.m. and got a recorded message telling me that the office closed at 4:30 p.m.

I stayed on the line. I listened to the phone tree offerings and waited. I felt the seconds ticking away, knowing that I had less than three minutes to reach someone before they went home for the evening. A receptionist answered. After I explained who and where I was, she asked me to hold while she tried to find someone who might be able to help me.

I felt like I was on hold forever, fear climbing up my spine. The realization of where I was and what I was doing finally hit me. I began to tremble. I reminded myself that I wasn't alone. The young firefighter on the dirt bike was just up the road.

"Ms. Williams?" It was a man's voice.

"Yes. Arleen Williams."

"Hello. I understand you have some questions about your sister, about Maureen. Let me introduce myself. I'm Sean O'Donnell. I was one of the prosecutors on the Ridgway case. How can I help you?"

"Thank you for taking my call, Mr. O'Donnell." My voice was shaking. I limited my words. "I'm sitting in my parked car on Highway 18 and 104th. I'm trying to find 105th, the spot where Ridgway left Maureen's body." My voice cracked. "There is no 105th."

He stalled for a minute or two, telling me that the document on the web didn't provide accurate details. It was deliberately vague because it was for public consumption. They were concerned, he said, about possible desecration of the sites.

"I don't think it's vague," I responded. "I think it's wrong."

He asked if he could call me right back. He needed to look up the facts. The case had closed over a year before, and it was an enormous file. I couldn't expect him to remember every detail.

True to his word, Mr. O'Donnell returned my call in less than the promised ten minutes. And he said the error was just a typo: 105th on page 105. A typo!

Again, I wondered about the judicial system that had allowed Ridgway to kill, to avoid capture for so many years. But I said nothing. I wanted to know whatever this man could tell me about my sister's death. I was again a child, desperate for information, but afraid to ask.

Referring to his notes, Mr. O'Donnell explained that Maureen's skull was found thirty yards off the end of the 104th pull-out on the opposite side of Highway 18 from where I still sat in my parked car. I heard the hesitation in his voice. He asked me if I was alone.

"It's okay," I told him. "I need to know."

He explained that the skeletal remains of three victims were found in the same area. In addition to the skull, other bones that were later identified as part of Maureen's scattered skeleton were also found, some as close as fifty feet from the highway. He was kind. He was gentle. He didn't want to tell me more than I could stomach. Again, I told him I wanted to know.

From fifty feet to thirty yards, he said.

I'm no good at math, but as I sat in my car staring at the pull-out on the opposite side of Highway 18, I could see the magnitude of the area he was describing. Feet and yards are quite different units of measurement. Somewhere in that space, my sister's decomposing body had lain for three years, exposed to nature's mercy. Her bones were spread apart by animals, both wild and domestic, as they sought nourishment from her body.

I wasn't just imagining this; I knew. The young man under the motorcycle helmet told me that one of his neighbor's dogs had found a bone. Thinking it might be human, the neighbor had turned it over to the police, and his suspicions had been confirmed. The young man wasn't being cruel or insensitive. He just didn't know who I was, or the pain he was causing. And I had no way of knowing whether that bone was part of Maureen or one of the other two victims Ridgway had dumped in the area.

I thanked Mr. O'Donnell for his help and ended the call. As I sat in my car, staring across the highway, I watched a red Subaru Forester stop at the pull-out. The driver, a heavy-set, middle-aged woman, unloaded four or five dogs of varying shapes and sizes. The woman began playing with her dogs and seemed in no hurry to leave. After another five minutes or so, I realized I could be waiting a very long time if I wanted to have the place to myself. I crossed Highway 18 and parked next to her.

Maybe it was her friendly smile, or maybe it was the reassuring presence of another living human being that gave me the courage to walk around that chained gate and up to the first bend in the logging road. Pacing it out, it felt like about thirty yards.

The air changed, becoming damper and mustier, as I distanced myself from the highway. The undergrowth deepened with salal, fern and blackberry. Vines and thick grass encroached on the edges of the narrow road. It seemed like the kind of place an unwary hiker could pick up a bad case of poison oak or nettle stings if she wasn't careful.

I walked just beyond the bend, just beyond sight of the highway, the cars, the woman and her dogs. It was as far as I could go. With each step deeper into the woods, my legs grew heavier. I didn't want to be alone in those woods, alone on the spot of earth where Maureen's young body had lain, consumed by the ravages of nature. I could feel the worms and maggots. I could smell the decay. And I wanted to turn and run.

I made myself stay. I stood still and quieted my breathing. I whispered my sister's name, but she wasn't there. I knew it was not the spot to leave the beautiful white chrysanthemum.

I didn't feel her presence the way I often do when I walk the Pacific beach in front of the last home my father built, the home where my mother still lives. Perhaps that was unsurprising: the beach is washed with the waters of the Pacific Ocean, into which my parents released Maureen's ashes from the stern of Dad's small fishing boat. In this place, I only felt a deep, evil sadness and an urgent desire to get the hell out of there.

Being there reminded me of Morrie Schwartz. Not long before, I had used Mitch Albom's *Tuesdays with Morrie* as a text in a college course I was teaching. It's the story of an elderly man, Morrie Schwartz, who is dying of Lou Gehrig's disease. Morrie called himself lucky, because he had time to prepare for death, and because he knew he would die surrounded by love.

My sister didn't have time to prepare for death. She didn't even have time to learn how to live. Ridgway robbed her of that time. Unlike Morrie Schwartz, Maureen died in violence and hatred. Perhaps it was this very contrast that drew me to Albom's book. It wasn't that it helped me come to terms with my sister's death, but rather it allowed me, it gave me permission, to again cherish my own life.

I walked back to my car as quickly as possible, said good-bye to the woman and her dogs, and got back in my car. I kept my head down, my eyes guarded. To her, I was probably just another woman who needed to stretch her legs or take a quick pee in the woods.

I decided not to return to Seattle the same way I'd come. Instead, I headed south on Highway 18, knowing I'd reach the turn-off to the Issaquah-Hobart Road within six or seven miles. I knew the area. I rode horseback there even before Highway 18 was cut through the wilderness. As I drove, I clocked the distance to the driveway entrance of the last house Dad built in Issaquah on Tiger Mountain Road, the house where Mom and Dad were living when Maureen disappeared. Nine miles. Nine point two miles, to be exact. Hiking distance.

I drove the twenty-mile-per-hour curves of Tiger Mountain Road, the blinding sun filtering through the dense canopy of alder, cedar and fir. I thought about another icy night when my mother had car trouble. She slid off the edge of one of these curves and ended up in the hospital. My old riding grounds had turned out to be a dangerous place.

When I reached the four-way stop in downtown Issaquah, I turned left, thinking I'd go into the new library and do some writing. Instead, I kept driving. Almost without volition, I pulled up the hill in search of Saint Joseph's Catholic Church, where Maureen's memorial service was held in 1986. It was the church where the nine of us kids were baptized, confirmed, and indoctrinated during Monday evening catechism classes and regular Catholic Youth Organization meetings. I could have found my way there drunk and blindfolded from anywhere in the state.

But I couldn't find the church I remembered, the church that had been such a big part of my teenage years. Instead, I found a church so completely remodeled that I no longer recognized it from either the outside or the inside. Gone was the long central aisle leading to the altar, lined by rows of pews. Now, there was a circular seating arrangement with a central altar. Staring at this new configuration, I wondered whether the priest would have seemed so all-powerful to me in my youth had I seen him surrounded by the congregation. The dark wooden pews felt familiar, but the crucifix that once hung over the altar seemed homeless, disoriented, off center on a far wall, the wall that used to stand behind the altar.

Had it been like this for Maureen's memorial service?

I didn't think so, but I couldn't be certain. I don't remember the memorial service, the words that were spoken, or the songs that were sung. Only the white chrysanthemums Mom had chosen to decorate the altar.

I left the potted chrysanthemum there in the church. I set it just inside the front door on the base of an ornate marble font of holy water, near the four original pillars that remained of the church I remembered.

Chapter Two: A Short Good-Bye

The first time Arturo kissed me, I knew it was something I didn't want. It was 1981, and I was living alone in Mexico City. What I wanted was companionship to soften my loneliness. To be loved, to feel loved, to feel love. But when Arturo kissed me, some part of my consciousness knew that by kissing him back, I had lost a wonderful friend. I ignored that gnawing voice. I allowed the relationship to develop. I felt loved, but I didn't feel love. I wasn't in love. But I married him because he blocked the demons of loneliness and despair, because he adored me, because he was a good man.

I married him because Mom and Dad didn't want me to marry him.

They never flat-out gave an opinion, of course—it was more of an opinion by default. When Arturo asked me to marry him, I wrote home to tell Mom and Dad about this loving, gentle man. This political science student at the national university, this intellectual, this friend who gave me comfort. And I asked if we could be married in their living room.

A few months passed before I heard back from my mother. The Mexican postal service was very slow, and I suppose Mom needed some time to mull over her response. She wrote suggesting that I come home for a long visit and think about the marriage idea. It was probably the best advice Mom ever gave me. But of course, I ignored it. I was furious that they could not be happy for me and would not allow me the joy of a family marriage at home. All my life, I'd felt judged by my parents, felt that I was never able to live up to their expectations. In Mexico, I was far enough away from them to allow myself to feel the anger I'd controlled for years. A whole lot of anger.

Blinded by fury, I insisted that we be married immediately. Arturo had no objections, so we set a date and sent out invitations. We were married by a Mexican judge in an ugly, gray, bureaucratic office on September 11, 1981. No one from my family came.

Arturo moved into my apartment, and we tried to build a life together. It was a small space for one person, and even tighter for two, but we managed. My mother's words echoed in my head as I organized our belongings: "A place for everything and everything in its place."

With urging from a college friend who was already living there, I had moved to Mexico City in 1979. Shortly after I got there, my friend returned to the States, and I found myself alone in the most densely populated city in the world. After a few years living in a tiny apartment and dating a musician of *la nueva canción revolucionaria,* a loosely-knit group of leftist protest singers and songwriters, I met Arturo. He was a friend of the musician I was seeing, so at first he kept a friendly distance.

At the time, we were both studying at the national university, so we ate lunch together now and again. He tried to teach me how to eat a mango. I never learned. To this day, I can't eat a mango without sticky juice running down my arms and strings of mango getting stuck in my teeth. Arturo could peel and eat a mango as easily as a banana.

Seven months after we were married, we decided to visit my parents. I wanted to go home to see my siblings again, and I wanted them to meet my husband. So in April 1982, I took Arturo home for Easter. As we landed at Sea-Tac International Airport, I was terrified. I had no idea what kind of reception Mom and Dad would give us. I didn't even know if we'd be welcome in their home.

I had good reason to fear. Dad had never accepted my older sister Laureen's husband. In fact, he had totally, completely, absolutely disowned her when she was nineteen. Arturo's skin was only a few shades lighter, his hair every bit as kinky, as Laureen's husband's.

I walked through the international arrival doors with Arturo's warm hand holding my trembling one. I felt my parents' presence before I saw them. Without a word, Dad wrapped me in a warm embrace.

"This is Arturo," I told them.

I watched as my father extended his hand to my husband. Arturo's English was very limited, and my father was always a man of few words, but they shook hands and smiled.

"Welcome, Arturo," my mother said, stumbling over the name.

"Call me Art," he told them both, as I watched in silence. He knew how difficult it was for most English speakers to produce the

Spanish *R* sound, and a name with two *R's* divided by a *T* was particularly difficult.

"Okay, Art. Let's go find your baggage."

With those words, Dad accepted Arturo. Over the next few years, perhaps he even grew to love him, but I never understood why. Maybe it was because Dad's sense of morality was even stronger than his determination that his six daughters all marry white men. Maybe being a good man, being an upstanding man of his word, was even more important to him than being a white man. Dad was an excellent judge of character. So he accepted Arturo, just as twenty years earlier, he had befriended the black bricklayer who had helped him finish our first Issaquah house.

Maybe the fact that we had adhered to one of my parents' rules made acceptance easier. We had gotten married, and thus were not "living in sin." Because we were married, I suppose, they decided to give Arturo a chance to prove himself. Somehow, Arturo knew what to do. He asked for work, for something to do to help out around the house.

Work was Dad's measure of character. If a man worked well and with dedication, he was a good man. So when Arturo offered to lend a hand, Dad put a paintbrush in it.

At that time, my parents and my youngest sister Maureen lived in the third house Dad had built in the Issaquah Valley, and they were preparing to put on the market. Dad had designed and built an intricate wrought iron gated entrance, as well as decorative iron fencing around the deck and patio areas, all of which needed a fresh coat of paint.

One morning after breakfast, I heard Dad say, "Come on, Art. We've got a job to do."

"What are you going to do?" I asked.

"Men's work," Dad responded, with a wink at my husband. Giving me quick glance and a shrug, Arturo followed my father out the back door. I watched as Dad set a tall ladder against the arch over the driveway and motioned for Arturo to climb it. With a paintbrush in one hand and a paint can in the other, so bundled up he looked as round as he was tall, his wire-rimmed glasses poking out from under his stocking cap, Arturo made his way up the ladder. He painted the arch with Dad, in jeans and a short sleeve T-shirt, standing below, steadying the ladder. Every so often, Arturo climbed down and they moved the ladder a few feet and repeated the process. By the end of the day, the arch gleamed fresh and black.

Arturo spent many long days with paintbrush in hand that early spring, wearing an old green Army surplus jacket and a bright green stocking cap. He couldn't stay warm in the cool Northwest spring weather.

But did they approve of my choice? One day, Mom and I were in the car together. I'm not sure what we were talking about, something about marriage and children probably, and she said, "Remember, Arleen, not everyone has to have children."

This struck me as odd, coming from a mother of nine. Maybe it was her gentle way of warning me, of dissuading me. Perhaps she feared the potential consequences. We were both painfully aware that Dad was capable of disowning me, just as he had disowned Laureen. Perhaps Mom was afraid of losing another daughter.

But I never asked, and it never happened. Instead, divorce happened, because I married a friend I should never have married. I wonder sometimes if I married Arturo to abate the all-consuming loneliness of my life in Mexico City, or if I married him as a deliberate challenge to see how Dad would react, to test my father's love for me. Dad passed the test. Not because of me, or even because of himself, but because of Arturo's willingness to engage in painstakingly tedious, slow work, climbing tall ladders and crawling around on his hands and knees. Dad's knee pain made this type of work impossible to manage with the ease of youth. By the time we packed to return to Mexico City, all the ironwork my father had meticulously wrought had several fresh coats of glossy black paint. Dad marveled that there wasn't a drop of spilled paint anywhere.

I have no doubt that he looked carefully, to make sure.

That visit was one of only a few times in the ten years since I'd left home that Maureen and I spent any time together. One morning early in the visit, I was alone in the kitchen when she came downstairs, rushing towards the back door.

"Good morning, Maurie." That was her family nickname—always Maurie, rarely Maureen. "Where are you off to in such a hurry?"

She muttered something under her breath.

"What was that?" I asked, not realizing I would offend her.

She stopped for a second and turned to glare at me. "What do you care? Why don't you just go back to Mexico, or wherever you came from, and leave me alone?" She turned, stomped across Mom's yellow linoleum, and slammed the kitchen door behind her.

Dad and Arturo were already outside working, and Mom, I quickly realized, was in the car, waiting to drive Maureen wherever she needed to go. Probably to classes at Bellevue Community

College, or to work at a childcare center. She was eighteen, but didn't have a driver's license, making her dependent on my parents for transportation. I was left alone in the empty house, trying to figure out what I'd done wrong.

When Maureen came home later that day, she handed me a small, tissue-wrapped package. "I'm sorry," she said. I opened the package and found a pair of wide colorful shoelaces with the words I LOVE YOU repeated in bright blue, red, green, and yellow along the entire length of each lace. I never asked her what was wrong, or what I'd done to upset her, but I still have those shoelaces, worn and tattered from much use, too cherished to ever throw away.

After that day, Maureen and I began to connect, to know each other as human beings. Arturo and I invited her to go to Vancouver, Canada, with us for a weekend. We were broke, so one night in a cheap hotel room was all we could afford. Still, we visited as many tourist attractions as we could cram into two short days, including the Capilano Bridge.

In a heavy brown coat, her short hair hidden under a red stocking cap, Maureen stood in the middle of the swaying bridge, suspended five hundred feet above the rushing river and rocks below. With her legs spread, her knees bent for balance, her hands gripping the bridge ropes for support, she challenged Arturo and me to join her.

"Come on, you big chickens," she taunted.

Arturo stayed on solid ground, but I stepped onto the bridge, unwilling to let my younger sister get the better of me. Maureen swayed and the bridge swayed. She was trying to frighten me, and succeeding. She grinned at me, a teasing, toothy grin filled with defiance, as I carefully backed my way off the bridge.

"Okay, whatever. It's your bridge!" I told her. "You win!"

Letting go of the ropes for a few brief seconds, she raised her arms in triumph, joy shining in her eyes.

Later that day, we took the gondola to the top of Grouse Mountain. Not to ski—none of us knew how, and we didn't have enough money, anyway. Just for the ride, the view, and an overpriced dinner we couldn't afford. We sat at a window table that felt as if it were suspended from the side of the mountain. The views from the three sides of the room overlooking the gorge were breathtaking. Elegant tables were set with fanned cloth napkins and crystal.

Maureen slouched in her place at the table, her arms looped over the back of the chair. The late afternoon sunlight streaming through the wall of windows behind us illuminated the left side of her face, leaving the right side in shadows. Her closed-lipped smile created the hint of a dimple in her left cheek. Her messy, brownish-blonde curls were almost auburn in the fading sunlight, and her soft gray wool sweater pulled tight over her small breasts. Just watching her face, I could tell she was trying to figure something out.

Grinning, she leaned forward and held up one of the numerous utensils in front of her. "Which of these are we supposed to use?"

"I think," my husband responded, "we watch the others."

My sister's eyes followed Arturo's around the room, and they both started laughing and mimicking the other restaurant guests. For a split second, I was jealous of them, of the easy, comfortable friendship they seemed to establish so quickly, but I pushed the feeling away and joined in the fun, insisting that we had to order dessert so we could use all of the utensils on the table. We splurged on elegance we were unaccustomed to, and I'm glad of the extravagance, for the memory.

We were in the middle of dessert, imitating the other dinner guests in the beautiful restaurant on top of Grouse Mountain, when Maureen first asked about our life in Mexico City. "So, what's it like there?"

"Boy, that's a tough question," I told her. "It's totally different. It's a huge, dirty, noisy city. There's poverty like you can't even imagine."

"God, it sounds awful. Why do you stay?"

"It's my home." I reached across the table to lay my hand on Arturo's arm. "Besides, it's also exciting and fun. The people are warm and friendly, and I love teaching English there." I was stumbling, struggling to find words to explain something I could not explain, even to myself. "Why not come and see for yourself?"

"Could I?" I heard the eagerness in her voice as she glanced back and forth between my face and Arturo's.

"Yes," Arturo said. *"Mi casa es tu casa."*

"Of course," I said. "When can you come?"

"I finish school in June, but I probably won't have enough money then." She paused for a moment, and I imagined her doing a few quick, mental calculations. "I could work through July and take some time off in August."

"What about Mom and Dad?" I asked carefully.

"I'm eighteen," she said, sneering. "I'm old enough to do what I want."

"Sounds good to me," I said, lifting my water glass. "A toast, to Maureen's August visit."

"*Salud.*"

"Cheers. Great! Something to look forward to."

That last comment struck me. At eighteen, my sister needed something to look forward to, something to pull her out of bed in the morning.

Now, I talk to my husband, to friends, to other mothers of other teenage girls, and I read an endless variety of parenting books in a feeble attempt to understand what normal teenage development and behavior looks like. When my teenage daughter screams that she can't wait to get away from us and live on her own, I remind myself that this is ordinary teen behavior. A breaking away, a development of self. I never experienced that process. As a teenager, I lost myself in my attempt to be perfect.

In my family, the only two options were perfect or gone.

I never understood why my three oldest siblings had been disowned. First, Marleen was taken away. Then, Laureen and Robert simply vanished, one right after the other. Three out of four of my older siblings disappeared mysteriously before I left childhood. Their very mention became taboo. I assumed that they had each done something horribly wrong, that they were really bad and needed serious punishment, but at that time, I had no idea what had happened or why. I just felt sorry for Mom and Dad, for having such rotten kids, and entered my own teenage years determined to protect them from further pain. I swore to myself that I would never do anything that would upset them or make them sad. I never smoked, drank, dated, or even had any close friends, girl or boy. I went to school, came home, did chores, and studied. When I graduated from high school at seventeen, I left home and never moved back.

I can't pretend to know how Maureen felt, how she navigated her early teen years. I was too far away. I do know that at her eighteen and my twenty-seven, neither of us had the emotional maturity and self-awareness of many younger teens. When I unwrapped those shoelaces, I didn't say, "Hey, thanks, but what was that all about this morning?" We didn't sit down or go for a long walk together to talk about what had happened and what was bothering her. We were both engulfed in the same superficial silence we'd always known.

* * *

Maureen actually did come to visit Arturo and me in Mexico City later that year, in August 1982, after she completed her first year in Early Child Development at Bellevue Community College. Her visit was special, I felt, because in her youth and innocence, she showed me that having a relationship with me was important to her. We had a wonderful time beginning, but only just beginning, to get to know each other. We hardly knew ourselves. But she seemed to be seeking me out, wanting to get to know this big sister who lived so far away and never seemed to have time for family. She didn't understand that I was running away from family, from myself, from the me I didn't even know. In our family, we didn't talk about deep things like this. So she reached out to me, as I reached out to her, to try to understand ourselves and the crazy, mixed-up, silent family of which we were both reluctant, frustrated members.

Maureen's visit to Mexico City was the only time I had an opportunity to get a glimpse of the wonderful young woman my kid sister had become. In her desire to get to know me, she allowed me to see her for the first time away from parents, family, and the constraints that had seemed to control our every breath back in Issaquah. We felt free to giggle and laugh and try to figure out who we were. It was like the initial introduction, the first date. And like most people on first dates, I suppose, we both felt very nervous and awkward. Arturo was our buffer, as he had been on our trip to Vancouver. He smoothed the rough spots, creating comfort and ease with his gentle humor.

In the three months between our visit to Seattle and Maureen's arrival in Mexico City, I redecorated our apartment. I wanted the tiny place to look as nice and homey as possible in order to impress my little sister. I painted the walls and trim, had carpet laid throughout, and reupholstered the second-hand sofa. The night before Maureen's arrival, I heard a loud knock at the front door. I opened it to find Arturo, his arms loaded with newspaper-wrapped packages, a shopping bag in each hand.

"*Qué es todo eso?*" I asked in surprise.

Setting down the bags, he handed me a huge bouquet of brilliant color. "*Para tu hermanita.*" Then, pulling another large bouquet from one of his shopping bags, "*Y otro para ti, mi amor.*"

He'd stopped at the local market and loaded himself up with fresh fruits and vegetables—Maureen was a vegetarian. With the apartment redecorated and full of flowers, we were ready.

I picked Maureen up from the Mexico City airport in my green VW bug and took her to the apartment. Arturo was at work, and we were alone together. We were awkward without our buffer, unsure of how to talk to each other. We were two people who were supposed to know each other, but didn't.

I showed her the apartment, and then, rather than sitting down for a long chat, I bundled her back into the car and raced across town to the neighborhood of Coyoacan with its wide, shaded avenues and vines trailing over ancient stone walls that encircled mansions built long ago. Bougainvillea worked its beauty up the ironwork fences of the newly-constructed luxury condominiums. Coyoacan was a neighborhood for the wealthy, and in my own political activism of the time, I swore I didn't want to live there, just on general principle.

But I lied. It was gorgeous.

I took Maureen to Coyoacan to meet Judi Bond. Judi was the closest thing to family I had in Mexico. We had met several years before, when we were both still single. We'd lived together off-and-on, when one or the other was between apartments, and we knew we could always depend on each other. Even though we had married very different Mexican men, from very different social classes, and who held opposing political philosophies, we remained surrogate sisters. She was the only child of British Protestants, and I was one of nine children of Catholic Americans, with an Irish-American father. Yet, on some odd level, we connected. When no one from my family came to my wedding, Judi's parents, visiting from England, stood at my side before the Mexican judge.

So, when my sister came to Mexico, I wanted to show her both ends of the Mexican socio-political spectrum: the dusty, working-class barrio where Arturo and I lived in our tiny two-room apartment, as well as the modern, high-rise condos set against the antique mansions that dotted the streets of Coyoacan. And I wanted my sister to know Judi.

We put Judi's baby boy, Moncito, into a stroller and started walking. Judi was in her long peasant skirt and cowboy boots, an eccentric, yet Euro-vogue look that was just chic enough to not offend her conservative husband. Maureen wore long dark pants and the cap-sleeved, button-up-the-front, permanent press blouse she wore for most of the visit.

For several months while working on an early draft of this memoir, I had old photographs spread over the dining room table. One day, my daughter sat down beside me and looked through the pile. She was fifteen at the time, and clothes were an important part of her developing identity. She held three or four pictures together and said, "My God, Mom, how long was she there? She wore the same clothes the whole time!"

"Believe it or not, she came for a three-week visit with only one small suitcase and a carry-on. Less stuff than you take for a weekend at Nana's."

"You've got to be kidding."

"Nope. She was a real tomboy, Erin. She didn't care at all about clothes, and she didn't wear make-up."

Erin dropped the photographs on the table and started to leave the room. I felt I needed to justify my sister's lack of style to my daughter. "Hey, it's just like when we went to Europe. Do you remember? We each carried just one backpack."

"Yeah, I suppose," she said, and walked away.

* * *

On that first full day of Maureen's visit, we strolled through the calm, tree-shaded cobblestone streets of Coyoacan in the warm August sunshine. We stopped at the plaza, a peaceful open space surrounded by colonial buildings that had an aura of history and culture which never failed to make me feel insignificant.

It was a good day. A happy day. Maureen was thrilled with everything she saw, including Judi's baby. Judi kept the conversation flowing, as I knew she would. We solidified a plan that Judi and I had already discussed: we would take Maureen to Teotihuacan, just outside of the city, to climb the Aztec pyramids of the sun and the moon, to steep her in a culture that seemed to run deep in my veins and Judi's as well. We arranged to pick up Judi and Moncito the next morning. Judi didn't have a car. Her husband Javier did, but the wives of well-to-do, conservative Mexican lawyers didn't. Cars meant independence, and independence was something Javier didn't want for Judi.

Early the next morning, we piled into my car. Maureen and baby Moncito in his car seat snuggled into the back. It was hot and tight. When we arrived at Teotihuacan, I offered to stay with the baby and let Judi and Maureen climb. Maureen's long, strong legs made short work of the pyramid steps, but Judi, a good ten pounds overweight, struggled to keep up. I followed their climb from below, with Moncito in his stroller at my side. I couldn't hear their conversation, but I could see them talking and laughing, and I watched as Judi's camera captured Maureen's shy grin at the top of the Pyramid of the Sun, with the Pyramid of the Moon as a backdrop. Far below, I felt a pang of jealousy for the ease with which Judi could make conversation with my sister.

* * *

Later in the visit, Arturo and I took Maureen to Vera Cruz. I have dozens of snapshots from that trip, all labeled with exotic names like Chachalacas, La Antigua, and Xalapa, small beach towns near the city of Vera Cruz on the Gulf of Mexico. The sand dunes of Chachalacas are now a sand-boarding destination, a sport unheard of back in the early 1980s. It was a road trip, again in the green VW bug, again with Maureen's long, slender legs crammed into the back.

We drove to Vera Cruz and stayed in a hotel with a rooftop swimming pool. Maureen loved to swim, and she loved the sun. As soon as we checked into our shared room, she closed herself into the bathroom and pulled on her swimsuit.

"Come on, you guys," she hollered. "I'll beat you to the pool." She and Arturo raced up the stairs to the roof and were swimming before I had time to find a spot in the shade to watch. I was never a sun-worshipper and usually wore long, white, gauzy cotton pants and a long-sleeved blouse if I had to be out in the sun for long.

Sitting poolside, watching Arturo and Maureen splash and play like a couple of overgrown kids, I felt old, like an outsider. Arturo had an amazing gift for making others comfortable, even Maureen who was so shy she didn't want to take off the T-shirt she wore over her swimsuit.

After a while, Arturo pulled himself from the pool and walked over to where I lounged, reading, under an umbrella.

"Hey, you're dripping all over me," I complained.

"Come swim with us, *güerita.* You need sun."

Maureen came up right behind him. "Yeah, Arleen. I don't know what he called you, but you look like a ghost."

"Look, I was cursed with Dad's skin," I said irritably. "If I get out there in the sun with you two, I'll be whining about sun rash for the rest of the trip. It's not worth it. Besides, I'm not even wearing a swimsuit under this."

What were those few weeks like? There were moments when Maureen and I were as uncomfortable together as strangers in a stuck elevator. There were other moments, like the day at the pool in Vera Cruz, when I felt jealous of my husband because he and Maureen had become comfortable together in so little time. Not jealous in the sense that I thought he was interested in her sexually, or vice versa, just envious of the ease and playfulness they shared. They could arm wrestle and have pillow fights and jump on the cheap hotel beds until they crashed to the floor. They had no emotional baggage. Nothing came between them. Nobody expected them to know each other already. Not like two sisters are expected to know, to share, to understand.

It felt like Maureen and I had no history together. I had left home before she reached double digits in age, and loss, silence, and confusion overshadowed my last years at home, my teenage years. At the time, I had been so self-absorbed that I had never bonded with any of the Little Kids, especially not baby Maureen. We were like two planets in a solar system, part of the same whole, but in different orbits. When she came to visit me in Mexico, our orbits came closer. We began to feel each other's atmospheric pressure and measure each other's temperature. But the visit was too short.

* * *

I wanted to spend some time alone with Maureen, just the two of us, so I took her to one of my favorite resort towns in Mexico: Puerto Vallarta. It was a town that Arturo had never visited. Somehow this was important to me. I wanted to show Maureen the Mexico I had known before I met Arturo.

I booked the best hotel I could afford for a three-day break from the city, a luxury beachfront hotel with a large swimming pool. Maureen loved to sit in the cowhide and wood chairs in the hotel bar, holding her drink with her right hand, the simple Mexican jade band I'd given her during my visit home a few months before on her ring finger. Sitting in a bar sipping a tropical drink with a colorful paper umbrella stuck into a piece of pineapple was a novelty for an eighteen-year-old from rural Issaquah.

She never reached legal drinking age in Washington State.

There she sat, in her green sports shorts and cap-sleeved blouse, just as I had sat almost ten years earlier on my first trip to Mexico. The only difference was that I had traveled alone, and I had drunk a *limonada* because I hadn't had the nerve to order an alcoholic beverage. Also, I hadn't been rosy pink from a day on the beach, like Maureen was, a day that included parasailing.

Maureen had never seen parasailing before and was drawn to it the moment she saw the beach spectacle earlier that day. We were sitting on the white sand, watching as clusters of barely-clad

Mexican men strapped harnesses and ropes on tourists and yelled to an offshore speedboat.

"Come on, Arleen," she exclaimed. "Let's do it!"

Even at the risk of once again being called a chicken, I refused to go with her. I knew I couldn't afford to pay for us both. I worked full-time as an English teacher in Mexico City, but I was earning pesos and being charged *gringo* prices. No matter how hard I tried, I never seemed to be able to get ahead. This was despite my parents' early teaching, "A penny saved is a penny earned."

Maureen spoke no Spanish, so I stood by and translated when it was her turn to be harnessed. My slender, blonde sister was quickly surrounded by three or four handsome, bare-chested young men, all teasing her and flirting in broken English: "*Oye chula*, you fly high!" "*Bonita güerita*, we drink later."

Unused to all this male attention, my sister trembled in her modest, one-piece swimsuit. No bikinis for this kid. She was always bashful, almost uncomfortable in her own skin. I was the watchful older sister, fearful that with all their joking and flirting, they wouldn't get her parachute safely fastened. Uncertain how she was going to land without breaking both legs, I imagined calling Mom and Dad to tell them that Maureen was laid up in a local hospital with multiple injuries. In contrast, she was as carefree as any eighteen-year-old should be. Full of life and vitality. Ready to conquer the world.

"*¡Ándale!*" The signal was given. She was off.

I lay back on the warm, white sand and watched my sister rising higher and higher, floating through the cloudless blue sky. Under my worries for her safety was a deep contentment. I was giving her a joyful new experience. Away from parents and siblings and lies and secrets, we could explore and experience together. I still didn't know the young woman flying above the bay as well as I wanted to, but I believed our relationship would grow in the years to come.

The boat circled and began to slow. Maureen floated back to me like a feather in the wind, a huge glorious smile on her lips and her bright blue eyes shining. As she dropped to beach level and her toes brushed the soft sand, three men surrounded her, one on each side and the third behind her, catching her as she landed. The one behind gathered the ropes and parachute. With more flirtatious teasing, they unharnessed her, and she threw her arms around me, overwhelmed with the glory of intense emotion.

That afternoon is etched in my memory. A beautiful August

afternoon over twenty years ago that I do not need photographs to remember. It may have been one of Maureen's final moments of innocent and intense joy.

* * *

I don't remember the details of my last day with Maureen. I want to remember. I want to know what she said, what I said. I want to know, with a desire that runs so deep it aches. But the simple fact is, I don't remember. I have only a snapshot, a hasty picture of Maureen and me together in late August 1982 at the Mexico City airport the moment before she boarded her flight back to Seattle and left my life forever. Two sisters, arms wrapped around each other, my right hand on her left shoulder, her left hand around my waist.

Two sisters, in a happy embrace. I'm wearing a bright yellow T-shirt with a Zihuatanejo logo, a souvenir from my honeymoon the year before, and ugly Elton John sunglasses. Maureen is in jeans and a khaki green "MASH 4077" T-shirt. Maybe a gift from Dad; he loved that show. Or maybe she bought it herself. Maybe she loved that show. I never asked, and now I'll never know.

That was the last time I ever saw my youngest sister. She planned to return, was saving money to return. I was as lonely as a lost child after she left, and only the promise of her return visit kept me going. Like Maureen, I needed a reason to get up in the morning. The sadness that settled over me after she left was like a suffocating blanket on a hot summer night. Sadness for the family I didn't have, a family that couldn't be replaced by the Mexican family I'd chosen.

Had I realized at the time that she wouldn't be coming back for that second visit, I would have been more vigilant, more attuned, more aware. I might have written her last words to me in my journal. But I didn't know that she'd be murdered thirteen months later, or that I'd never see her again. So I wasn't affixing her face, her voice, her smell in my permanent memory. I wasn't present in the moment, and the moment was lost.

All I have left is a snapshot. Two slender, smiling young women, their arms holding each other, a younger blonde and an older brunette. My sister's shy smile and childishly pudgy face attest to her youth. We were two sisters who had managed to come together, despite a lifetime of confusion and silence, trying to find what was missing in our solitary lives by reaching out to each other.

I wish I had never let go.

Chapter Three: Missing!

August 17, 1983: one year after visiting us in Mexico City, Maureen moved into her first apartment. It was a tiny place, only a one-room studio, just barely large enough for a twin bed. There was a kitchenette on one side of the room and a door to a half-bath on the other. But it was hers, a home of her own, and she was thrilled.

Her studio was in a yellow brick building on East Madison in the Capitol Hill area of Seattle, close enough for an energetic teenager to walk downtown to the west and into the Central District to the east, where she hoped to find a job in the Health and Human Service's Head Start Program, working with underprivileged inner city kids. She'd put in applications, but in the meantime, she kept her job at a Bellevue childcare center in the Eastside suburbs. She'd been there for the past year, and wasn't eager to quit, despite the long bus commute. She'd never learned to drive.

Ten days later, on Saturday, August 27, Maureen crossed the street to pick up a few groceries at 7-Eleven. Convenience is everything when you don't have a car. A young black man with a bright smile began making small talk with her. I don't know what he said; I don't know his routine. I do know, however, that Maureen had little experience with guys, smooth-talking or otherwise. She had never dated in high school.

Whatever his line was, evidently it worked. Within the next two weeks, she fell in love with Tobey Hicks. Later, too late, we learned that she'd told her friends Kathy and Marcie about this "great guy" she was dating, someone who always seemed to have money and friends, but no job. She told them that she and Tobey would drive around Seattle, stopping at different places to buy cigarettes, and everywhere they went, Tobey had friends who hung around the car and were "real friendly" to her. One time when they were out cruising, the car "sort of blew up," so Tobey just walked off and left it.

Maureen never mentioned her new boyfriend to anyone in the

family. Maybe the relationship was just too new, and she wanted to get to know Tobey better before introducing him, but I doubt it. Dad would have been furious if he had known she was dating a black man. Maybe Tobey's race and his lifestyle were even part of his attraction for her. Maureen knew he was somebody our parents wouldn't approve of.

Dad never considered himself a racist. He just didn't see it that way. In addition to his strong sense of morality and intense urge to protect his daughters' honor (and thereby his own name), he did not believe in mixing breeds, regardless of the species: canine, bovine, equine, or human. Almost every animal he bought was purebred, with registration papers to prove it. I never heard him express attitudes of racial superiority; he simply did not believe in interracial dating or marriage.

Two weeks after Maureen met Tobey, all the money she'd been saving for her return visit to Mexico was gone. She had drained her bank accounts. Three withdrawals were noted in her bankbook, which my sisters found on the floor of her apartment after her disappearance. The police verified that one withdrawal was from an ATM on Sunday, September 11, 1983. Two more were made on Monday. One was from savings, the other from checking. Bank video footage showed a young black man at Maureen's side each time she made a withdrawal. The total amounted to only $390, but she was left with nothing. In her bankbook, her childish handwriting noted "withdrew for T".

That bankbook was held in one of the large binders in the offices of the Green River Task Force for over twenty years before I was able to retrieve it, along with her other personal documents, after Gary Ridgway's confession in 2003.

With no knowledge of the new developments in Maureen's personal life, our sister Doreen picked her up on Sunday morning, September 18, and they drove to Redmond, a suburb to the east of Lake Washington, to visit Marleen, our eldest sister. These weekend visits were quite normal. Either the sisters got together at Marleen's place, or they all converged at the family home in Issaquah for Sunday dinner. Later, when Marleen and Doreen tried to remember this last visit, they agreed that Maureen was moody, but then she was often moody. Nothing seemed out of the ordinary.

At the time, Marleen was seven months pregnant. She had hoped Maureen would accept her offer to be her live-in nanny after the baby was born, but Maureen made it clear she wasn't interested in the job offer. She also told them she wasn't returning to Mexico to visit me in November, as planned. When Marleen and Doreen pressed her, she told them she didn't have enough money for the trip.

On Monday, September 26, only eight days after this visit, Maureen didn't show up for work at the childcare center in Bellevue. The following day, she called in and quit her beloved job. She gave no explanation. She never picked up her final paycheck.

That same Monday, a Seattle police officer gave someone using the name Kris Tammy Ponds two consecutive jaywalking tickets at the corner of South Jackson Street and Maynard Avenue South, in the International District of downtown Seattle. Twenty years later, I first saw the tickets in the Green River Task Force files. Two sixteen-dollar citations: Incident #3221011 and Incident #3221012. The ticketing officer wrote the following comment on the second ticket: "W/F crossed against red 1 minute after I wrote her ticket #3221011." It wasn't Maureen's name, but it was her address, phone number, and date of birth on both tickets. The physical description was close: "Height 5'4," Weight 135, Eyes Blu, Hair Brn."

The officer was moving prostitutes out of the area by harassing them with tickets—not an uncommon practice. The Seattle Police Department and Gary Ridgway shared a common goal: they were trying to clear the streets of Seattle of prostitutes. At some point during the five months of interviews following Ridgway's plea agreement in 2003, he made the following statement:

> ...I was doing you guys a favor, killing, killing prosititutes, here you guys can't control them, but I can...I was doing uh, like I said, doing you a favor that you couldn't, you guys couldn't do. You couldn't uh, I mean if its illegal aliens, you can take 'em to the border and fly 'em back out 'a there. But if it's a prostitute, you'd arrest 'em, they were back on the street as soon as they get bail and change their uh, name, and you guys, you guys had the problem. I had, I had the answer... (*Superior Court of Washington for King County, State of Washington vs. Gary Leon Ridgway, Prosecutor's Summary of the Evidence, p. 131*)

Twenty years before Ridgway made this statement, two months after her disappearance in November 1983, Maureen's case was turned over to the Green River Task Force. At that time, Task Force detectives questioned the officer who ticketed Kris Ponds and showed him a picture of Maureen. The officer couldn't make a positive identification; he'd given out too many similar citations. Handwriting comparisons of the signature on the ticket and writing samples collected from Maureen's apartment were also inconclusive. Still, there was enough circumstantial evidence to convince the Task Force that Kris Tammy Ponds and Maureen were one and the same person.

That Wednesday, two days after Kris Ponds was ticketed, Mom decided to give Maureen a call to see how she was adjusting to her new life in the city. It was 10:00 a.m. She and Dad were at their beach home in Grayland, Washington, an isolated retirement community on the Pacific Ocean. Three or four streets, like strings of black pearls, lying parallel to miles of endless gray sand. It was late September, and many of the neighbors were packing up to head south for the winter. Mom dialed Maureen's number, and a man answered the phone.

"He's a friend," Maureen told Mom when she eventually got on the line. "His name's Fred."

Mom hesitated, not wanting to intrude, but concerned all the same. It was the concern, I suppose, of any mother of a nineteen-year-old living alone in a big city for the first time. "Be careful," Mom said. "Be careful, Maureen."

That was the last time anyone in the family spoke with Maureen.

After hanging up the phone, Mom called Doreen at work to tell her about the conversation. She mentioned the defensive tone in Maureen's voice and asked Doreen if she knew anything about a guy named Fred.

A mother's intuition. Something was wrong.

At the time, Doreen was working full-time days and attending classes every evening at the University of Washington, but busy as she was, Mom's phone call was still churning in her head the following evening. At 10:00 p.m., she called Maureen's apartment to check on her. Tobey Hicks answered the phone. He said Maureen wasn't there, but he expected her anytime. He'd have her call when she got in or, if it was late, the next day. Doreen never got a call.

Instead, the following morning, my parents had a phone message from Tobey Hicks. He'd found the number in Maureen's address book, he said. He wanted Maureen to call him; he didn't know where she was. Later that day, sometime around noon, Doreen called Maureen's apartment again. And again, Tobey answered the phone. "I just called your parents' house looking for Maureen," he said. "She left Wednesday afternoon and never came back."

Doreen was shocked. According to this stranger, Maureen had been missing for almost forty-eight hours. "How'd you get into her apartment?" she demanded.

"I was here when she left. She was headed for a job interview. Said she'd be right back, so I decided to hang here for her."

"Do you have a key to my sister's apartment?" Doreen was uneasy; she didn't like the idea of this stranger in her sister's space.

"Naw, there's an extra here in the apartment. I'm using that."

"Okay, I'm coming over. Please leave the apartment and leave the key on the table."

"Sure. Okay. Oh, yeah, I called the cops. They told me to call your folks, so I did. I left a message on their machine."

Doreen repeated that she wanted him out of the apartment by the time she got there and hung up the phone. Then, with fear crawling up the back of her neck, she called Mom and Dad's Grayland phone number. Mom's intuition had become her own.

"Mom, did you get a phone message for Maureen from someone named Tobey?"

"Yes, it was here on the machine when your Dad and I got back from the post office," Mom said. "He asked us to have her call him. Do you know who he is?"

"All I know is that he was in Maureen's apartment when I called. He said Maureen left for a job interview Wednesday afternoon and never came back. We need to call the police."

In our family, Doreen has always been the Rock of Gibraltar, the one with a solid head on her shoulders, the one who could handle any situation with calm determination. Like Mom, she rarely shows emotion, but it runs deep, just like her strength. Mom followed her advice and immediately called the Seattle Police Department to file a missing person's report. She was told the police could do nothing until three days had passed. At nineteen, Maureen was considered an adult.

About half an hour after talking with Mom, Doreen called the apartment again. Tobey was still there. She asked him to look in Maureen's address book for her friends' numbers. That done, Tobey said he was leaving the apartment. He gave Doreen his number as well as his dad's name and number. He asked her to call him if she heard from Maureen.

Doreen didn't go to the apartment that evening. She had called Marleen, who convinced her not go to the apartment alone, or at night. They agreed that it might not be safe. They didn't know who Tobey was, but he obviously had access to Maureen's apartment. They arranged to meet outside the apartment early the next morning, which was a Saturday, a rare day neither of them had to work.

Doreen made a few more calls that evening. She called Maureen's two closest friends, Kathy and Marcie. They both confirmed that Maureen was dating a black guy named Tobey, but neither of them had met him.

At 8:00 a.m. on Saturday, October 1, 1983, Doreen again called Maureen's apartment, hoping to hear her younger sister's irritated voice on the line. Instead, she heard Tobey's voice. She asked him what he was still doing there, and he claimed to have just arrived from his dad's house in West Seattle. He said he had taken the extra key the night before, when he left. She told him that she and Marleen were on their way over.

The two sisters met on the street in front of Maureen's apartment and entered together. Tobey was still there. As they walked through the door, he looked behind them, as if checking to see who they'd brought with them. The apartment was littered with fast food trash and Tobey's clothes. He said he had just brought them over from his dad's place that morning, but Doreen counted six pairs of men's shoes on the open closet floor, as well as several pairs of pants and shirts on hangers lying over the back of the only chair.

Tobey told my sisters that he was worried because Maureen hadn't returned from her job interview on Wednesday, and that's why he had stayed all night in the apartment waiting for her, and why he'd been coming back off and on to look for her. He said that she was wearing blue jeans and an old, brownish-gray wool jacket when she left. She wasn't carrying anything. Not even a purse.

None of Maureen's clothes seemed to be missing, and a tidy pile of her identification cards lay on the small table in the kitchenette. Next to the cards was an envelope addressed in Maureen's loopy script to my apartment in Mexico City. Opening the envelope, my sisters found the following undated letter:

Dear Arleen,
I'm sorry, but due to an unfortunate mistake I can't afford to come to Mexico after all. I know that in my last letter I said I was definately coming, but it just didn't work out. Don't get me wrong, I want to come and I sincerely apologize for getting your hopes up and changing your

plans etc. Never-the-less, its impossible. I guess thats all I really need to say. I'll write again later. Again, I am sorry, for you and for me.

> With love,
> Maureen

P.S. Send mail to Mom & Dads address.

Next to the letter and pile of ID cards, Maureen had also left a to-do list. It included an 8:15 a.m. appointment on Thursday at Planned Parenthood. When Doreen asked Tobey about the appointment, he claimed he'd known nothing about it. He said he had called Planned Parenthood when he saw the note, but they wouldn't tell him what the appointment was for, only that Maureen hadn't shown up or canceled.

"Are you and Maureen dating?" Doreen asked. Already certain of the answer, she was expecting a denial, and Tobey's answer didn't surprise her.

"Naw, we're just good friends," he said, looking down at his feet. "I don't think she's dating anybody. She's too shy. And, you know, it's like she doesn't know her way around at all. It's like I'm her tour guide or something."

As he was talking, Doreen saw Maureen's bankbook lying open on the floor among the scattered newspapers. She motioned to Marleen, not wanting Tobey to notice, and they both saw the withdrawals with the notation "withdrew for T."

At that point, Doreen and Marleen just wanted Tobey out of the apartment. They were worried about Maureen and growing suspicious of Tobey's possible involvement in her disappearance. They took the extra set of keys from him, offered him a ride, and drove him to his grandmother's house in the Central District, a small, gray house with pink trim. They went in and met his elderly grandmother. Tobey called to someone he referred to as an uncle upstairs; he asked if Maureen had phoned. The uncle didn't come down.

Doreen and Marleen returned to Maureen's apartment. From there, they called Mom and Dad at the beach house and called Maureen's friends, as well. There was still no sign of her.

They made another call to Missing Persons and spoke with Detective Gordon of the Seattle Police Department. He was the same officer Mom had spoken with the day before when she attempted to file a missing person report. They told him about the identification cards, about the bankbook, and about Tobey Hicks.

When he heard the name Hicks, Detective Gordon's response was chilling. "She's not mixed up with him! He's got a record a mile long for drugs and extortion. We know the whole family down here. Prostitution's a very real possibility if she's mixed up with the Hicks."

Not a piece of news anyone wants to hear about her sister.

Our family has always used a combination of absolute denial and excessive activity to cope with the unbearable. So, when Detective Gordon mentioned prostitution, my sisters refused to believe that Maureen willingly chose to prostitute herself. The only alternative explanation for her disappearance, and the one they immediately embraced, was that when she realized she was in trouble, mixed up with a guy like Tobey, she ran away, and she was hiding somewhere. After discussing their options, they set to work to find her. There was no time for tears. Tears were for alone time, at night in the darkness, with nobody around to watch.

They left a note in Maureen's apartment, urging her to call home. They also mailed her a letter, in case she checked her mailbox or arranged for the post office to forward her mail. They left their phone numbers with the assistant apartment manager, who assured them he would call as soon as he saw her. They took her ID cards, bankbook, to-do list, address book, and the letter to me. Then they began their search. They spent the weekend checking the YWCA and all the women's shelters in Seattle. They found no sign of our little sister.

On Sunday, October 2, Doreen again called Maureen's friend, Kathy, and learned that Maureen had told her that she and Tobey were planning a trip together. Where, she did not know. "I'm sorry," Kathy said. "I probably should've said something sooner, but I didn't want to violate Maureen's trust or anything."

"I understand," Doreen responded in her careful, clipped business tone. "So that's why Maureen couldn't work for Marleen or go to Mexico again. She wanted to go on a trip with Tobey."

"Yeah. I wanted to talk to Tobey myself, so I tried to reach him at the numbers Maureen gave me."

"No luck?"

"None."

On Monday, October 3, Mom called the Bellevue daycare center where Maureen had worked. The owner told her that during the second and third weeks of September, Maureen was a changed person—edgy, irritable, argumentative—not at all the happy-go-lucky Maureen the kids adored. She was supposed to have worked on Monday and Tuesday, September 26 and 27. The owner had called Maureen's apartment when she didn't show up for work, and Tobey had told her that Maureen was sick at Providence Hospital. The manager called the hospital to verify, and was told that Maureen had never been admitted.

That evening, Mom, Dad and my youngest brother, Andrew, went to clear out Maureen's apartment. This is one of those family mysteries I doubt I will ever understand: only five days after Maureen's disappearance, my parents were packing up her belongings and terminating her lease. I'm not certain those directly involved understood it even when they were in the midst of it. When I first learned of this, months after the fact, I was shocked. Why so soon, I wanted to scream. But I was too busy trying to be the perfect prodigal daughter to ask the difficult questions.

As I look back on it now, I realize that it makes sense on several levels. For Mom, closure was needed. By then, she knew in her heart that her youngest child was dead. She felt it. Years later, she called it a mother's intuition.

For Dad, it was an opportunity to get his daughter, or at least her belongings, out of a dumpy apartment building in a seedy neighborhood that he had never wanted her to move into in the first place. With Tobey hanging around, there was even more of a reason, in his mind, to terminate the lease.

And for Andrew, it was just a chance to help out, to do something. The sense of helplessness was overwhelming for all of them. By moving Maureen's belongings out of that apartment, they closed that part of the story and did not have to return to it. Perhaps they thought they could erase a bit of the shame that even the suggestion of prostitution brought down on the family.

As my parents were entering Maureen's apartment, a neighbor named Bobby approached them in the hall and told them he had heard a fight there the night of Wednesday, September 28, the night Tobey said Maureen had never come home. Bobby said he was visiting another neighbor, a friend who lived across the hall from Maureen's apartment. "I heard some loud noise in the hall, so I looked out through the peephole. There was at least one black guy, maybe more, and I heard a girl's voice."

"What'd she say?" Andrew asked.

"I think it was something like, 'What are you doing here?' Then they moved into Maureen's apartment. The fighting and screaming continued until about three a.m."

None of the neighbors had bothered to call 911.

The next morning, Mom called Detective Gordon and reported what Bobby had told them. Detectives questioned Bobby, but daylight had changed his story. Now, it was an argument he had heard, not a fight. He said he didn't see anyone well enough to identify them. He also said the argument was around midnight, not at 3:00.

Wednesday, October 5, 1983: Maureen's twentieth birthday. That evening, Mom and Doreen went back to the apartment to move out the last of Maureen's clothes. While they were cleaning out the apartment, another neighbor, Shane, came over to tell them about the fight on Wednesday night.

"It started at about 11:30. At first, it just sounded like a normal argument, you know. But then it sounded like they were knocking each other around in there. And then, the screaming started, and that went on for a long time."

"Another neighbor, Bobby, told my parents the same thing," Doreen said between clenched teeth, trying to control her tears of anger and frustration. What I'm sure she wanted to scream was, "Why the hell didn't you call 911?" Instead, she said, "When the police questioned him, his story changed. What about you? Will your story change too?"

"No," Shane assured her. "I'll tell the cops exactly what I heard. And by the way, I saw Tobey go into Maureen's apartment again on Sunday. He wasn't in there for more than a few minutes. And then he left."

"Just this last Sunday, October second?"

"Yeah, I thought it was kind of weird."

If Shane saw Tobey on Sunday, the set of keys Tobey gave Doreen and Marleen on Saturday, October 1, wasn't the only set he had. Tobey had secrets he wasn't telling. Again, my family reported what they'd learned to the Seattle Police Department.

Finally, on Thursday, October 6, the SPD called Tobey in to answer some questions. Tobey didn't show up for his 9:00 a.m. appointment the next day. It took another three days for the police to track him down at his father's house.

In his statement, Tobey denied getting money from Maureen or having plans to go on a trip with her. He mixed up his stories by saying Maureen had plans to go to Mexico to babysit for her sister. He also denied having had a fight with Maureen in her apartment. They asked him who she had been screaming at if it wasn't him. He said he may have gone out for a while, insinuating that Maureen may have had another visitor. He also denied going back to the apartment on Sunday, October 2.

There were holes in Tobey's story, but the SPD was done with him. They had nothing to pin on him, no proof of criminal wrongdoing. With Hicks's criminal record, they assumed Maureen was just another young prostitute. Unless she filed some kind of complaint against Tobey, there was nothing more they could do with him.

The following weekend, Doreen and Maureen's friend, Kathy, plastered the Capitol Hill neighborhood with posters of Maureen's smiling face and a detailed description. "MISSING PLEASE HELP US FIND: MAUREEN... REWARD OFFERED FOR RELIABLE INFORMATION." Since she had Kathy's help, Doreen convinced Marleen to stay at home. Her pregnancy was too far along to handle any more physical and emotional strain.

For the next month, my family heard nothing from the SPD.

On Friday, November 4, my eldest brother, Robert, arrived from his home in Hawaii. He and Andrew conducted a two-week search of every sleazy hellhole in the Seattle area, distributing pictures, asking questions, offering rewards. But it was as though the earth had swallowed Maureen, erasing all trace of her existence. For months afterwards, Doreen continued to receive phone calls from contacts Robert had made, from people claiming to have seen Maureen, but none of them led anywhere.

As Robert and Andrew continued their search, the SPD also cranked up their investigation. On Thursday, November 17, the local KING-5 television evening news aired a broadcast about six missing girls that Detective Gordon was "listing as being possibly connected with the Green River case." Detective Gordon showed pictures and gave names, including Maureen's. He asked that anyone having information about these young women contact him at the SPD Missing Persons office.

For the 11:00 p.m. broadcast, reporter Aaron Brown expanded the story, saying that some of these missing women were involved in prostitution, and explaining that the vice squad was cracking down on prostitution along the airport strip.

Doreen was furious. The next morning, she called Detective Gordon and demanded to know why he had not told the family in advance about the Green River connection or the television coverage. Detective Gordon apologized, explaining that he had agreed to the broadcast for publicity, in case someone in the viewing audience might have information on any of the six missing young women. He said the 5:00 p.m. news had covered the story well: these girls were missing, and the police were looking for any possible leads. But the 11:00 p.m. reporter had rewritten the script to tie it into the story of prostitution on the airport strip. Detective Gordon had received other angry phone calls, and he suggested Doreen complain to Julie Blacklow at KING-TV, who had written the original story.

Detective Gordon also told Doreen that he had turned over a list of all of the missing women in the SPD's files to the Green River Task Force. He said that, as far as the police knew, there was no connection between Maureen's case and the Green River investigations; they were just being thorough. At the same time, though, he requested a copy of Maureen's dental records.

Doreen promptly called Julie Blacklow to complain about the prostitution focus of the 11:00 p.m. broadcast. Ms. Blacklow apologized, saying she'd been getting calls all morning from relatives and friends of the missing girls. No one wants a relative, missing or otherwise, labeled as a prostitute, even if it is true. Ms. Blacklow said she'd known nothing about the rewritten script, but the station was planning on airing a correction on both the 5:00 p.m. and the 11:00 p.m. broadcasts that would make it clear that Maureen and others were not involved in prostitution. Doreen thanked her and hung up.

That evening, Doreen watched as KING-5 reporter Jean Enersen clarified: they had made an error in their broadcast the night before. She said that Maureen and another girl had no record of prostitution, and that police had no reason to suspect they had ties to the notorious airport strip. She apologized to family and friends for the mistake.

Still, the tie to the Green River Task Force, and thus to prostitution, had been established in the public mind. Maureen became a public commodity with a label.

And the label read: disposable.

November passed with the birth of Marleen's only child, a healthy, beautiful son, born in the midst of confusion and pain. Robert returned to his home in Hawaii, and the family settled into a waiting mode, waiting for some kind of news, some kind of resolution. It was a long wait.

There were no Christmas celebrations that year.

The new year began with a five-part series in *The Seattle Times* on the Green River murder case, entitled "Deadly mystery: 46 young women missing over 3 years." In the first of the series, which was written by staff reporters Carlton Smith and Paul Henderson, all of the young women were listed. Maureen was included as number forty-two.

Since January 1981, 46 young women ranging in age from 13 to 38 have either been killed or have been reported missing under suspicious circumstances.

Although many of the 32 dead and 14 missing were active in prostitution—at least half had records of convictions for prostitution, or contacts with police—a sizeable number had no known records at all.

More than half were under 19, with the average age being just over 20. *(The Seattle Times, January 15, 1984, page D2)*

Prior to Maureen's disappearance, my family had been extremely private. My parents raised their children on an isolated farm in the Issaquah Valley, as far as they could get from the dangers of city life while still being able to commute to the city to work each day. Now, it felt like the family morals were being examined under a microscope, with images broadcast on the nightly news. We felt watched and judged by everyone in the Seattle metro area.

Reading and watching media speculation about the secrets and whereabouts of your nearest and dearest is an experience no one should have. To hear the press tell it, Maureen had broken all the family rules. My family could only stare at the headlines and ask themselves: my God, how did we get here?

Chapter Four: The First Myth

It's odd how a word can become part of one's personal lexicon without thinking about it, without understanding, without even questioning. The word is just there. It just exists, a bit like the homeless people living under the overpasses along Interstate 5. The word (like the homeless) is there, but you don't think about it. You don't notice it. It just is.

Throughout my childhood, and even as an adult, I'd heard the words "cadet nurse" as the reason my mother had come to Seattle in 1946, but I had no idea what they meant. I knew my mother had gone to Mounds-Midway Nursing School in St. Paul, Minnesota, straight out of high school, completing her training in an intensive, what today would be called fast-track, nursing program during World War II. I also knew that she was a registered nurse, of course, but I hadn't known what "cadet" meant. Moreover, it took me almost fifty years to finally realize I had no idea what my mother was talking about when she said she was a cadet nurse. To be specific, it took me almost fifty years to realize that I had never asked.

Just recently, I tried to ask Mom a different question. I knew she'd been a cadet nurse working at the U.S. Marine Hospital in Seattle. I also knew that she'd been a flight attendant working for United Airlines, based in Seattle. I didn't know which was first, or even how she came to be in Seattle. What had brought her from St. Paul to Seattle, where she crossed paths with my father, fell in love, and stayed for the rest of her life?

But it was too late. She couldn't remember.

So, I googled "cadet nurse." I learned at the click of a computer key what I had not known my entire life. In 1943, there was a severe shortage of nurses both at home and abroad, due to American involvement in World War II. Between 1943 and 1948, close to 125,000 nurses graduated from accelerated nursing programs affiliated with the Cadet Nurse Corps. They were required to complete their program within thirty months, as opposed to the standard thirty-six months, and work either in the U.S. military or civilian service for the duration of WWII.

I don't know if my mother chose the Marine hospital in Seattle for her work training, or if she was assigned there. She found herself working in a sixteen-story, orange brick, Art-Deco tower crowning the northern edge of Beacon Hill, overlooking downtown Seattle. She and the other cadets lived on-site in dormitory-style accommodations in the hospital. The building now houses the corporate headquarters of the online retailer, Amazon dot.com.

It was in the U.S. Marine Hospital that my parents first met. The story goes like this: my father was dating a friend of Mom's, another cadet nurse. One night, he brought Mom's friend home from a date after curfew, and Mom was mad. She was a diligent, hard-working young woman who followed the rules. She didn't want her friend getting in trouble because her date didn't bring her home before curfew. I can see this pretty, petite blonde with bright green eyes and a tiny waist shaking her finger at Dad as he towered over her with a cocky grin on his face, a jet black curl falling over his forehead and his bright blue eyes twinkling. They were married on December 6, 1947, and they were inseparable for over fifty years, until the day Dad died.

World War II had ended, and the country was still celebrating. My father was never in military service, though. He had bad eyes, bad knees, and served as his mother's sole support, so he was never a candidate for the draft. Instead, he worked at Seattle's Todd Ship Yards as a welder. Todd Ship Yards had been a landmark on the Seattle waterfront since 1916. By 1940, the shipyard was designing, building, and repairing destroyers for the U.S. Navy. At the peak of World War II, Todd employed over 20,000 people in its waterfront construction and repair facilities between downtown Seattle and the small West Seattle peninsula where Dad grew up, and where I now make my home. Seven days after Japan bombed Pearl Harbor, Dad turned twenty-one, and he was already developing his talents as a welder, steamfitter, and craftsman, skills he would use for the remainder of his life.

After standing before a judge to be married, Mom and Dad moved into a shack on Marine View Drive in West Seattle. Dad expanded the footprint of the shack by pouring a new foundation. He put up new exterior walls, rebuilt the roof, and divided the new interior space into rooms, thus turning the shack into a house. When the Big Kids—Marleen, Robert, Laureen and Charleen—reached school age, Dad and Mom moved their growing family into a larger house on Walnut Avenue, where the kids could walk the few blocks to Lafayette Elementary School.

Despite having grown up in Seattle, Dad wanted to raise his growing family in the countryside. So, in 1959, my parents bought ten acres of undeveloped land on the side of Tiger Mountain in the Issaquah Valley, about twenty-five miles southeast of downtown Seattle. Today, this valley and the entire east side of Lake Washington have been developed into suburban cul-de-sacs. But in 1959, Issaquah was nothing more than a sleepy, one-street town. The Issaquah-Hobart Road had so little traffic that we rode horses along the shoulders. My father spent every weekend and holiday for the next year putting in a rough access road, clearing the land, finding a water source and preparing a building site for our new home.

The following summer, we moved into a large green army surplus tent with a tall center pole, which was naturally a circus tent to my infatuated, five-year-old eyes. At that point, I had six siblings: Marleen, Robert, Laureen, Charleen, Doreen, and Michael. Marleen, the eldest, turning twelve in July, was tall and thin, with dark hair and Dad's vivid blue eyes. Robert would be eleven in September. He was wiry and thin, with the same blue eyes, but wild, curly blond hair. Even at age nine, Laureen was different from the rest of us. She was a soft, pudgy child with bright red hair, the only redhead in the family and the only one unhappy about leaving the city. Charleen had just celebrated her eighth birthday in April. Small, thin, and allergic, she was inquisitive and full of energy. Then there was me. Born cross-eyed, at five I was a dark-haired ball of mischief with thick, Coke-bottle glasses. Doreen was a sweet, curly-headed blonde who wouldn't be a two-year-old until August, and Michael wasn't yet six months old. Later, Andrew and Maureen would join the family, making us a family of eleven.

We were named and raised Irish-American—this despite Mom's German heritage. The girls were all "eens," tied together with a suffix by parents who seemed to believe that we were as similar as peas in a pod. In their strong sense of fairness, they tried to treat us all the same, without realizing that in doing so, they were compromising our individuality. Somehow the "eens" made me feel less important, an incomplete part of a larger whole, ill-equipped to stand alone.

By contrast, each of the boys was unique, different, special from the moment of birth. Each was given a name of his own. I always wanted to be a boy. If I were a boy, I'd be special. I'd get more attention. I felt I was a disappointment to my parents: just another girl. I was the fourth girl at a time when Dad still had only one son, one helper. I should've been a son. Instead, I was a tomboy, trying as hard as I could to keep up with my older brother.

One day, shortly after starting elementary school, I was walking up our long dirt driveway with Robert, who was a lanky adolescent at the time. I was struggling to keep up with him. At one point, he stopped, looked me up and down, and said, "You've got long legs, Arleen. Use them." And then he started walking again, fully expecting me to keep up with him despite the difference in the length of our legs. It was probably that guy-walk I developed to copy my older brother that convinced my parents to send me to "charm and modeling school" years later, when I was a teenager.

Despite my insecurity, I never heard a single complaint from my parents about all their daughters, never a word of disappointment from either of them. Still, I felt it.

That first summer in the tent was an adventure: ten acres of wilderness to explore. A deep, wooded ravine ran along one edge of the property, the Issaquah Creek at its base. Dad had bulldozed a rough road down the hillside to the creek and dug a well. He had also built a pump house around the well and laid water pipes up the ravine to the building site. The foundation poured, Dad was ready to start construction of our future home. Before we knew it, we had a framed-in basement and running water.

But at five, who cares? All I was interested in was the creek at the base of the ravine. My older sisters and I wandered to our hearts' content, both parents too overwhelmed with the magnitude of their adventure to do much supervising. Mom used the buddy system, so each sister was responsible for at least one younger sibling. We were never assigned an explicit buddy. Instead, we were all responsible for each other; the eldest on any adventure was always in charge. We never went anywhere without Mom's words ringing in our ears, "Keep an eye on (insert name of youngest sibling)."

Siblings raising siblings. Children responsible for children. A responsibility now, in my mind, burdened with deep, unbearable pain. And Robert, the eldest son, was Dad's shadow, always working, always learning, always excited about the next project.

As we roamed the dark, wet ravine, we cut trails through the thick undergrowth, imagining ourselves brave explorers, charting new and exotic lands. The scent of the Northwest woods never left me, even during my years living on the arid plateau of Mexico City:

the damp of fern and blackberries and moss and Oregon grape, of rotting leaves and fallen logs, a musty, moist fragrance that never dissipates, even in the heat of August. An ancient, rich aroma of decomposition intermingled with new growth that reminds me, still, of our tenuous existence on earth. Even as a young child, I was aware of the miraculous cycle of life that engulfed me.

One day in our wanderings, we discovered the Big Rock. A boulder the size of a small house with a large, rotting old-growth snag on top, its roots draped down one side of the rock to the rich earth below. To this day, mention the Big Rock to anyone in my family, and it conjures memories of cool retreats on hot summer days. The rock was lodged into the hillside and loomed over the creek below. From the upper hillside, we climbed down to the top of the rock, where we could lie on our bellies to watch the creek water flow below us. On energetic days, we scrambled down into the creek itself, to work on our swimming hole. Using old pails or coffee cans, we dug rocks and endless quantities of mud and sand from the creek bottom, trying to make the water deeper so that we could swim. We carried logs from the wooded hillside to build a dam in hopes of slowing the flow of the creek water. No amount of adult logic could convince us of the futility of our project.

That first summer in the tent was before the silence and taboos, before my family created myths to ease our pain. The adventure of roughing it appealed to both kids and parents, like some kind of Swiss Family Robinson fantasy, only our isolation was by choice. At least by our parents' choice.

When we weren't down in the ravine, we were playing in the woods, staking out territories and building rival camps. As we played and explored, Mom kept house in the tent, taking care of baby Michael. Dad continued working full-time as a steamfitter in Seattle, but evenings and weekends were dedicated to building our new home, until daylight faded and he was forced to stop. I can still hear his jovial words, "Time to call it a day."

He closed in the basement foundation with the creative energy and master craftsmanship of a gifted artisan. He put up floor supports and laid plywood for the first floor, and we had a ceiling for the basement. He plumbed a bathroom and laundry sink, and Mom set up kitchen in the future laundry room. She still used a large Coleman stove, one of those green metal suitcase-looking things with four burners inside, but at least there was running water and a bathroom with a toilet and a hot shower.

My older siblings claim that we did not live full-time in the tent, but instead, we only spent weekends there, Friday night to Monday morning, until the basement was finished and we could move into the house. Perhaps they're right, technically, but to me, the summer of 1960 will always be the summer of the tent adventure. I danced around the tent pole, stumbling over folded sleeping bags and boxes of supplies, imagining myself a famous circus dancer, until Dad or Mom yelled at me. "Stop messing around before you knock down the whole tent."

By the time school started that fall, we moved into the unfinished house. As preparations began to enter a new school seven miles away in the town of Issaquah, the huge army surplus tent, our home for the summer, was packed away for future camping trips.

I was only five in September of 1960, but my birthday is in October, so Mom was able to convince the school to let me skip kindergarten and start first grade, thus making it possible for me to go to school and return with my older siblings. Every morning, we trekked down our long, rutted dirt road, dusty in the summer and muddy in the winter, to catch the school bus on the Issaquah-Hobart Road. There was an old metal box for shoes at the bottom of the driveway. We wore old shoes for the hike and carried our school shoes to change into before getting on the bus. Mom always wanted us to look nice for school, and besides, she knew our "school shoes" would last longer if we only wore them at school. Keeping so many kids in shoes was expensive, even in the early 1960s.

I remember racing to catch the bus and, at times, not having time to change shoes before boarding. What to do with the old, stinky barn shoes? One day, when I was still in elementary school, I left them on the school bus. I didn't have a bag to hide them in, and I was too embarrassed to carry them into school with me. I dumped my lunch out of my brown paper sack onto the empty seat beside me and tried to cram my dirty shoes into it, but all I managed to do was rip the sack. In frustration, I changed into my school shoes on the bus, stashing the barn shoes, the ripped sack, and my lunch under the seat. I never retrieved them. After school, I walked up the long, dirty driveway as carefully as I could, determined to keep my good shoes as clean as possible. I avoided the mud puddles, despite the urge to splash and play. When I reached the house, I snuck straight to the furnace room, found an old rag, and rubbed my brown and white saddle shoes until they shined.

I never told Mom what I had done. I knew she'd be mad at me for losing a perfectly good pair of work shoes just because I was worried about what the other kids at school would think of me. I never wanted my parents to be mad at me. Their anger frightened me. Dad's anger was loud, and then he'd turn and walk away like I didn't even exist. Mom's anger was quiet and disapproving. She was always busy with the youngest child, so making trouble meant making more work for her. I kept my secret, and my silence protected me. They never found out. Because we were so many kids, there was a large box full of old shoes and cowboy boots of various sizes in the furnace room. Some of them were worn-out school shoes, shoes that had been handed down so many times they were no longer presentable for school. That was Mom's word, "presentable." She always wanted us to be clean, neat and presentable, no matter how tight the family budget. So after I left the shoes on the bus, I made do with whatever I could find from the furnace room shoebox. Even though I was never caught, never scolded or punished, and even though there were plenty of old shoes in the furnace room shoebox to protect my silence, I never left shoes on the bus again.

* * *

By the time our first Christmas at the new house arrived, we were settled into our new life. We still didn't have a chimney, or even finished interior walls, so I worried that Santa Claus would never find us. But Mom and the Big Kids solved the problem. My mother was resourceful, and in her quiet way, she found solutions to our concerns, often times without our awareness of her intervention. That first Christmas, Mom and the Big Kids used a large piece of butcher paper to create a chimney, complete with red bricks and a fireplace full of red and orange Crayola flames consuming a large pile of logs. They hung the paper chimney on an unfinished wall and hammered nails into a two-by-four stud above it. The unconcealed, silver-foiled, wall insulation only added to the illusion of flames. On Christmas Eve, we ceremoniously hung our Christmas stockings on the bare nails, and Santa did, indeed, find us.

The following morning, as each of us made our way one-by-one from the upstairs bedrooms to the basement family room, Dad took family movies with an old reel-to-reel camera. We each clowned down the unfinished stairs to find what Santa might have left us under the tree. That first Christmas celebration in Issaquah was meager. In fact, all our Christmas celebrations were simple, with homemade gifts supplemented with necessary items such as pajamas and warm socks. I still have a few of those homemade gifts: a collection of news clippings and pictures memorializing the civil unrest of the 1960s, a burlap wall banner with the words "Stand beside your brother and take his hand" in hand-cut, felt lettering, and a hanging mobile made of driftwood and sand dollars with letters spelling out my name burned into the wood.

It was only when I went to school that I realized the orgy of gifts that Christmas meant to other kids. Only then did I feel inadequate answering the endless litany of, "What did you get for Christmas?"

It was usually on the playground, during the long lunch recess. Groups of girls stood in tight knots, comparing their Christmas hauls. I liked to listen, to hear the lists of treasures, but then they turned to me. "What about you, Arleen? What did you get?"

"Some pj's and some socks."

They laughed and turned their backs. I was no longer part of the group. After a few Januarys of humiliation, I learned to stay inside during recess, away from the groups of girlfriends and gossip. The school library became my refuge, the librarian my friend.

Walking through the library doors, the checkout desk was along the right wall, where the librarian always sat. In front of her was the fiction section, and just inside the doors, to the left, one or two shelves up from the floor, were the books whose authors' names began with the letter *F*. I read every book in Walter Farley's *The Black Stallion* series while sitting on the library floor, hidden from the playground questions and gossip. Hidden from friendship, lost in the wonderful silence of books.

During my elementary years, Dad built the house up around us, brick by brick. We had contests to see who could carry the most bricks to help him. Three or four was my limit. Robert always won, with stacks so high he struggled to see over the top. Bricking the house was one of the few times I remember Dad hiring someone to help with a construction project. Usually, he did everything himself, or with Robert's help, from foundation to finishing. Later, Michael and Andrew were his helpers. But to brick that first Issaquah house, he hired a skilled bricklayer, a man he respected. A man who happened to be black.

The day that Dad laid the last chimney brick was a day of jubilation. He stood on the high, pitched roof as we kids climbed the elaborate yellow scaffolding that stood alongside the house like some kind of jungle gym. We had the agility of little monkeys, learning to climb anything, without fear. We heard Dad's joyous, bellowing "Yaa Hooo!" echoing through the hills. And we watched as his dirty cowboy hat floated through the air to the ground far below. The chimney was finished. By the time our second Christmas rolled around, we were ready for Santa Claus.

Those first half dozen years in Issaquah were good years. I couldn't seem to make friends at school, but I had siblings to play with and we were as free as the wild animals that filled the woods around us. We didn't even have any close neighbors, but we had each other. For me, that was enough.

We built a large, three-story house as a family project, and we were all expected to do our share of the work. The top floor was the girls' dormitory, with enough floor space, despite the sloping ceilings on both sides, for six twin beds, two large closets, two built-in desks, and a bathroom for us all to share. From the front windows of the third floor dormitory and the second floor living room, we had an unobstructed view of Mount Rainier, marred only slightly by the distant lines of the Bonneville Power Administration. Our mountain. She watched over us day and night, even when we couldn't see her, which was a good part of the year in the cloudy, rainy Pacific Northwest. But on a clear day, we could almost reach out and touch her.

As Dad and Robert continued to fell trees and clear away the underbrush to create pastures, huge piles of wood debris formed, some as large as small houses. In time, these piles became bonfires that we tended for hours, but until then, they were a haven for a new kind of adventure, a forbidden adventure. The temptation was greater than our fear of danger or punishment. We crawled deep into the center of these woodpiles and made mazes of trails, building camps and hideouts in their bowels. Each of us staked claim to our own woodpile, or at least a particular area of one, and we played our own version of king-of-the-mountain until we heard Dad's booming voice yelling, "If I've told you kids once, I've told you a million times, stay out of those wood piles."

Every summer, I found a special place in the woods and marked off a small area as my camp. I built tiny rock walls or just lines of pebbles for the walls and doorways. I don't remember playing house, or even playing with dolls in my wooded camps. It was more the process of building and the sense of ownership that was important. In a large family, having a private space was rare. Building camps each summer was a way to define a sense of fledgling individuality in a family were clanship was taken to such an extreme that at times, when we were very young, the girls, Mom included, even dressed the same: red jackets, red pants, white scarves. Only size gave us individual definition.

On October 5, 1963, ten days before my ninth birthday, the ninth and final child was born, the fourth of the Little Kids. I was used to babies coming home from the hospital. It was just part of my life. Maureen was the last of a long string, fifteen years younger than Marleen, the first of the string. With her birth, the month of October was no longer mine. I had to share my month. In a family of eleven, it was important to own a month. A birthday was a time to be special, to be the center of attention, if only for a few hours.

With twelve months available, no one in a well-planned family should have to share one, even if it is a family of eleven. But our family was not well planned. It just happened. The first four kids— Marleen, Robert, Laureen and Charleen—the Big Kids, were all born about a year apart and all in different months: July, September, February, and April. There is a six-year gap between the four Big Kids and the four Little Kids—Doreen, Michael, Andrew, and Maureen. When the Little Kids started arriving, they took August, March, December, and my month of October. I don't remember any resentment about sharing my month, though. Sure, having your own special month was important, but for some reason, I didn't mind Maureen's arrival or having to share October with her. Perhaps I was already beginning to lose that sense of self that is so easily lost in a large family. This sweet little bald baby just seemed like an early birthday present.

I was the middle child, two and a half years younger than the last Big Kid and almost four years older than the first Little Kid. Too young to be one of the Big Kids and too old to be considered a Little Kid. The cheese in a toasted cheese sandwich, melted just enough to stick to both slices of bread, but alone all the same.

By the time Maureen reached her second birthday, she had turned into Goldilocks. That's how I came to think of my little sister—Goldilocks with beautiful long, golden curls. Even after she convinced Mom and Dad to let her get her hair cut short, she was still Goldilocks in my mind. I found an old, faded photograph taken in the mid 1960s. Mom and Dad are standing in front of a large red and white International Harvester pick-up truck. Dad is so thin I don't recognize him at first glance. Mom is petite and slender, not the typical image of a mother of nine kids. She wears a yellow and orange plaid, button-up-the-front, sleeveless cotton blouse.

I remember that blouse. Mom never gave clothes to charity.

"Charity begins at home," she used to remind us. When a piece of clothing had been passed down from sibling to sibling so long that it had too many holes in it for decency, it was used as a rag. If we absolutely refused to wear something because it didn't fit or was out of style, she still kept it, insisting that it would come back in style sooner or later and somebody could use it. As my own daughter, Erin, reached my mother's height when she was about ten years old, Mom put together bags of her old clothes to pass on to her, including that yellow and orange plaid blouse.

In a large family, nothing is wasted, not even words. In my family, words were never wasted, not in conversation, not in parenting. Mom and Dad used and reused old sayings to teach, to instill values, to replace conversation. "Waste not, want not" was a favorite.

We used and reused everything. With three older sisters, hand-me-downs made up the bulk of my wardrobe. But I wasn't the only one. We all shared. Maybe that's why later, as a young woman, deciding what I liked and didn't like, finding my own style, was hard for me. As a kid, I never had the opportunity to decide if I liked something or not. If it fit, I wore it.

It was different from the way my teenage daughter and her friends share and trade clothes. By comparison to the meager collection of clothes my sisters and I shared, Erin and her friends have vast wardrobes that they share because they want even more variety, because they want something new and different. Because it's fun to share, to trade.

Growing up, we were our own charity. Erin has no siblings. I had eight. Our clothes were worn to rags, and then used as such. Nothing was wasted, nothing was thrown out. In Mexico, they call it *el valor de uso*. As I look through family pictures, I laugh at the number of clothing items that reappear through the years, each time worn by a younger sibling.

* * *

Off and on throughout my childhood and adolescence, we had horses. Never more than a few at a time, and never enough for all of us to ride simultaneously, but we shared and it was wonderful. The first horse was Duchess, a large, powerful chestnut with a broad back and heavy legs. Robert would hitch her up with an old harness and use her to pull stumps or piles of brush. The Big Kids took turns riding and leading Duchess as she pulled. I was too little to participate much, so I wandered on the periphery, playing my own games, gathering my own piles of sticks, and imitating my older siblings. Where other kids played with toys, we learned to play with work. We had no toy horses, bulldozers, or dolls. Instead, we had the real thing, and we made a game of work. Duchess was just part of the game. As I grew older, there were different horses through the passing years. I remember Lady, Persnickety, and my favorite, Misty.

I also remember the first calves we owned, Chocolate and Cinnamon, food references that described the color of their coats. There was another as well, a sweet little white-faced heifer we named Calico. They wore little halters, and my sisters and I would attach lead ropes and try to take them for walks as though they were puppies, but it was more like playing a game of tug-of-war that we could never win. The calves were much stronger and always did what they chose, which was usually to graze. I loved those calves almost as much as any horse we ever owned, at least while they were small and playful—before they grew large, docile, and smelly. Before I realized we were expected to eat them.

My father never slaughtered any of the cows at home. Instead, he loaded them up in a truck or trailer and disappeared with them. The next time we saw them was on a dinner plate. A few weeks after the first cow disappeared, we were sitting down to dinner and someone asked, "Is this Chocolate?"

"It's roast, and we're lucky to have it," was Dad's stern answer.

There were a few times when I simply refused to eat, but hunger can be very persuasive, and so could Dad's angry face.

Dinner was always family style. Serving platters were put in the middle of the table and then passed around. We were allowed to serve ourselves, but we were required to eat everything we put on our plates. I learned the delicate balance between taking enough to satisfy my hunger, but not too much, in case it was something I just couldn't get down. In a large family, seconds were not always an option, so if you didn't take enough the first time the serving platter went around the table, there might not be anything left on it the second time. Dinnertime was a competitive time among the siblings—competition for food and for attention. We were a bit like baby birds in a nest, begging for food. The loudest, the most assertive, got more attention, both good and bad. No matter how badly I needed Mom and Dad's attention, if there was beef on the table, I usually avoided it and kept as quiet as I could.

I used to play a game under the big fir tree beside the house. I built my own slaughterhouse with scraps of building lumber. I filled my slaughterhouse with furry, black and orange caterpillars. I loved those caterpillars, just as I loved the cows, but I kept them in pens, and fattened them up for the slaughter. I could never actually bring myself to kill them, any more than I could understand how Mom and Dad could let anyone kill our cows.

Because a whole cow couldn't fit in our home freezer, my parents rented a cold storage locker in town. I hated going there and seeing the shelves full of white butcher-paper packages. If I happened to be with Mom when she went the locker to pick up meat for the week, I couldn't bear to go inside with her. I'd wait at the door until she came out.

Dad and Mom were city people. It never occurred to them to teach us to distinguish between pets and livestock. Or maybe they tried, and I just didn't get it. Maybe I refused to get it, stubborn denial already showing his demon head. We never owned a real working farm, only a few cows and chickens to enhance the family diet with fresh meat, milk and eggs. And a few horses, when we could afford the pleasure they offered.

In the early Issaquah years, when the family economy was extra tight, we rode the cows. We never actually saddled or bridled them. We rode bareback, with nothing more than a halter and a lead rope. We had no control. The cow wandered and grazed as it pleased, or bucked and ran. I remember sitting on their broad backs, my skinny, adolescent legs sticking straight out in opposite directions, clinging to the flesh on the ridge of the cow's neck and trying to stay on. Usually, I didn't. Falls were a common part of growing up on the farm. Nothing to get upset about. Nothing to worry about.

When we weren't riding the cows, when there were enough horses for two or three of us to ride, my favorite game was "fern war." The house Dad built faced Mt. Rainier and the high voltage power lines of the Bonneville Power Administration. In the sixties, it was still only one line. The second line, twice the size of the first, came after my parents sold that house and moved into another Dad built on the same property, the summer between my junior and senior years in high school. But even one line of domineering steel scaffolding, huge structures with wide arms holding three heavy wires, distracted from the natural beauty. They were imposing soldiers, marching with outstretched arms right over the top of Tiger Mountain and through the Issaquah Valley, soldiers that were stopped by nothing or no one, and who commanded an easement of land through every farm in their path—land and a service road. That endlessly long, narrow strip of land ran adjacent to our property. Our long, rutted, dirt driveway ran parallel to the service road. The area under the power lines afforded us kids an open space for horseback games, and right along with them, a lifelong love-hate relationship with the omnipotent Bonneville Power Administration.

Bonneville came through every few years to spray the encroaching blackberry vines and undergrowth and to rip up any new growth trees that could eventually threaten their precious wires, and thus the comfort of tens of thousands of Seattleites, but most of the time, the easement, or what we called the right-of-way, was a long, narrow summer meadow of Shasta daisies and ferns. I spent a large part of my childhood riding along the right-of-way road under the power lines. I loved the access Bonneville provided, but I hated the crackling electrical static I could hear in the lines above me, and I hated the way they marred our view of Mount Rainier.

Several kinds of ferns grew among the daisies in the cleared land under the power lines, but my favorite, by far, were bracken ferns, or what I used to call spear ferns. They had a feathery top, one sturdy stem, and a root that grew straight into the soil with only a question mark shaped hook at the end. When you pulled them out and ripped off the tops, you had a perfect spear.

My sister, Charleen, and I used to ride through the meadow, reins in our left hands, our bodies leaning to the right, pulling up the ferns. We stripped them of their lacy, leafy beauty and collected them until we had a handful of small spears. Then we aimed and threw them, racing towards each other on horseback in a wild game of fern warfare of our own creation.

I learned to ride on Misty's side with my left foot in a stirrup and my right barely over the top of her back for balance. I held the reins and a hank of Misty's long heavy mane in my left hand and kept my right free to throw fern spears at my opponents, shielded from their attack by Misty's broad body. I'm sure it wasn't a game she enjoyed.

Sometimes, a neighbor girl who lived above us on the Tiger Mountain Road joined us, a girl named Cookie who rode a horse named Candy. Or was the girl Candy and the horse Cookie? I could never keep it straight. She was Charleen's friend, not mine. Two and a half years younger, I was just the pain-in-the-butt little sister who was always tagging along. But Charleen was good to me, and we shared our love of horses.

We also loved to "sleep out." Every summer when the weather was warm enough, we would drag sleeping bags into the yard and sleep under the stars. Charleen was a great storyteller. One summer she told me a continuous adventure story, night after night, as we lay under the stars. She created a fantasyland and used her voice to help me escape there.

Because our long driveway ran parallel to the power line easement, Bonneville was a source of all kinds of childhood adventures. The driveway was about a half mile long, hot and dusty in the summer and full of ruts and mud puddles in the winter. Heading up the driveway from the Issaquah-Hobart Road, about mid-way from the road to our house, there was a steep incline. We called it the Big Hill. Like most of our favorite places, the name stemmed from usage. We got tired of saying things like, "Let's go down to that big rock by the creek," or "There's a huge mud puddle at the bottom of that big hill in the driveway." So, we had the Big Rock, the Big Hill, and later, when we noticed that the horses often grazed on the steep incline behind the barn, we had Horse Hill.

One exceptionally cold winter, the large mud puddle froze. That was the winter we dug Mom's old, white leather ice skates with their shiny silver blades out of the unfinished attic space under the eaves in the girls' dormitory, a space that was inhabited by mice that scampered around keeping me awake at night. To this day, I'm terrified of mice, even little field mice.

Mom grew up in South Dakota, where ice-skating was a regular part of winter life, but in the Pacific Northwest, weather cold enough to freeze a pond, or even a very shallow mud puddle, solid enough for outdoors ice-skating, was a rarity. The ground was covered in several feet of icy snow as we stomped down the driveway, the four Big Kids and me. I'm not sure how we figured that one pair of skates from our petite mother's high school days could possibly fit all of us, but we knew how to take turns, and we were determined to try. Marleen and Robert were out of luck. We learned early that too small just didn't work, but if a pair of shoes or boots were too big, you could always stuff the toes with old socks or crumpled paper to make them fit.

As the youngest, my turn to try the skates was last. One of my older sisters tightened the laces, and I was off. Balance has never been one of my strengths. I was an absolute failure, spending more time falling and trying to get up than upright and moving forward. I have a vague memory of a bad fall, of Marleen and Robert standing over me, unlacing the skates and pulling me to my feet. I couldn't breathe, and they supported me on both sides. Slowly we made our way up the Big Hill and home. Nobody mentioned the fall to Mom. I still have an ever-so-slightly deformed rib on my left side from that afternoon of self-instruction in the fine art of ice-skating. But mostly I have a wonderful memory of an afternoon of laughter and fun with my older siblings.

As the good years, the years of exploration and adventure, piled one on top of another like the tree stumps and brush on Dad's clearing piles, he and Robert built fences, a riding ring and a barn. But it wasn't just a barn. It was a ten-stall horse stable, a beautiful two-story structure with a concrete walkway up the center aisle and five large box stalls on each side. The walls between the stalls were built with solid four-by-twelve beams, so solid even the wildest colt or bull couldn't fight its way out. The five stalls on one side nestled into the base of Horse Hill, the hill rising like a wall behind the barn, but those on the opposite side of the aisle had doors that opened into large, fenced paddocks. The loft was huge and full of baled alfalfa we got in eastern Washington by the truckload each summer. Dad had a friend with a ranch outside the small town of Cle Elum. I remember spending a few long, hot summer days in the dry eastern Washington winds while Dad worked the alfalfa fields. As I look back, I wonder how often Dad relied on the barter system.

Like most, our barn was painted red with white trim, but that's where the similarity ended. Using a stencil Marleen drew, Dad used a jigsaw to cut a horse head into every door. He also welded horseshoe hooks to hang bridles and halters outside each stall door and in the tack room. I still have one of those hooks, bright yellow, the color I painted the baseboard and trim of the tiny apartment I rented in Mexico City years later. Like those handmade Christmas presents, I've carried it with me through the years as a reminder of my roots.

My family never had much money. Still, my father created our home with ingenuity, determination, and just plain hard work. He also used surplus building materials that he was able to get for a song from his job sites. He drove off to his job in the early morning before we left for school, and went straight to work on the current project when he got home in the evening. He worked every weekend from sunup to sundown, determined to build economic security for his large family. But it was more than work for my father. Building was also his hobby. He loved the process of creating something from nothing. He'd stand back to survey his latest project with a smile on his face, lost in thought, planning the next phase. He was a man of few words and a bright whistle. Bright in those early years, the good years.

But Dad wasn't alone in his adventure. Without Mom, he could never have done it. She was the backbone of the family, and she was in charge of the family finances. She fed us, clothed us, and kept us as safe as she was able, with nine kids to supervise. Like my father, she never stopped working. There was always a meal to plan or prepare, laundry to do, housecleaning, and then later, when we were all school aged, she went back to nursing to supplement the family income.

On rare occasions, I'd see Mom and Dad walking off together after dinner, hand-in-hand, with our dog, Laddy, following at their heels. They'd be gone until dark. It was their time together, alone.

The home my parents built was a large, three-story brick box with a daylight basement. The front basement rooms were at ground level, but the house was built into a hillside, so the back basement rooms were below ground. From the back of the house, the second floor was at ground level. The back two basement rooms were separated by the stairwell going up to the main floor. On one side of the stairwell was the furnace room, and a bedroom was on the other side. Later, as we became teenagers, that was the coveted bedroom of the eldest kid still living at home, coveted because it was far away from everybody else. In a family of nine kids, privacy was a rare and highly valued commodity. Still, there was never any sibling conflict about the basement bedroom. Our parents always granted privileges on the basis of seniority. The eldest kid got the bedroom. That was it. End of story.

Across from the bedroom, the furnace room was spacious, maybe fifteen or twenty feet square. Two walls of the room were lined with floor-to-ceiling locked, wooden cabinets. On the opposite side of the room was a large workbench, and in the corner sat a huge oil-burning furnace. It was larger than an average bathroom. It would fill my current kitchen. It was a noisy, stinky monster that intrigued me. Somehow, I always expected it to come alive. I guess in the winter of the root beer, it sort of did.

For several years, Dad had been experimenting with winemaking. After endless hours of pulling out blackberry vines to clear our land, he decided to make use of some of the berries. He spoke fondly of his mother making berry wine when he was a kid and wanted to try it himself. So, Mom gave each of us an old coffee can with a shoestring handle, and sent us off to pick berries.

There were two kinds of wild blackberries growing in

abundance on our land. Again, with great creativity, we called them the Big Berries and the Little Berries. Years later, I learned that there are actually two kinds of "Big" berries, Evergreens and Himalayas. On our land, we only had Himalayas. The Little Berries were our favorites, full of sweet, tart flavor, but they were miserably hard to pick because they grew on fine vines in tangled underbrush. It would take half a day to get enough for one pie.

The Himalayas were different. They grew on large vines that tried to take over our pastureland as fast as Dad and Robert could clear it. You see them all over the Pacific Northwest, even in the cities. We never liked their flavor, but they were the berries of choice for wine or commercial jelly. What we didn't pick for Dad's winemaking, we could sell by the pound at the local Hobart market for money to buy school clothes.

When we brought back our cans full of berries, Mom spent hours pressing and straining them to get the juice ready for Dad's winemaking. After washing the large, seedy berries, she dumped them into an old pillowcase. She tied the end shut and hung the bag from a water pipe above the laundry sink in the basement. Under the hanging berry-filled pillowcase, she placed a large, clean bowl to collect the juice as it dripped from the bag. Then she started squeezing the bag to smash the berries and release their juice. The bag hung for a day or two until it contained little more than dried pulp and seeds. Then she took it down, turned it inside out, rinsed it clean and started the process all over again.

At some point we all began to protest, Mom included. She saw the imbalance of the system—nine kids who couldn't drink wine, and she didn't even like it. She knew we wanted to sell all of our berries at the Hobart market. That made more sense to her than wasting the time, effort, and money on winemaking. One year, someone came up with the idea of making root beer instead of wine, and Dad agreed. Apparently, the wine wasn't all that great anyway.

Making root beer is really pretty simple, and even the bottling wasn't too bad. Unfortunately, we made at least two serious miscalculations. The first had to do, I think, with the yeast-to-sugar ratio. I'm no chemist, but I do know that too much of one or the other can be pretty volatile.

Then there was the storage issue. Even though our house was spacious, we were a big family, and finding a safe place to store dozens of glass bottles was problematic. Robert and Marleen decided that putting the newly-capped root beer bottles in the empty space between the basement foundation and the back of the furnace would be perfect.

The space they chose was unused, out of the way of potential accidents. What they didn't consider was the heat factor. The furnace room was the warmest place in the house. The closer you got to the furnace, the warmer it was. Those yeasty bottles of root beer were snuggled up to that burning box all winter long. Well, really only part of the winter, only until the explosions began.

I was up in the third floor dormitory when I heard the first blast. I thought the whole house was blowing up. As I went tearing down the stairs to the basement, Mom blocked the way. She'd already figured out what was happening.

Most of that winter, my parents declared the furnace room off limits. The following spring, after the furnace was turned off for the summer, there was a serious root beer and shattered glass mess to clean up. It was another group project, with Marleen and Robert in charge, and Mom supervising. We used large pieces of cardboard to scrap the broken glass into piles and pick it up. Once we got rid of most of the glass, we had to scrub down the entire room: ceiling, walls, and floor.

That was the only year we made root beer.

Our old coffee cans had another use, in addition to blackberry picking: nail picking. I hung my can around my neck and scrambled through the construction site of our house, and later our barn, in search of nails, any nails, used or new. We'd make a contest of it to see who could find the most nails in a certain amount of time. Once, I came across a small, crumpled brown paper bag of shiny new nails. Glancing over my shoulder to make sure I was alone, I dumped the bag into my coffee can and shook it thoroughly to get the new nails dirty.

That was one of the few days I actually had the most nails. And I never confessed.

It was not my only childhood deception. One of the chores my siblings and I shared was to carry firewood from the woodpile to stack next to our large open fireplaces, both in the basement, and later, as the house was built up around us, in the living room on the main floor. More than one cold, rainy winter day, I stood under the downspout as the rainwater drained off our large roof and allowed myself to get soaked to the bone, in hopes of convincing Mom that it was raining too hard to make me bring in firewood. I wonder how many times these childish deceptions really convinced my parents of anything.

The nail-collecting job, like carrying firewood, was an ongoing chore, but finding the nails was only the first part of the job. After that, we had to sort them, separating the new from the used. Then my father would straighten the used nails. He would take one nail at a time, examine the angle of the bend, put it on his anvil and hammer it straight. As a child, I don't think I knew that my father's grandfather had been a blacksmith. Now, as I look back, I can see the smith in my dad. The only things missing were the tongs and the furnace to heat the nails before pounding them straight.

Every nail was valuable, every screw, every piece of wood, every brick, every pipe. Just as nothing was wasted in our daily lives of chores and school, nothing was wasted in the construction of that house. We ate whatever was put on the table, or we went hungry. No questions. No complaints. We used and reused paper and plastics, bottles and cans. And what we couldn't reuse, we recycled, not because we were conscientious environmentalists, but because there was money available in aluminum and glass.

The summer before I entered junior high school, I was eleven years old, and I earned enough money picking blackberries to order a brand-new jumper from the Sears catalogue. It was soft, pale blue, green and cream plaid wool, with three pairs of gold buttons on the front and a delicate chain connecting the two lowest buttons. I'll never forget ripping open the package when it arrived in the mail, pulling the jumper out of its plastic wrapper, and burying my face in the wool to smell its newness. I hung it carefully in my area of the closet and waited anxiously for the first day of school.

That little scrap of memory helps me understand, helps me accept, my daughter's aversion to buying used books. Erin loves the smell, the touch, of a new book. She loves to open a new cover and turn the crisp, fresh pages knowing her eyes, her hands are the first to touch them. In contrast, I love to browse used bookstores. I imagine the stories each book could tell of the places it has been and the people who have held it. But still, I understand the pleasure of the new and fresh.

Maureen was three years old during my first year in junior high. She had changed from a bald baby to a blonde toddler with long ringlets, and for the next few years she was our beautiful little Goldilocks. Every Saturday night Mom washed Maureen's hair in the big yellow bathtub on the main floor of the house. Then, they sat together on the tile hearth with Mom holding Maureen tightly between her knees as she worked the tangles out of Maureen's long, wet hair and combed it into locks. Maureen squirmed with impatience, but Mom's stoic German determination always prevailed.

By the time she started school, Maureen hated her hair. She wanted to chop it off so she looked more like her bowl-cut older sisters, so she wasn't different from us. And, more important, so she didn't have to endure the grooming ordeal each week.

But we all loved our little Goldilocks, and we didn't want her beautiful ringlets cut off. So every week, Mom held Maureen still while she combed and separated her hair in sections. With care and patience, she wrapped each section around her finger to form a curl, and then released it. She repeated the process at least a dozen times, and then, if it were wintertime, Maureen would have to sit in front of a blazing fire until her hair was dry. There were times when Mom was too busy, and the job was passed off to Charleen or me. I can still feel Maureen's silky hair wrapped around my index finger and see its golden sheen glisten in the firelight.

By the time Maureen was six or seven, she was old enough to insist on getting her own way, at least as far as her hair was concerned. And by then, we were all tired of the struggle to tend her ringlets. She had her hair cut very short and kept it that way for the remainder of her short life. When she came to visit me in Mexico, I envied that short, curly haircut that always looked cute and comfortable in the tropical heat.

Twenty years later, as I was reading through Maureen's Green River files, I came across transcripts of the numerous interviews Task Force detectives had conducted with Maureen's co-workers at the childcare center where she was working until she disappeared. One co-worker spoke of a conversation in which Maureen angrily accused Dad of chopping off her beautiful, blonde curls.

> DET.: Okay, can you tell me about her background in terms of her family life, anything like that?
>
> WIT: I think she loved her fam...she really loved her mother - I don't know really the relationship with her dad. She had some bad feelings towards her dad, of things that happened in the past, you know, when she was little. I mean by bad feelings her experience, like discipline, the way of discipline. She mentioned one time where she had cut off her sister's hair or at least done... then her dad would put something on her head and cut off her long blond hair, and this was kind of a devastating experience for her. *(King County Department of Public Safety Statement, File 01.00049, Section 29, R 2016130)*

I remember it differently. I remember Maureen hating her long hair, squirming and complaining during the endless brushing, begging to cut it off. As I read the transcripts, I questioned the tangles of memory and perception and truth.

But there were some aspects of those transcripts that made absolute sense to me. Maureen's co-workers described a teenager frustrated with parental control, with a fierce desire to be free of that control. They also described a naïve young woman with low self-esteem who showed radical changes, both positive and negative, during the early fall just before her murder.

DET.: Okay. Now, we talked a little bit too, and you mentioned that you saw a change in her. Can you tell me aout when that was and what the change was?

WIT: Well, I think that was in late summer or early...early fall. The change was MAUREEN was the kind of a girl that was not as attractive as she, as I expected that she could be. To me she did not have a good feeling about herself as a person, and then during this summer, or some time during this summer, she just started acting happier and looking better and wearing nicer clothes and wearing make-up, which she had not done before, and you just felt that there was... someone had come into her life and made her feel good about herself. And I believe I even accused her, I said, oh, do you have a boyfriend, or is it some guy in your life! And she kind of laughed and said yes. (*King County Department of Public Safety Statement, File 01.00049, Section 29, R 2016138*)

DET.: You mentioned just before I turned the tape on, about how you thought she could be sweet talked...and I don't want to put words in your mouth, but if you could explain that to me...

WIT: Well, there are certain people I think as you get older , there are certain people that you can pick out that to you seem like victims wiating for something to happen to them...they have an attitude about them. Or a way they walk, and I think that with MAUREEN I felt that because she was a plain, plain girl... not, I mean she could be a very attractive girl. I had the feeling that if someone talked, or sweet talked her, that she, she would be naïve and she could be duped into something that was not good for her - might be harmful. That's really what I, I really think about when I think about her. (*King County Department of Public Safety Statement, File 01.00049, Section 29, R 2016140*)

DET.: Okay. YVONNE, as you've been talking, is there anything that you can think about or have thought about that I ahven't asked that you feel we should know?

WIT: ... I, I really, the thing that concerns me most, you know. like I said, she just was a sweet kid. She really was. She was a good kid, you know, and I don't really think, knowing what I know about MAUREEN, that she was living a double life at the time. You know, where sh would do one thing during the day and, she was a good kid. And I think that she just made the wrong ...somewhere along the line, you know, something or somebody she met got her into a wrong thing, obviously, but you know, I mean uh, I know the changes all started when she moved to Seattle, you know... and, ...

DET.: The major changes.

WIT: I mean, there must have been some unhappiness down here that we weren't aware of, or whatever, you know, but...

DET.: Did...

WIT: Uh, she doesn't fit the pattern at all as far as, you know, when you hear about all the other things going on... it's not like her at all.

DET.: Okay. All right. Is there anything else?

WIT: No, I just wish the crime would get solved...

DET.: Okay. I'll turn the tape off. It's 10:36. (*King County Department of Public Safety Statement, File 01.00049, Section 29, R 2016135 and R 2016136*)

When Maureen began elementary school, Mom returned to work as a registered nurse. She worked the graveyard shift, so she was at home to get us off to school in the morning and to feed us dinner at 6:00 p.m. every evening. She slept during the day while we were at school. We learned to be silent. When we came home, there were no loud voices, laughter, or music in the house. We changed from our school clothes and headed outdoors, rain or shine. In the summertime when there was no school, we lived outdoors in the mornings while Mom was sleeping. There were always chores, lots of chores. Ever since that first summer in the tent, we had chores. We cared for the animals, tended a huge strawberry patch and a failure of a vegetable garden, and carried firewood. When Dad got home each day, Robert worked at his side while my sisters and I took turns cooking, washing dishes, doing laundry, and cleaning the house. I always wanted to do outside chores, but found myself stuck doing "girl's work" more often than I care to remember. Years later, a married woman and a college instructor, I tried to help Dad chop and stack firewood.

"Oh no," he said. "This isn't teacher work."

In the years when Maureen was still our little Goldilocks, horses brought more chores, but also endless adventure and happiness into my life. I began to ride when I was very young, always determined to keep up with the Big Kids, and I learned a sense of independence normally experienced with a first driver's license. After I came home from school, I could saddle up and leave. As long as my chores were done and I wasn't supposed to be watching any of the Little Kids, I could ride for hours.

Although my parents didn't socialize much, Dad started a 4-H horse club. Marleen and Robert were thrilled. They were teenagers, and for them, the farm was already getting too small, too isolated. A 4-H club meant friends and activities. Charleen and I were too young to join, but we went to the meetings anyway. But Laureen hated the farm. She stayed in the girls' dormitory as much as possible, transported through books to a world beyond the limited confines of the Issaquah Valley.

Under Dad's leadership, the 4-H club sponsored a few Play Day events in our riding ring. For the first time, there were strangers on our farm, crowds of people and noise and fun. It was wonderful.

Even though I couldn't be in the club, I practiced. I rode daily, perfecting my skills, looking forward to the day when I would be able to join and compete in the Play Day events. Although I was surrounded by Western-style saddles, barrel racing, and pole bending, I loved English riding and jumping. I didn't like the heaviness of the Western saddle with its roping horn that inexperienced riders so often clung to as if it were designed for that purpose. I hated the cowboy hats and cowboy or cowgirl shirts and garb. Besides, you can't jump with a Western saddle, and jumping was what I loved best.

At the time, we owned a horse named Misty. She was a tall, high-spirited chestnut, with a long, white blaze down her face. She never walked flat-footed under saddle. She pranced. And for some unknown reason, she hated men. If Dad or Robert tried to ride her, she would rear and buck or take the bit in her teeth and run, but with Charleen or me, she was as gentle as a lamb. I was determined to teach Misty to jump, but I was an English rider without an English saddle, so I rode and jumped with a bareback pad hooked up with some lightweight metal, English-style stirrups.

Those afternoons of riding and jumping were exquisite, even when things went wrong. On short winter days, I'd ride after school into the early twilight, long after it was safe for either horse or rider. At the end of each run of jumps, I'd pull Misty to a stop and, holding the reins in my right hand, stretch forward with a carrot in my left. Misty would turn her neck in a tight *U* and nibble the carrot from my outstretched palm. I'd learned young to feed a horse while holding my fingers and thumb pressed tight together, forming a slight cup of the hand, in order to avoid accidents.

One winter evening, I wasn't careful enough. As I reined Misty to a stop after an especially rewarding run of jumps, I could see the lights twinkling in the house windows on the hill above the ring. It was getting too dark to be riding, too dark to be jumping, and definitely too dark to be stretching my arm around Misty's neck to treat her with a small piece of carrot.

When her teeth clamped down on my middle finger, I felt no pain, only confusion, hers and mine. For a split second, I didn't understand why I couldn't withdraw my hand. I slid from her back, my middle finger still held firmly in Misty's mouth. I stood before her, a towering chestnut, her beautiful brown eyes ringed with fearful white, trying to get her to open her mouth and release me. I pried at her mouth with my right hand. I slapped the side of her beautiful head. This bizarre behavior on my part only startled her, causing her to pull away from me, dragging me right along with her, my finger still clamped between her teeth. Despite my pleading and hollering, it was Misty's first taste of blood that saved my finger. She opened her mouth with more of a snort than a release, and I was free.

It was too dark to see the splatters of blood on my sweatshirt and jeans. I don't remember what happened next. I don't remember if I walked Misty back to the barn, took off the bareback pad, wiped her down, fed her and let her loose in the pasture. Or if, instead, I left her tied to a rail as I hurried to the house, the end of my left middle finger gaping open on both sides and dripping with blood. I do remember running up the hill to the house, screaming for my mother at the top of my lungs.

"What's wrong, Arleen?" Mom was standing in front of the stove making dinner when I burst through the kitchen door. I held up my left hand, my bloody finger dangling in front of her. Without a word, she grabbed me by the shoulder and walked me into the bathroom. Silently and efficiently, she washed and bandaged my finger.

"Misty didn't mean to do it," I cried. "It wasn't her fault. It was my fault. It was too dark. I shouldn't have fed her the carrot."

"Shush," my mom said. "It's okay." But I felt the throbbing pain, and I knew it wasn't going to be okay, at least not for a while.

Dad came home a little while later, and I could hear them talking in the kitchen as I stretched out on the sofa in the adjacent living room, my hand elevated per Mom's instructions. "Does she need stitches? Do we need to get her in to see Dr. Anderson?" Dad asked.

"I don't think so. Maybe a few. But the office is closed now. We'd have to take her all the way to the Emergency Room at Overlake. I think it'll heal all right without them."

In the end, I didn't see a doctor. Mom was a nurse. I healed, and to this day I have scars on both sides of my middle finger, the side nestling against my ring finger with a perfect horseshoe-shaped scar. It's my lifelong token of Misty, the horse I later wanted to run away with, never knowing if I wanted to run for me or for Misty, to prevent my parents from selling her. But even as a young teen, I was rational enough to know I could never run far enough.

My years of practice, my many falls, my scarred finger weren't enough. I never belonged to the 4-H club. By the time I was old enough to join, the club no longer existed. Marleen and Robert had become older teenagers, Dad didn't know how to loosen his control over them, and our 4-H club died. By the time Maureen turned ten, the horses and the joy they had brought to our family were little more than a faded memory.

In the beginning, we were a happy family. There were a fourteen or fifteen wonderful years, the years before Maureen's birth and those while she was still a very young child. Later, we wanted to believe that Maureen was a normal, happy teenager from a large, close-knit family, so we clung to this myth, our first family myth. We refused to acknowledge that our family had changed even before Maureen reached adolescence. She never knew the happy family adventure of those early Issaquah years. We were no longer the same family by the time Maureen was a teenager, but I still clung to the notion that we were somehow special. I still took pride in our family adventure, in the home we'd created in the wilderness, despite the financial hardships. I still believed that we were somehow smarter and more creative, bigger and better, than every other family in the world. I believed that we were special. And I suppose we really were, in the same way that all families are special and unique.

As a young teenager, I hadn't even begun to see our fault lines.

Chapter Five: Unraveling

Mom was the daughter of a Southern Baptist church deacon; her parents were first generation German immigrants. As a teenager in the small town of Herreid, South Dakota, she was a cheerleader and a flautist in the high school band. At a very early age, after her father took her up in a biplane at a county fair, she decided she wanted to fly. But in the early 1940s, women were stewardesses, not pilots, and to be a stewardess, you had to be a registered nurse. So after high school, Mom went to nursing school. She graduated as World War II raged in Europe and the Pacific, and she came to Seattle as a cadet nurse to work at the U.S. Marine Hospital until the war ended. After the war, she fulfilled her dream of flying when she was hired by United Airlines. She moved out of the Marine Hospital dormitory and into a basement apartment she shared with several other United stewardesses. Despite her early religious training, religion wasn't a part of her adult life.

Dad was raised Catholic, the youngest of four children and the only son. His father was a redheaded Irish-American Merchant Marine who was often away at sea. Grandfather died when Dad was in his early twenties. Mom met him only on his deathbed at the U.S. Marine Hospital; she still worked there at the time. Dad was a hell-raiser who was kicked out of parochial school, and a West Seattle High School football star, notorious for flipping his Harley on Charlestown Hill, a steep incline only a few blocks from the high school, where the senior class tradition of graffiti painting the hill on graduation night with "Seniors Rule" or "Class of (insert year)" still endures. It's become such a tradition that the city puts up roadblocks at the top and bottom of the incline to protect the kids from oncoming traffic while they deface the street. My dad went to work at Todd Shipyards right out of high school.

Mom and Dad were not practicing Christians, but they were stubborn, and neither wanted to convert to the other's religion. For sixteen years, they raised us kids as free thinkers, devoid of any religious training. But when Marleen and Robert and Laureen began questioning Dad's authority, demanding the new freedoms and privileges that all teenagers demand, Dad couldn't relinquish control.

In his frustration, the same frustration that parents around the world experience, Dad's childhood upbringing surfaced and he turned to the Catholic Church for parenting advice. St. Joseph's Catholic Church stood on a hill just above the only stoplight in downtown Issaquah.

"With the help of the church," Father O'Connor told my parents, "your children will learn to respect your rules." Mom and Dad were willing to try almost anything, and they took his advice to heart. What they weren't willing to do was to reconsider their rules or adjust them as the older kids became teenagers.

Instead, Mom converted to Catholicism. She and all nine of us kids were baptized Catholic in a group ceremony at St. Joseph's. Father O'Connor scored: eleven new parishioners at the same time. We began Monday night catechism class and Sunday morning Mass immediately.

For me, it was an interesting change in routine, a rare time to be with Mom and Dad together when nobody was working. Some Sundays, we went to a pancake restaurant in the small town of North Bend after Mass, just up Interstate 90 towards Snoqualmie Pass in the Cascade Range. More often, Dad bought a newspaper and we went home to read the funnies. We were a house full of readers with piles of school library books everywhere, but the comics were special. My parents weren't daily newspaper readers, so the Sunday paper was a new treat.

* * *

My parents didn't entertain often, but one summer day in the mid-60s, they held a large picnic. Several of Mom and Dad's Seattle friends and relatives came to spend an afternoon in the country. We set up tables under the huge old-growth cedars and firs in the side yard on the knoll above the riding ring. At the end of dinner, the Big Kids disappeared into the house to get away from the adults. After all, they were teenagers now, ranging in age from thirteen to seventeen.

Mom said to me, "Arleen, go tell Marleen and Laureen to come help clear up for dessert." I did as I was told.

Laureen was in rebellious teen mode. "Go tell Momma to go to hell."

I ran back out to the picnic area. Part of me knew that what I was doing was wrong, but Marleen was chasing behind me, yelling at me to stop, knowing that what I was about to say would be devastating. But to me, it was just another game, and I wasn't about to lose the race to my big sister. Right in front of all her guests, I told my mother, "Laureen says to go to hell!" Gasps, followed by stony silence.

Dad stood quickly and started for the house. "No," my mother said quietly. "I'll go." I started to follow Mom back to the house when I heard Dad's voice.

"You stay right here, Arleen. You've done enough for one day."

That was the day my world began to fall apart, and I felt responsible. Dad started calling me "Big Mouth." Throughout my early teens, he told me I had a big mouth and that I never knew when to shut up. Until finally, I shut down completely.

Sometime before the picnic fiasco, or maybe because of the picnic fiasco, my parents decided we needed religion. This was just before Dad started yelling at the television. He roared until his voice filled every corner of the house. Dad didn't agree with government policy and didn't want his taxes used to support the war effort in Southeast Asia. He didn't want his eldest son drafted. He was a strong man accustomed to being in control. Now, he felt powerless. He could not change the course of history, and he was losing control of his teenage children.

It wasn't that Marleen was doing anything any normal teenage girl of the sixties wasn't already doing, but one Sunday morning she refused to get up to go to church. Like most teenagers, she just wanted to sleep in on the weekends. She was in the area of the girls' dormitory closest to the stairwell, the special place reserved for the eldest.

That Sunday morning started out like any other. Mom called up the stairs to wake us for church. We took quick turns in the bathroom and got dressed. All but Marleen. She turned to the wall, refusing to get out of bed.

When I saw Dad at the top of the stairs, I knew something was very wrong. Dad never came into the girls' bedroom except for construction purposes. Time stood still. Silence fell over the house.

We didn't go to church.

I was hiding behind the chimney, listening. "I'm not going, and you can't make me," Marleen screamed. Mom and Dad called the police. They came and put my big sister in a patrol car and drove out of sight as I watched from the bedroom window.

So Marleen was taken away, the first of the falling dominos, and I never asked a single question. The dinner table that night was silent. No teasing, mimicking, or fighting. No kicking each other under the table. None of us said a word.

Once, a few months after she was taken away, the family went to visit her at the Catholic girls' school in Seattle where she was living. We sat on concrete stairs at the entrance to a large brick building. I didn't understand where we were, why Marleen was in that place, or why she couldn't come home with us. There was only that one visit, and we never spoke of her at the family dinner table or otherwise. There was no explanation as to why my big sister was taken away. No show of emotion. She was just gone.

And I was afraid. I sensed that something had gotten the better of us and taken control, but I didn't understand who or what this demon was. So I remained silent, Dad's words ringing in my ears. "Children are to be seen and not heard."

I had gone through early childhood like a big, dumb workhorse with heavy, black blinders limiting my vision. If we saw an accident along the side of the road, we were told, "Look the other way." If we complained about something said to us, we were told, "Just ignore it." If we criticized someone, we were told, "If you can't say something good, don't say anything at all." We were taught to be just like the little wooden monkeys sitting on top of Grandma's old piano: See no evil, hear no evil, speak no evil. It was so deeply ingrained, at least for me, that I never even learned to confide in my siblings.

Before Marleen was taken away, I was unaware of the developing struggles between my parents and my older siblings as they became teenagers. With the rare exception of the picnic disaster, I remember no other conflict. But even at eleven, I didn't think Mom and Dad called the cops and had Marleen taken away just because she refused to get up one Sunday morning to go to church. Still, I didn't have the whole story, and the silence was pervasive.

* * *

One evening, less than year after Marleen was taken away, we sat down for dinner. The table was set for ten, but Robert's place was empty.

"Where's Robert?" one of the kids asked. With seven kids crammed around a large table, it was often hard to know who was saying what.

"He's not here," Mom responded, quietly.

"Where is he?" somebody else asked.

"That's enough," was Dad's stern reply. We ate in silence. The next night, Robert's place at the table was, again, empty. This time his plate was not set. Nobody said a word.

Robert had disappeared, and from my point of view, it was even more mysterious than Marleen's departure. I didn't see him leave. I didn't hear the words. I didn't learn the whole story until forty years later.

He simply vanished. Like Marleen, he was just gone. We never went to his graduation. His name was never mentioned. Again, I didn't ask questions. But I began to feel uneasy about the nature of Mom and Dad's love for me.

* * *

Laureen's turn rolled around next, only a year behind Robert's. That's how I began to see it, as turns. In a big family, you learn to take turns. I wondered when my turn would come to disappear, to fly off the family merry-go-round, which was spinning rapidly out of control. By the time it was Laureen's turn to be a teenager, my parents' resources, both emotional and financial, were already spent.

At the same time, Dad and his older sisters had just moved their aging mother out of her home and into a small apartment in the Highpoint housing community in Seattle. She was lonely without her neighbors and her garden. Mom and Dad thought it might be good for her to have some companionship, and they were determined to get Laureen away from a circle of friends of whom they didn't approve. The problem was that it seemed impossible to have friends that my parents liked. They just didn't understand teenagers. Their solution was to pack Laureen off to live with Grandma.

Highpoint had been built in 1942 as temporary housing for the tens of thousands of war workers rushing to Seattle to fill job openings at Todd Shipyards and Boeing. By the early 1950s, it had become low-income housing, providing homes for the elderly and minorities, particularly blacks. During one six-month period in 1956, occupancy rose from 800 to 1,200 families. By the mid 1960s, it was a well-established low-income housing project.

At the time, my parents seemed unaware of the changing demographics of the area. You'd think that a West Seattle native like my father might have taken a closer look at the community and the high school where they were putting Laureen. But either they didn't, or they saw no other alternative.

I remember only one visit to see Laureen while she was living at Grandma's house. Then, for reasons that Mom and Dad never explained, we were not allowed to speak her name again. Another sibling vanished with no explanation. All I knew for sure is that she disappeared from my life when I was still young. The fine threads that once held together our fragile family unraveled as completely as a spider web across a hiker's path on a dewy spring morning. And just as that spider web disappears when it is brushed aside, so did Laureen.

* * *

Years later, as adults beyond Dad's control, Laureen and I were reunited. During our infrequent visits, I began to piece together my second sister's story. Once, she told me that when she started attending her new high school in Seattle, she was terrified. She was accustomed to an all white, middle-class, rural school environment, and totally unprepared for the inner-city dynamics of the one she was thrown into. She said she was lucky that one black girl befriended her, took her under her wing and taught her to survive. Slowly, she adjusted, and black friendships led to black boyfriends, something Dad could not tolerate.

When Grandma, thinking it was one of Laureen's high school friends, opened her kitchen door one afternoon to a young black man, and was assaulted and robbed in broad daylight, Dad blamed Laureen. When Laureen ran away from Grandma's apartment and disappeared, Dad didn't call the cops, nor did he go after her. Instead, he refused to speak to her, or even about her, for the remainder of his long life.

* * *

Still, I didn't have the whole story. I only had fragments. Bits and pieces, because I was afraid to ask questions, because my own siblings were strangers to me. I didn't understand what had set off the chain of events that led to the disappearances of my three eldest siblings. And I didn't find out the truth until a few years ago, almost forty years after watching from the bedroom window—a testament to how well my family keeps its secrets.

Robert and his adult daughter stayed with us for a week. Now a salty old sailor, tanned to leather, his hands so calloused and cracked from years of hard labor in the Hawaiian sun that they're scratchy to the touch. Though his body is worn, his mind is sharper than ever.

It was Christmas time. The traditional tree stood in the corner, the fireplace mantle in the adjacent living room was aglow with soft candlelight, and the house was fragrant with evergreen. It was late in the evening, and Robert and I were alone with a blue bottle of Skyy vodka.

Finally, after thirty-eight years of silence, I worked up the nerve to ask. "So what happened? What did Marleen do that was so horrible?"

"Yeah, her refusing to go to church—that was just the final straw. I guess all the trouble really got going about the time when I started sneaking off to that under-aged dance club in Eastgate. All the kids from the local high schools used to hang out there on Friday and Saturday nights. And Mom and Dad forbade us to go. I suppose they were afraid we'd get into some kind of trouble. Alcohol, sex, you name it. It was the sixties, and that shit was all over the news. Anyway, Marleen got caught trying to sneak out of the house. At that point, I think Mom and Dad were just zapped."

"What do you mean?"

"You know, burned out, exhausted. Too much work and not enough money. We were teenagers in the sixties, and they were losing control. They didn't know what to do."

"So what did they do?" I got up to refill our drinks. (Cocktail onions for him, olives for me.)

"I'm not sure. I think they went to that Catholic church up on the hill above Issaquah. Do you remember? What was that priest's name? He wasn't such a bad guy. Remember how he used to walk the power line right-of-way? He found Laddy's grave marker one weekend. Dad had to do some fast talking on that one."

"Yeah, he sure did. The Catholic church sort of frowns on putting crosses on dogs' graves," I laughed. "Father O'Connor. Saint Joseph's Catholic Church."

"That's right. I think they went and asked Father O'Connor what they were doing wrong, and he told them we needed religion."

"What else would a priest tell them?"

"I suppose." My brother laughed softly, lost in his own

memories.

"What about you? You disappeared too. It was like poof," I said, adding the appropriate hand movements for emphasis. "One day you were just gone."

"Oh, it didn't happen that quick," he said. "I ran away so many times, I guess Dad just got tired of dragging my ass home."

At the time, I knew nothing about the numerous times that Robert had run away or that Dad had dragged him home. My blinders were very effective, and it was easy to hide secrets on ten acres of land. Finally, Robert left and Dad didn't go after him.

"Why did you keep trying to run away?" I asked him. "What was so very wrong at home?"

He paused, lost in thought for a long time. I thought he might not answer, but finally he said, "I don't know. I guess it was just time for me to be on my own."

As we sat in the twinkling light of the regal Christmas tree, he told me the story of how he had wanted to buy a car. He made money chopping cord wood and selling it throughout the Issaquah Valley, and even as far away as Bellevue and Seattle. After he saved enough, he bought a car even though our parents had forbidden it. His motive, as he tells the story now, was that he "didn't want to waste two hours on that damn school bus every day." He wanted to get home, eager to get back to whatever project he and Dad were working on and get a lot done before Dad got home from work.

That desire to impress our father, to make him happy, controlled our lives, both as children, and for me, even as an adult. A couple of years after my father's death in 2002, the summer after that late night conversation with Robert, I was having a picnic lunch in my backyard with a good friend who'd met my parents several years earlier. She, too, is from a very large family, so we often compare stories. I could hear the hesitation in her voice when she said, "There's always been something that's bothered me about that visit to your parents' place."

"Really? What?"

"Oh, I shouldn't say anything."

"Look, you can't backpedal now. Come on. I'm intrigued."

"Okay," she said, pausing to find the right words. "I was surprised, shocked really, by how hard you kept trying to please your dad the whole time we were there. It bothered me so much I even went home and told Ron about it."

I was silent for a moment, listening to the birds in the cherry tree overhead. "I didn't even realize I was doing it," I finally said.

Even though I wasn't aware that I was still behaving like a child, it made absolute sense to me when Robert told me of his childhood desire to impress Dad with his hard work. It was our way of life. It was all we knew. Still, Dad did not want Robert buying a car. He was afraid for him. Afraid of the increased mobility, of accidents, of losing control over his eldest son. But he lost him all the same.

Robert finished high school sleeping in the backseat of his car, parked in the school parking lot. He told me that the principal was the first to arrive each morning and woke him before the buses pulled up. He managed to graduate, earning a full scholarship to the University of Washington. But Vietnam was raging, and destiny took Robert in a different direction. It took some creative solutions, but he found his way out of the U. S. Army and never completed his university education. He moved to the Hawaiian Islands and never again made his home on the mainland.

* * *

A formal family portrait hangs on the wall in the hallway Mom calls her picture gallery. It was taken in 1966, when all the siblings were still living at home. We're lined up in front of the fireplace with its mosaic tile hearth that Dad designed and built. The Big Kids are standing with Mom and Dad behind the tattered sofa. From left to right, we first see Charleen, who was allergic to dairy at a time when soy was still unheard of in our part of the world. Charleen got off to a slow start, but she made up for her small stature with spirit and determination. Next is Laureen, a full head taller than Charleen and always a bit chubby. Her wonderful auburn hair is chopped into a short 1960s hairdo that does nothing for her. Marleen, the eldest, stands next in line in her perfect model pose. She was always the beauty of the family, even at sixteen. Dad and Mom stand side-by-side, united as always, she beautiful and he handsome. But deadly serious. They seemed to be tired, the weight of life, of us, their nine kids pulling them down. To the far right is Robert, in his Malcolm X glasses which can't block the piercing blue stare that looks as if it could burn ice. Dad's eyes. Beautiful, powerful, intense eyes.

The Little Kids sit on the sofa. Again from left to right, is Andrew, then Michael. Andrew is five and Michael six. Andrew is dark-haired and Michael blond, both in short-sleeved white shirts and bow ties, both sitting with their legs sticking straight out from the sofa, the bottoms of their worn shoes visible to the camera.

Doreen sits beside them wearing white, horn-rimmed glasses. At eight, she's the eldest of the Little Kids, always the responsible one, always taking care of the little ones. Michael sits to Doreen's right, and Maureen, a toddler of three with long, blonde curls, to her left.

I'm not one of the Big Kids and not one of the Little Kids. The middle kid doesn't belong. I'm tall enough to be standing, certainly taller than Charleen. Too tall to be on the sofa with the Little Kids, but there I am, stuck in at the end of the sofa, messing up the perfect symmetry of two sets of four kids. As the middle kid, I didn't belong anywhere. Maybe I was the only one who saw it that way, but surely that doesn't invalidate my feelings.

Mom has another large portrait on her wall, but it's only the kids, without her or Dad. We nine kids are lined up in front of the fireplace, all dressed up, the girls in spring Easter dresses, the boys in white shirts and ties. After we started going to church, we always got new clothes for Easter Sunday. That was the best part, the new dress. In this picture, Maureen and I are on the hearth with the four Big Kids. Marleen is holding Maureen tight in her lap. The other Little Kids—Doreen, Michael, and Andrew—are on the floor.

Unlike the family portrait, this photograph of the siblings isn't dated, but it must have been taken at about the same time, just before the unraveling. It is the last picture of all the siblings together.

There will never be another.

In that photograph, Maureen is still our little Goldilocks, her long blonde ringlets intact and her bright blue eyes shining. Too young to know her older siblings.

I have only a few clear memories of the next six years, the years when I was eleven to seventeen. They're a blank. A blank because no words were used to explain what was happening to my perfect family. Only stony silence.

I felt stifled, censored by the realization that I had to be perfect. Perfect by Dad's definition, or I would disappear like Marleen, Robert, and Laureen had. The problem was that I didn't understand his definition of perfection. To me, the words, "silence is golden," did not ring true.

When we were very young, Mom and Dad raised us to think for ourselves, to be strong-willed, determined, pragmatic individuals. Dad used to tell us about the best teacher he ever had— a high school teacher who got fired for encouraging her students to think for themselves and to question everything, even authority. But when Marleen, Robert, and Laureen became strong-willed, defiant teenagers who questioned Dad's authority, he couldn't cope. Despite his determination that we should learn to think for ourselves, it never occurred to him that our thinking, our way of seeing the world, might differ from his own.

And Mom remained silent.

As I tried to understand what was happening to my family, I could only blame my older siblings. I had to believe that it was their fault, that they had each done something very bad that caused them to lose Dad's love, because if I allowed myself to blame Dad, my whole world would be a lie. Dad was like the center pole of that army surplus tent we lived in our first summer in the Issaquah Valley. He held the world up around me. If the pole collapsed, so too would my world.

So there was pain, the pain of love withdrawn if we didn't behave the way Dad expected us to behave. Pain because Dad saw life in black and white, and he demanded that his children see it the same way. He was blind to the gray. He had no tolerance, no acceptance, no understanding of the gray. The gray of communication, negotiation, compromise. The gray of love.

*   *   *

Dad stood in the middle of the family room, holding the black and white bathroom scale in his large, gnarled, calloused hands. Strong hands, with wisps of dark hair on his fingers, but no rings. Rings are dangerous for a working man. They can cut off a finger. When Dad retired, Mom gave him a beautiful gold and jade ring. He wore that ring to his death, a visible symbol of his newfound leisure.

He was a tall, barrel-chested man with wide shoulders who towered over me.

"Were you playing with this scale, Arleen?"

I felt his anger more than I could see it. As I gazed up at him, I saw only the hair of his nostrils and the lower rim of his black-framed glasses. "No, Daddy. I didn't touch it."

"Well, who did, then? Who broke it, if it wasn't you?"

I was stunned. I had no idea why my father was blaming me for something I hadn't done. "Honest, Daddy, it wasn't me. I don't know who broke it, but it wasn't me."

"Look me in the eye and tell me that. Look me in the eye and tell me the truth."

But I couldn't. Even though I knew I hadn't played with the scale, I couldn't look Dad in the eye. I felt his piercing blue eyes bore into me. Even through his thick glasses, I knew my father's stare could burn my soul. I was scared by the intensity of that stare, by the judgment it held. Scared because I knew that by not looking him in the eye, I was convicting myself. I looked down at my feet, shuffling back and forth, one foot to the other foot, one dirty sock to the other dirty sock on the cement floor of the basement of the first house Dad built in the Issaquah Valley. Cool cement floors, with warm hand-hewn alder log walls. Dad and Robert cut each of those trees, split them, peeled the bark off, and varnished them to a soft · gleam.

Dad turned and walked away, muttering, "Don't you ever touch this or any other scale in this house again. You hear me?"

For him, it was black and white. I couldn't do what he wanted. I couldn't do it his way. I was guilty.

Such a simple, little memory: my father not believing me because I could not look into his stern, blue eyes. A memory of when my word meant nothing to the most important man in my life.

* * *

Marleen was seventeen when Mom and Dad called the cops, Maureen wasn't yet two, and I was still eleven. I had almost a dozen years of family bliss, first in Seattle, and then in the paradise of the Issaquah Valley. I had happy, if exhausted, parents who were building a dream together. But the dream was elusive, and the workload overwhelming. I watched as the dream collapsed, as Marleen was put into a police car, as Robert's space at the dinner table remained empty, as Laureen moved into Grandma's tiny apartment and then disappeared. I watched without understanding, without explanation, but at least I had memories of these older siblings. Of horseback riding and berry picking, of carrying armloads of bricks and tending huge brush fires.

Because she was only two, Maureen had nothing. She grew up not knowing her three oldest siblings. Of course, it's not uncommon in large families for there to be distance between younger and older siblings. In my family, the distance was of epic dimensions, supported by heavy walls of silence. Silence supported by competition for attention from parents who were too busy to provide any. It's normal for older siblings to move out, go off to college, get married, move on. It is far from normal to see your oldest sister carted off in a police car, or your oldest brother's place at the dinner table remain empty, or to have another sister totally, completely, absolutely disowned, all for reasons that are never explained or even mentioned.

In retrospect, I don't think we ever learned to communicate among ourselves because we never learned to communicate with our parents. We imitated the silence that they modeled. Maureen was not a happy girl growing up in a happy, close-knit family. Instead, she was a very confused and frustrated girl, moody and at times explosive. I wonder how many times she was asked questions she found herself unable to answer.

When my daughter was in the fifth grade, she had to create a family tree. For over a month, butcher paper covered our dining room table as Erin mapped out five or six generations. Her father's side was easy, just a matter of a few long-distance telephone calls to her paternal grandmother. She called my mother once, trying to learn more about her extended family, but the answers were so evasive that she gave up. Mom couldn't or wouldn't remember. But Erin worked hard to trace her roots because at ten, understanding your roots is essential to understanding who you are and how you fit into this enormous and confusing world.

I'm haunted by the image of Maureen trying to complete a family tree when she was in fifth grade. My daughter had trouble putting together past generations; my kid sister would have struggled trying to map out her immediate family. Before she reached her seventh birthday, she was already an aunt to a granddaughter Mom and Dad hadn't acknowledged because by then they had disowned Laureen. Dad died never knowing, or even having met, Laureen's two daughters. He died without having spoken to his own daughter for over thirty years.

Chapter Six: High School

I struggled through my high school years, awkward and lonely. Through the Catholic Youth Organization, I was introduced to the world of boys and the anti-abortion movement of the late sixties. One year, I attended a CYO convention in a downtown Seattle hotel. There was to be a dance one evening, and I was nervous, having never danced with a boy before. I remembered an earlier conversation I'd had with Laureen. "When you dance with a guy," she had told me, with all the worldly confidence of an older sister, "just rub the back of his neck with your fingers. Guys really like that."

I wasn't at all certain that it was good advice, but knowing nothing better, I did as instructed. It was a formal dance, and the boys were all wearing suits and ties. When the boy I liked best finally asked me to dance, I tried to follow my sister's advice. The boy stopped in the middle of the dance floor and asked, "Why are you scratching my neck?" Mortified, I escaped to the ladies room.

It was also at the CYO convention that I was first told of the horrors of abortion and the impending doom should abortion be legalized. I was taught to take a stand against abortion in any way possible.

Catholicism taught me little else. I never read the Bible or memorized the scriptures, but I did learn not to rub a guy's neck while slow dancing and that it was my moral obligation to fight legalized abortion with all my strength—a lesson that caused me an unbearable moral dilemma only a few years later.

Maureen was just starting elementary school then, so this was the childhood she knew: Mass on Sunday mornings, catechism class on Monday evenings. She also knew when Mom and Dad gave up, when the Sunday morning routine was dropped, and Monday night catechism forgotten. By then, I had moved out. Only the Little Kids were left at home. Maureen was entering adolescence, and religion had failed to save our family.

By the time I reached my junior year in high school, there were only four other kids still at home: Doreen, Michael, Andrew and Maureen. Charleen had graduated from Issaquah High School the year before, earning a scholarship to a small Catholic university in Spokane, Washington. Spokane was a good five or six hour drive, so visits were rare, but I visited her in the dorm. I remember thinking, "This is how moving away from home is supposed to be. You're supposed to be able to visit them when they leave."

It seemed miraculous to me.

I spent three troubled years at Issaquah High School, 1969 to 1972. I can see the layout of the buildings even now. The school was big and open, with patio and garden spaces, covered walkways connecting modular buildings. It was a great architectural design for warm, dry climates, but totally impractical in the Pacific Northwest rain.

As you entered the front gates, there was an open area with clusters of square, cedar-plank platform benches. I hated walking through those gates every morning, past the groups of kids clustered in tight groups, like the benches. You were either in or out, and I was always out.

I was gothic before Goth hit the American teen scene in the late eighties and early nineties. I habitually wore a long, black raincoat, a shiny black wide-rimmed hat, and black, fitted boots that zipped to the knees. Heavy black liner circled my eyes, and my hair hung as straight as I could get it to my lower back. I carried a black guitar case in one hand and a black bag in the other. When I see teens walking the streets of Seattle in black trench coats, I understand, and my heart bleeds for them—and for a much younger me. I remember the pain.

Heads turned the first time I walked into the front patio dressed in black from head to toe. Heads turned, kids snickered, but most just stared, trying to figure out what I, myself, did not understand. I didn't fit in, and never had. Just as I had never fit in at home. But I'd reached a point in my life where being seen, at any price, was more important than being invisible.

The Christmas before Charleen left home, she gave me one of those homemade gifts: a collection—collage, really—of newspaper and magazine clippings and poetry, cut, typed, and glued together on a series of unbound pages. Memories of the sixties, the war raging in Southeast Asia, the civil rights movement at home, Neil Armstrong's "One small step for man…" Now it's a collection worn with years and travels. Somewhere in my many moves, I bound the loose pages together into a small booklet with a plastic worm spine and a vinyl cover, a cherished reminder of the hopes, worries, and dreams of one teenage girl. It was Charleen's gift that introduced me to Ralph Waldo Emerson. "Who so would be a man must be a nonconformist... What I must do is all that concerns me, not what the people think..." And she introduced me to Henry David Thoreau, too. "If a man does not keep pace with his companions, perhaps it is because he hears a different drummer."

I stood at the front of the classroom, shaking. A wooden podium and my classmates' bored faces were in front of me. It was 1971. The Vietnam War continued to escalate, and President Nixon had just eliminated the student deferment program that the majority of the male students in my high school had counted on to keep them safe from the draft. Still, there were no anti-war protest marches or demonstrations at Issaquah High School. The anti-war buttons I wore brought nothing more than a few stares and wisecracks.

I spent days listening to James Taylor and Carole King's lyrics reassure me, through the trembling voices of my terrified classmates, that all I had to do was call out to friends, and they'd instantly be at my side to assist me. As I stood before that speech class and began to speak, my own voice echoed the tremors I'd become familiar with in their voices. Yet within moments, Emerson, Thoreau and I were alone in that silent classroom:

A common and natural result of an undue respect for the law is, that you may see a file of soldiers, colonel, captain, corporal, privates, powder-monkeys, and all, marching in admirable order over hill and dale to the wars, against their wills, ay, against their common sense and consciences... They have no doubt that it is a damnable business in which they are concerned; they are all peaceably inclined. Now, what are they? Men at all? Or small movable forts and magazines, at the service of some unscrupulous man in power? (*On the Duty of Civil Disobedience*, Henry David Thoreau, 1849)

When I finished speaking, there was no applause, none of the good-natured cheering that had followed my classmates' stumbling recitations of insipid pop lyrics. Only silence accompanied me back to my desk. The bell rang, and alone, I made my way to the next fifty-minute class.

The only class I loved in high school was Spanish. Miss Crelly will never know how her class touched a chord in my being. She was an elderly spinster who traveled extensively. She was tall and spindly with curly, gray hair, and she always wore loose, floral "grandma" dresses. Most of the students thought she was a crazy old bat, but I thought the world of her. I loved the silly songs she played on her classroom piano, and I loved the slides she showed of her worldly adventures, particularly those when she was in Latin America and Spain. I remember one slide where she was shown wearing pants and riding a donkey. That was when I first realized that teachers are real people with lives outside of school. I thought she must have a perfect life. I didn't even mind too much when I had to speak in front of the class. When I spoke in Spanish, I became a different person, someone nobody knew.

Miss Crelly introduced me to the struggles of Latino farm workers. She taught us about the efforts of Cesar Chavez and the United Farm Workers Union. I spent hours standing in front of the local Safeway grocery store with handmade posters, trying to convince shoppers to boycott the store as long as they continued to sell non-union California grapes. Dad was a strong union supporter, so I thought he'd support my efforts. Years later, he still couldn't drive past a Safeway without chuckling. "That's where Arleen tried to change the world," he'd say, smirking at whoever was in the car. I never knew if it was with pride or scorn. Probably a bit of both.

It was the same look, the same chuckle I got when he caught me watching *Little House on the Prairie*. I loved that television show, even as a teenager. I wanted to be Laura Ingalls, and I wanted my father to be loving, understanding, and communicative like her father was. Instead, he called it sappy and made fun of me for watching it.

I did well academically, and I even participated in some school activities, but I never learned how to make or keep friends. I never had a boyfriend. To this day, I'm astounded and envious of people who maintain high school or even college friendships well into their adult lives.

That old black guitar case is still stashed in my attic somewhere. I can't seem to get rid of it. It was the first thing I ever bought for myself, other than school clothes. But my guitar was my first non-essential purchase. I'd been saving what little money I made picking blackberries and later doing babysitting to buy an English saddle, but my father sold Misty and I no longer needed a saddle.

Mom came with me to a music shop in downtown Seattle near Pioneer Square. I fingered the nylon strings, choosing the cheapest six-string folk guitar they had. In retrospect, I don't know why Mom would have driven me all the way from Issaquah to Seattle to buy a guitar. I never even learned to play more than just a few songs. I never had private lessons, but there was a guitar class offered at the high school. I learned little in that class. I wasn't at all interested in group strumming. Determined to learn more, I found myself a how-to book and kept at it. I saw myself as the Joan Baez of the Issaquah Valley. I was making some kind of statement, but I didn't know what it was.

I didn't know who I was.

* * *

A few years earlier, Marleen had started college at Seattle University and moved into the dormitories there. Her evil ways were forgiven and forgotten, polished with the enamel of a good Catholic education. I remember one Sunday afternoon she drove out to Issaquah with her boyfriend, later her husband, in a bright red convertible with a white leather interior. We had a family dinner as though nothing odd had ever happened. Mom and Dad welcomed her back into the family. Marleen even started to do some professional fashion modeling; one year she was the Seattle Boat Show queen. A few years later she married into her boyfriend's family of white-collar professionals. She's the only one in our family to finish a doctorate.

My lost identity was tied in part to my attempts, or Mom and Dad's attempts, to make me as successful as Marleen had become. Because we looked more alike than any of my other sisters did, I became her copy. That last year living at home, after my Goth period ended, I became the Frederick & Nelson department store fashion representative for Issaquah High School, while also taking modeling classes at Elizabeth Leonard's Finishing School in downtown Seattle, the same school Marleen had attended before me. I don't remember if Mom and Dad encouraged me, or if I begged for the classes in an attempt to get the attention that Marleen got, but I do remember sitting in front of the large make-up mirrors and learning the secrets of applying foundation and eye shadow. I learned to walk with my shoulders back and my pelvis out.

It must have been financially difficult for them, as well as being a complication to get me to and from downtown Seattle one evening a week. But they were proud of the successful university student that Marleen had become, and they were trying to reinforce the idea that I could also be successful like her. I don't think they ever realized how clearly I remembered watching the police take away my model sister only five years before.

The financial strain on my parents of trying to boost my self-confidence through modeling classes paled in comparison to the physical strain life in general had become on me. I suppose we all deal with stress in different ways, holding it in different parts of our anatomies. For me, it's always been my gut. Today, it's got a name: Irritable Bowel Syndrome. Today, I know what to do about it, how to eat, how to manage stress. But not as a teenager. Not as a young woman. There were many times when I was doubled over in pain, not knowing what was wrong with me or what to do about it.

I was hospitalized once when I was in high school. Lying on my side on a gurney, wearing a faded hospital gown, I was having an enema. I was being cleaned out, emptied, purified. My body had shut down and was storing more than emotional waste. I was mortified, of course. What teenage girl wouldn't be? I was shy. I was a virgin. And some stranger was touching my private parts. I wanted to die. Instead, I sat on a toilet afterward and felt just like the accumulated waste the doctor was trying so hard to eliminate from my body.

Despite the fact that my mother was a nurse, she never discussed my issues with me, never explained what was happening to me or why. But when the doctor wanted to do exploratory surgery to find out if anything was physically complicating my body's ability to eliminate waste, my parents refused. Not that they told me this; I must have overheard a conversation with the doctor. I was relieved and ready to get the hell out of that hospital; the last thing I wanted was for some doctor to cut me open and dig around inside. In my naïveté, in my ignorance about my own body or about human anatomy in general, I couldn't even imagine where they'd cut me open. I just wanted to go home. After a few days of laxatives and enemas, that's exactly what happened. I went home, and life went on as before. Without discussion, as usual.

As I look back on my parents' decision to refuse surgery, I don't think it was financially based. Dad had decent medical insurance through his union, and I believe that they would have done whatever was medically necessary for my physical health. No, I think Mom knew that my problems were stress-related. I think she and my dad did everything they knew how to do to relieve my stress. But their approach was distraction, with activities such as the modeling classes, rather than facing, rather than talking about, the issues causing the stress.

In retrospect, it's pretty obvious why my body didn't want to get rid of things. I had lost my older siblings. They had disappeared. I didn't understand why, and I was afraid that Mom and Dad would stop loving me, just as I thought they had stopped loving Marleen, Robert and Laureen. I was afraid of stepping out of line, of doing something wrong that would make them stop loving me, but the line I had to toe kept moving.

During my last years at home, thick clouds of self-absorbed identity crisis engulfed me. I was oblivious to the Little Kids. As the middle child, I had always wanted to see myself as one of the Big Kids and never had much to do with the Little Kids, so after the Big Kids were gone, I felt lost and very alone. There were times in high school and those first few years of college that I thought about suicide, but I never acted on those fantasies—the way Maureen did later, in one of her more desperate teen moments. A suicide attempt I only learned about much later, much too late.

* * *

Dad sold our home and half the property, then built a second house on the remaining land. Mom said the first house was too big, that they wanted something smaller, but later they built a third house that was even bigger than the first.

I don't know at what point a home became nothing more than a house, an investment, to my father. Maybe it had always been part of his life plan to build, sell, and build again. By building one mortgage-free house after another, he created a comfortable retirement for Mom and himself, all the while working full-time and raising nine kids.

Unlike most of my siblings, I lived in the same home, a home I loved, from the time I was four years old until the summer before my senior year in high school. In other words, for most of my childhood. I loved that house. It felt solid and safe when everything else in my world was swirling out of control. I had childish notions of keeping that house, our homestead, in the family. I never figured out which of the nine siblings would live there when we were grown, but that didn't stop my fantasies. I just wanted us to all come together again and live there forever.

From the day Marleen was taken away until the day we moved

into the second Issaquah house, I worked on my own running away schemes. These schemes usually involved finding my three older siblings and moving in with them. But when I realized that Dad had plans to sell Misty, my schemes intensified and included her. I never knew why he sold her. She was a high-spirited horse that hated men, a horse that only Charleen and I could handle, and Charleen had left for university. Maybe my parents were afraid for me. Maybe they couldn't afford to keep her. I only know that when I watched the creature I considered to be my best friend being loaded into a trailer and driven off, I was heart-broken. I felt punished for something I hadn't done, and I regretted not having run away.

One afternoon before Misty was sold, I did try to run away. I came home from school and changed my clothes, just as I always did. Mom was still sleeping, and the Little Kids weren't home from school yet. Now that I was in high school, I always got home a few hours before they did. It was my time alone, my time to feel the feelings that were too painful to feel.

I made a decision. I pulled on my warmest jeans and an extra jacket. I knew that even with these warm early spring days, the nights were still cold. I knew I would need warmth. I knew I would need food and water. I knew Misty would need the same. And I knew I'd be caught. I knew Dad would find me and bring me back, because I couldn't ride far enough or fast enough to get away, to run away. I was too rational to really believe that I could ride out of my life and start a new one, but for just one afternoon, I wanted to live the fantasy. So, I executed my escape. After I changed clothes, I stole a loaf of bread from the bread drawer, filled an old milk jug with water, and headed to the barn. I filled two groceries bags with grain and stuffed them into saddlebags.

I saddled Misty and rode away from home, riding the Bonneville easement road until I reached my hidden meadow at the foot of the Big Hill, deep in the forest. I was a brave kid. Maybe all kids are brave before they learn fear. I had explored the woods, sometimes with Charleen, but often alone. And alone I had found my hidden meadow, tiny and round, though I doubt that I was the only kid in the family who knew about it.

The woods surrounding the meadow were dense fir and alder, deep with Pacific Northwest undergrowth of Oregon grape, fern, and blackberry. Deep in this wooded area, there was a tiny clearing, possibly the site of a long-ago cabin, just large enough for a spotlight of sun to filter through the light canopy that parted in the center above the meadow. There, tall grass was sprinkled with white and yellow Shasta daisies and the pink, lavender, and purple spikes of foxgloves.

I unsaddled Misty and threw myself onto the grass. The sky was a deep, Northwest blue, with cotton-candy clouds. I tried to find shapes in the clouds, animals or objects, but I found none. Only fluffy white comforters. I wanted to be up there, to float away, protected by the cotton fluff. Rousing myself from my fitful daydreams, I began to unpack my saddlebags.

The sun was warm on my shoulders as it began its late afternoon descent. As a child, I never cried, so the wetness on my cheeks stunned me. I rolled into a tight ball, pulling the saddle blanket over me. I shook, despite the warmth of the day and my extra layer of heavy clothes. I knew the Little Kids were home from school by now; it was time for evening chores.

As the sun began to set, I saddled Misty and headed home, a deep sadness settling in my heart. I felt trapped, helpless to change the direction of my life. I was the perfect, obedient teenager, and even though I fantasized about running away, I couldn't do so.

I don't know if I was more devastated and heartbroken by the sale of my childhood home and the loss of the stables and riding ring, or by the loss of my best friend, Misty. But move we did, into a house with only three bedrooms. Doreen and Maureen shared one bedroom, Michael and Andrew another, and, of course, Mom and Dad had the third. I spent my senior year in high school sleeping on a fold-out-sofa in the living room.

By then my sense of identity, of space, of belonging, of security, were all shot to hell. I didn't even know who I was. Again, I felt punished, but never had the nerve to ask what I'd done wrong. In five years, I'd lost my older siblings, my horse, and my home. The fold-out-sofa was a blatant reminder that it was my turn to disappear.

* * *

I smelled the rain before I heard it: a gentle rain in the summer of 2005. I climbed out of the bed in my mother's guest bedroom and stuck my head under the curtains covering the only open window in the house. Whenever I visit, I always open a window after my mother goes to bed and close it before she gets up. Even before my father died, my mother always liked her house closed up tight. Now it's locked up like a cell every night, and the windows are never opened, day or night.

So I stuck my head out the window like a dog with its head hanging out a car window on a country road. It was an early, wet dawn on the Pacific Coast. I made my way to my mother's kitchen without a sound and made a small pot of rich, hot coffee. I was waiting for the rain to stop, waiting to take a long walk alone on the Pacific beach in front of my mother's home, hoping I'd be able to get it in before Mom woke up. Once she was awake, I knew I wouldn't be able to get away. I see her only once every three or four weeks. My sister Doreen and I alternate weekends twice a month to check in on Mom. It's a two-hour drive with no traffic from my home in Seattle, but Mom refuses to move closer, to leave the last house my father built. So she's alone most of the time in a beach community of vacation homes and a few retirees, only a handful of whom are full-time residents as she is. I feel guilty if I go off alone when I'm visiting her, but she can't keep up when I walk, so I try to go out while she's still asleep. Later, when she's ready, we stroll at her pace. If I've had my exercise, I'm better able to slow to her speed.

Mom's table is always covered with an accumulation of dated cards, letters and photographs. It's her way of staying connected with her large, disconnected family. Thumbing through a pile of family photos as I waited for my coffee to brew, I found a folded sheet of lined notebook paper. A letter. I glanced at the upper right corner. "August 21, 1971," written in flowing blue script. The handwriting of times past. It was addressed to my mother and father. I scanned the letter, and I saw my name mentioned, but not my name. My name spelled wrong: "e-n-e." A common mistake. The Anglicized spelling. I turned the paper over. The letter was unsigned. Intrigued, I began to read: "Just a word We are fine and enjoyed Arlene stay with us and the 2 weeks passed fast Will take her to Bismarck to get her plane back home."

I scanned the rest of the letter. Farming news, crop sales. Then, with the imperfect spelling of a second language learner, "How is the home comeing working hard I spose."

I set the unfolded paper on the tiny kitchen table, poured myself a cup of coffee, and sat down hard. I read each word, the way a child reads, trying to grasp the meaning, trying to understand. 1971, the summer of my sixteenth year, when my parents sold the home I grew up in and half the property on which it sat. I had no memory of them sending me away that summer. What had I done? I have no memory of flying alone for the first time, or of those two weeks in South Dakota with grandparents I hardly knew. In fact, I have no memory of the summer of my sixteenth year, the summer it was my turn to disappear.

I finished my coffee, put on my running shoes and headed for the beach, leaving the photographs and the letter on the kitchen table. I wanted to ask my mother who wrote the unsigned letter. My grandfather? While my grandmother's spoken English was good, she never learned to read or write it well. There was no other feasible explanation. It had to be from my grandfather.

I went to the beach with my head in a fog thicker than anything the Pacific Coast could muster. How could I not remember? Could my grandfather have just confused our names, which all looked and sounded the same? Could he have written the wrong name? But who else could it have been? Marleen and Charleen were university students at the time, Laureen disowned, and Doreen and Maureen were too young to travel alone. I knew the letter was about me. I must have been sent away, I reasoned, disappeared just like my older siblings for something that I had done, for some reason that I didn't remember.

When I returned from the beach, my mother was up. The envelope and the photographs were still there in the middle of her kitchen table where I'd left them, but the letter was gone. I heard Mom moving around in her bedroom. Had she seen the letter on the table, picked it up and moved it, as she often does these days? She moves things around, sorting, organizing and forgetting where she's put things. Mail, magazines, memories. Maybe she had seen it on the table and moved it to a place where she felt it would be safer.

I took a shower and decided to confront her. I'd never asked or told my mother much of anything before, so I was nervous.

When I came back into the kitchen, my mother was searching for the cereal bowls. I took the envelope of pictures from the center of the table and began. "Mom, I was looking at these photos earlier this morning and I found a letter mixed in. I left it here on the table because I wanted to ask you about it, but now it's gone. I think it was from your dad. Where did it go?"

She looked confused and paused for a moment before saying, "Oh, yes, I found that a while ago."

"But you moved it just this morning. While I was gone to the beach. I left it right here on the table because I wanted to ask you about it, and now it's gone. Where did you put it?"

"This morning?" She began to shuffle through the piles of papers and photographs on the kitchen table, and then on the adjacent dining room table. I could see her growing confusion and frustration. She had no memory of moving the letter less than an hour, maybe a half hour, before.

"Maybe you carried it into the bedroom," I suggested. She continued to wander around the small house, shuffling through piles of photographs and outdated greeting cards. After about five minutes, I knew it was pointless. I tried another approach.

"Mom, the letter was dated August 1971, and my name was mentioned. Apparently, I was in Herreid that summer. Do you remember sending me to Herreid alone when I was sixteen?"

"Oh no, that was a long time ago." She shook her head, sadly. "I can't remember so long ago. I get confused sometimes."

We sat down and ate our Cheerios in silence.

Several hours later, I was noting some future visits and doctor appointments on Mom's large calendar next to the telephone. It's one of those calendars with pockets, and there I found my grandfather's letter for the second time that day.

I held the letter out to my mother. "Mom, look. I found Grandpa's letter right here in your calendar."

She took the letter from me and held it to her chest in both hands. "It's from my father. He was a wonderful man." That was all she remembered, yet who was I to criticize? It was more than I remembered of that summer.

Chapter Seven: Leaving Home

I was a twenty-year-old university student when I had my first serious confrontation with Mom and Dad. Up to that point in my life, I had been the perfect daughter, doing everything humanly possible to please them. Even my attempt at running away was a complete failure, one they knew nothing about. I saw their pain, and in my innocence, I blamed my older siblings. I sheltered my parents in silence, just as they had done when I was younger. And when I found myself in trouble, my silence only deepened.

I graduated from high school at seventeen, in June 1972, earning a scholarship to the same Catholic university where Marleen had studied years before. Just as I had done with modeling school, I was following in my eldest sister's footsteps. In September, I moved into Bellarmine Hall dormitory at Seattle University and began classes. The classes themselves were fine, but I felt lost in a dormitory full of girls I didn't know how to relate to. They all seemed to know how to giggle and tell stories and have fun together. My clothes weren't right, my hair was wrong, and my glasses were ugly. I just didn't belong. I didn't know how to make friends, and I felt stifled and claustrophobic in the tiny room I had to share with another girl. I felt uncomfortable and embarrassed using the bathroom down the hall that I had to share with a whole floor full of strangers. My sisters and I had shared at home, but we had shared a very large bedroom and bathroom in a big house in the middle of a spacious piece of land. We weren't crammed together in an overcrowded high-rise.

My sophomore year at Seattle University, I was determined to get a private room. Again, I was running away from an uncomfortable situation, and this time I was successful. At first, I was told there were no private rooms available; the dorms were full to capacity. But I did some checking and learned that upper class male students were being allowed to have single rooms in a dormitory on the southern edge of the campus called Campion

Tower. When I asked for a room there, I was told that it was an unsecured building and female students weren't allowed. Furious, I kept digging and learned that a private English language school for international students was housed in Campion Tower, leasing several floors for both classroom and dormitory space. I went to their administrative office and asked to rent a room. They agreed, figuring that a native speaker on the same floor would be beneficial for the foreign students living there who were struggling to learn English. I settled into my second year within the ivory towers of Seattle University, determined to adjust.

Unfortunately, the university administration caught wind of what I'd done. Or maybe it was fortunate. For me, at least. SU threatened to terminate the lease agreement with the language school if they continued to rent to me. Rather than kick me out, the language school hired me as a resident assistant, so I lived rent-free for the remainder of my sophomore year.

During those first two years in college, I went home on weekends and holidays as often as I could. One visit I was surprised by a new puppy in the family. He was a small sheepdog mix, shaggy and ugly. Maureen named him Shugly. He was a Christmas gift from Marleen, the sister who always said she'd have a dog if she could find a hairless, shitless breed.

During one of my visits home, the Little Kids, with the exception of Doreen who was never crazy about dogs, decided it was time for Shugly's first bath. They filled a large blue wheelbarrow full of soapy water, and together they lifted a struggling Shugly into the cold, from-the-hose water. Maureen stood on one side of the wheelbarrow and Andrew on the other. Laughing and splashing, they held the wet, bewildered, gray and white puppy while Michael poured water from a large stainless steel pitcher over Shugly's head. I stood at a distance, snapping photographs and laughing with them. Almost thirty years later, I saw that metal pitcher in Mom's backyard, rusted and forgotten. I asked her if I could take it home with me, and she put it in the back of my station wagon.

So many memories from one oversized wide-mouthed metal pitcher. Dad said that it was a milk pitcher from a dairy where his father had once worked. But with nine kids, my parents couldn't afford fresh milk. Instead, they bought restaurant-sized boxes of Carnation Non-Fat Instant Milk powder. I remember mixing it by the gallons in that huge pitcher—the awful smell of the powder and the tiredness in my arm as I whipped and whipped with a wire whisk trying to get rid of the horrible lumps. One of the greatest treats I discovered when I started eating at the Seattle University cafeteria was "real" milk.

Still, Seattle University was not for me. It was small, quiet and Catholic. I wanted something bigger, broader, more liberal, more political. The United States was still in Vietnam and SU was protest-free. I decided to transfer to the University of Washington, the largest public university in the area and a hotbed of anti-war activities.

In September 1974, I signed a six-month lease for my first apartment, a large third-floor studio in an old brownstone, one block from the University of Washington campus. I had always wanted to live alone, in my own apartment. Maybe it was all those sitcom episodes of Marlo Thomas in *"That Girl"* that fueled my fantasies of living alone in a big city apartment, or maybe it was growing up with so many siblings that fed my craving for a space of my own. I rented an apartment within easy walking distance of both my classes and my part-time job, and I was thrilled. At least in the beginning— at least with the idea of it—before the unbearable loneliness and sense of isolation set in.

For six months, I floated between Political Science classes, visits to Campion Tower to see a few old friends, and sitting in my solitary apartment trying to make sense of what life was all about. Once, I crawled under my desk and stayed there for a day or two, banging my head against the wall until I was exhausted. Curling myself into a ball, I would fall into a fitful sleep, only to awaken and begin the cycle again. But even then it wasn't my personal life I was questioning. I hadn't managed to take off the blinders of my childhood. Instead, I questioned the state of the world, or the meaning of life in general. Ever since my high school protests against non-union produce, and even junior high, when I first understood what Vietnam meant, I'd used politics as a distraction from looking inward and trying to figure out who I was and what was making me so lonely and unhappy.

I never found any answers. Instead, I found a Venezuelan physics student named Eduardo. He came from Caracas, on government oil money, to get an American university education. Like most foreign students coming to the States, he had to improve his English skills and pass the dreaded TOEFL (Test of English as a Foreign Language) exam, the language exam required of all international students entering American universities. He was a competitive chess player with intelligent brown eyes, curly black hair and warm brown skin. He was my first love.

I was a confused twenty-year-old virgin, brainwashed by Catholicism. I believed sex before marriage was a sin. I believed abortion was a sin. I believed my own raging hormones were a sin. I was crazy in love and burning in my own self-induced hell.

Before I met Eduardo, I had already bought a month-long Greyhound bus pass to travel around the country and arranged a quarter's leave of absence from the University of Washington. My six-month lease was up, and I had decided to give up my apartment. Eduardo had applied for admission to several universities around the country and would be leaving Seattle. I hadn't made any definite plans. The only thing I knew for sure was that I wanted to be with him. I was my parents' daughter, however, and I wasn't going to waste the money I'd spent on the bus pass.

On St. Patrick's Day 1975, I sat on the front steps of my apartment building waiting for my dad to show up to help me move out of my apartment. I didn't have much—no car and few belongings, but I still needed some help getting what little I had out to Issaquah for storage. I had asked Dad to help, and he agreed to meet me in front of my building after he got off work. We set the date and time without realizing that the day we chose was St. Patrick's Day.

I sat on the cold, concrete steps of my apartment building, waiting as though frozen in space and time. I couldn't move. I just sat there on the steps. Three cold concrete steps. I sat on the top step with my feet on the bottom step, waiting. I waited much longer, much later, than any logic could justify. I kept expecting my dad to drive up to the front of the building with his usual gruff apology and fix-it attitude. But he didn't.

Finally, I gave up, unlocked the front door, and went up in the elevator to my now-barren apartment. It was spotless. The phone was disconnected and there was no food in the kitchen. I slept on the floor that night, surrounded by boxes, crying, lonely, forgotten. I realized for the first time that my father was not the mythical god I had thought he was. He was flesh and blood, and he had forgotten me.

Dad showed up at my apartment the following morning, apologetic. He'd gone for a rare after-work drink with some union brothers to celebrate Saint Patrick's Day. He wanted to know why I hadn't called home. I couldn't answer him. Sure, I could've walked up the street to the nearest pay phone and called. Sooner or later, he or Mom would have come to help me. But that wasn't the point. I didn't want to have to remind my father to think of me, to remember me.

I had planned to jump on a bus and leave town the same week I moved out of my apartment. Six weeks later, I was still in Seattle, living out of a backpack, sleeping on the tiny sofa in the lobby restroom of Campion Tower or with Eduardo in his Campion Tower dorm room. My parents thought I was traveling. My older siblings knew nothing of my whereabouts. I don't think my younger siblings, Maureen included, gave me any thought at all.

It was crazy, hanging around Campion Tower like some homeless runaway. Fortunately, the building manager, the front desk clerks and many of the residents still knew me. After all, I'd lived there for two years. I was in love for the first time. I didn't want to begin my bus trip and leave Eduardo until I knew his plans. He had passed the TOEFL exam, but was still waiting for university acceptance letters. I was afraid that I'd return to Seattle and find that he was gone.

Finally, one Sunday evening, I boarded a Greyhound in downtown Seattle and headed east towards Spokane, and north from there into Canada. I was relieved to know that Eduardo had been accepted at the University of California in Santa Cruz, but it was still hard to leave. I began to feel ill, in a way I'd never felt before. At first, I thought I was just homesick for Eduardo. I missed him more than I'd ever missed anyone before in my life, even more than I had missed my older siblings when they disappeared from home. I hadn't known love could hurt so much. Then I started having dizzy spells. I was nauseous. Naïve as I was, I knew I was pregnant. On Wednesday, I got off the bus somewhere in central Canada.

The bus station was cavernous, with concrete floors and rows of hard wooden benches. A large institutional clock hung high on one wall, a white accusing face with large black numbers staring down at me. Shaking, I huddled on one of the benches and pulled a heavy cotton sleeping bag from the backpack leaning against the bench beside me. It wasn't one of the high-tech, super lightweight backpacking bags available today, of course. This bag was huge. I wrapped myself, cuddled myself, tried to comfort myself. I couldn't stop shaking. Below the clock on the wall was a huge schedule of arrivals and departures, eastbound and westbound buses.

I looked at the clock: 7:20 p.m. Almost four hours until the next westbound bus. The next eastbound would roll out within the hour. I sat frozen in time and indecision. I heard the crackle of the intercom system, a bored voice announcing the eastbound bus. I sat paralyzed.

At 11:00 p.m., I boarded a bus headed west to Spokane. I felt numb. A zombie unable to feel or think, I was acting on instinct. When I reached Spokane, I found the Youth Hostel, left my backpack, and asked for directions to Planned Parenthood. I found my way as if in a dream. I sat at a receptionist's desk.

"How long has it been since your last period?"

"About four weeks."

"It's too soon to test you. The result will be inconclusive. Unless, of course, it's positive."

"It'll be positive." I spoke with calm determination.

"How can you know?"

"I know. Please, just test me. Please."

They did, and I was right. The women at Planned Parenthood were kind, supportive and gentle. I told them I needed to return to Seattle, to my boyfriend. They gave me the name of a doctor to see: a legal abortion clinic.

I climbed back on another bus, but not without calling Eduardo. I told him we had a problem. I told him I was returning. As I rode the endless hours from Spokane to Seattle, I relived every anti-abortion demonstration I had participated in, every pro-life button I had worn, every Catholic Youth Organization meeting I had attended. I knew my parents would disown me for my sins, any of them, all of them, no matter what I decided to do, unless I kept them a secret. Another family secret.

The only other choice I had, the only way I could avoid being disowned, was to get married, but marriage wasn't an option. Eduardo was on a national scholarship, under contract to get an education and return to Venezuela to repay the loan by working for the government. He had no interest in marriage. The last thing he wanted was a wife and a kid. I had called Eduardo before I left the Spokane bus depot.

"I'm pregnant. I'm coming back."

"Are you sure?"

"I just tested positive."

"I'll get the money to take care of it."

That was it. No discussion. He didn't want a kid, but he was willing to solve the problem. It was so easy for him. His scientific mind made life simple, clear-cut, precise. As I stepped off the Greyhound at Eighth Avenue and Stewart Street in Seattle and into his arms, I let him take over. I let him make the decisions and solve the problems, just as I'd been raised to do. Let the man make the decisions. That's the way I thought Mom did it. Dad made all the decisions. Mom and all nine of us kids followed along without questioning, without conflict. Conflict meant being disowned.

I knew I couldn't raise a child alone without family support. I had no financial resources to even get through the pregnancy, let alone raise a child. I considered adoption as well as abortion.

Funny how those words are so similar, how they play in the mind. They dueled in my consciousness from Spokane to Seattle, with stops at every tiny town along the way. Adoption, abortion, adoption, abortion, as the wheels of the Greyhound went round and round, gobbling up the miles.

The doctor's office was just south of Seattle, near the airport, convenient for those coming to Washington State for this purpose. A quick procedure, maybe an overnight stay in an airport hotel, maybe not. An easy secret to keep. From Capitol Hill, where Eduardo was still living in his dorm room, however, the clinic was anything but convenient if you didn't have a car. More buses.

He was with me. He took charge.

I sat in the reception area, waiting for my name to be called, fearful and trembling. The examination room was clean, professional. I remember a doctor telling me it was over, but that they would need to give me an injection to prevent future birth defects. I had no idea what he was talking about. I only nodded.

Many years later, when I again found myself pregnant, I understood. I have O-negative blood. Eduardo did not. Our blood types were not compatible. My body would create antibodies against his, against the fetus if it had his blood type instead of mine. These antibodies could cause birth defects in a future child.

After we left the clinic, Eduardo was attentive, almost joyous. He took me to dinner at a Mexican restaurant in downtown Seattle. He wanted to celebrate. We walked down a short flight of steps into a brightly lit, underground restaurant. The vibrant colors—orange, red, yellow—of the crepe paper streamers and flowers assaulted my tired eyes. Eduardo supported me on one side, holding my right elbow. I knew I should be home in bed. Home? Eduardo's dorm room. But this celebratory dinner was what he wanted.

"Are you sure you're up to it?" he had asked on the bus ride back to Seattle.

"Sure," I responded, in little more than a whisper.

We sat in a corner table that soon filled with Eduardo's friends from the English language school he attended, the school where I used to live. Had he planned this? A party to celebrate his freedom from premature fatherhood? Or was this just one of his regular hangouts, a place where he could always run into a Latino friend or classmate? I never asked.

Eduardo was charismatic, the center of every party. As I sat in the corner, watching him laugh and talk with his friends, a feeling that something wasn't right began creeping up my spine. I ignored it, assuring myself that things would be different when we got to California.

I tried to be happy, but I could not forgive myself for what I had done. I had taken a human life. I knew I would never have children; I knew I didn't deserve children. I moved to California with him, and we shared a life together for a few more years, but it didn't last. Nothing lasted.

Exactly eleven days after I left Seattle the first time, I climbed back on a Greyhound bus and rolled out of the city again, still determined to use my bus pass. This time I headed south to Arizona, crossed the southern states, and looped the county. I returned to Seattle twenty days later to find Eduardo packing to leave the city forever.

I couldn't fathom being left behind, so I decided to pack my bags, extend my one-quarter leave of absence from the university to a full year, and follow Eduardo to California. I figured if everything worked out, I'd establish California residency within a year so I wouldn't have to pay out-of-state tuition, and then I could afford to finish my degree there. If not, I could always return broken-hearted to Seattle and complete the degree I had left pending at the University of Washington. But first, I had to tell Mom and Dad of my plans.

We were in the second Issaquah house, the one where I had slept in the living room. I'd called and told Mom that I was coming out for a visit and that I needed to talk to her and Dad. After dinner was over, Mom scooted the Little Kids off to their rooms and called to Dad and me. "Let's go into our bedroom to talk."

I'd never had such a serious conversation with them. I'd never had a private, in-the-bedroom, closed-door conversation. I wonder now what they thought I was going to tell them. I was nervous, but determined to tell them the truth.

"I came to say good-bye. I'm moving to California."

"California?" Mom asked. "Why California?"

"Because Eduardo's going to the University of California in Santa Cruz. I want to live there. I'll work for a year to make some money and establish state residency. Then I'll go back to school."

I was sitting on the edge of their bed, with Mom beside me. Dad stood in front of me, looking down on both of us. "So you're going to shack up with him, then?"

"I really don't know if I'll live with him or not, Daddy." I rushed, the words tumbling out of me, trying to get them out before he cut me off. "He'll have to live in the dorm, at least for the first year, and since I won't be a student right away..."

"Then you are saying good-bye. Forever."

With that, he stomped out of the room, slamming the door behind him. For him, it was as simple as that. I wasn't living up to his expectations of me. I was no longer the perfect image he created and controlled. I no longer existed for him. Shut out. Forgotten.

I was stunned. I'd always told myself that the earlier disappearances of my older siblings had been their own faults. They'd each done something terribly wrong, hurting Mom and Dad so deeply that they'd deserved to be rejected. I loved my father deeply, profoundly. I had him so high on a pedestal that he had to fall. Still, I was taken aback by his reaction. At the same time, I felt I deserved it because of the abortion I'd had that they knew nothing about.

I sat in my parents' bedroom, shocked by my father's absolute rejection, and for the first time it occurred to me that maybe it was Dad, and not my older siblings, who was causing so much unnecessary pain in our family.

For Dad, it was always his way or the highway. But we were the ones hitting the pavement, with the doors slammed and locked behind us.

In my mind, he didn't just fall from the pedestal. He crashed and shattered into a million fragments. Half of me wanted to pull on a pair of old, manure-covered cowboy boots and stomp the fragments of my father into dust. The other half, like a deer in headlights, was too stunned to move.

Mom called after Dad, but I don't remember if she stayed with me, if she tried to comfort me, or if she rushed after him. I do know that I cried for a long, long time before I could move. And then I decided to follow my dreams, with a hole in my heart no longer filled with my father's love. But I didn't let go. I lived with hope. Sometimes, Dad came around. It would take time, but sooner or later, he might accept me again, as he had Marleen just a few years before.

I followed Eduardo to California and to Caracas, Venezuela, as well. But when he returned to California to continue his studies, I stayed in Caracas to gain some teaching experience, supporting myself by teaching English at the British Embassy School for six months.

Caracas in the mid-seventies was a strange place, awash in oil money and growing so fast that the proverbial head of the collective population was spinning, unable to keep up with the changes. Everywhere you looked, huge construction cranes marred the skyline. Traffic, both motorized and on foot, was congested by roadwork. And without contacts, it was almost impossible to find a place to live. I was lucky. One of my wealthy, older students had just married and moved out of her downtown condo. She offered it to me rent free, knowing it would be safer to have it occupied rather than sitting empty.

With my American accent and ways, I was definitely an oddity at the British Embassy School. It was one of my first formal teaching jobs, and I was young. The bulk of my teaching load was made up of after-school enrichment classes for wealthy Venezuelan teenagers whose parents wanted them to go beyond the level of English offered in their high schools. I was only a few years older than some of my students.

The Embassy ran a tight ship. I taught back-to-back classes most of the afternoon and into the evening, with only short bathroom breaks between classes. During one of those bathroom breaks, I was rushing to get back to class. Like many people, when I rush, my brain can't seem to keep up with my body. The normal, the routine, sometimes gets lost in the confusion.

When the break ended, I hurried back to the classroom. Promptness is the rule of order in a British Embassy school, so I tried my hardest to always be on time, or even a few minutes early. I must admit, it was against my nature. I usually run late, always trying to cram too much into too little time. But it was a new job; I was young, I wanted to look good, to stand out, to impress the Director. I should have known you can't mess with human nature.

I was punctual, standing erect in front of my class just as the bell rang. I began the lesson. I noticed distraction among my usually quiet, respectful group of students. They were whispering. Something wasn't quite right, but I continued talking.

There were a few snickers, followed by a shushing noise. Then, a young girl with deep brown eyes and thick black hair that reached to her slender waist stood and approached the front of the room. She cupped her hand around my ear, whispered her message, and returned to her seat. I turned my back to the class, pulled my pants zipper closed and began writing on the dusty blackboard.

I was wearing pink panties that day, a bright contrast against my severe black pants. The gaping opening just below my belt had been at eye level to every student seated in front of me. By the next day, it was unlikely that there was a single person in the school who didn't know about my foolish blunder. At least that's how it felt to me, when I forced myself to go to work the following day. I walked into the school with my head in the air and a smile on my face, as though it were a day as normal as any other.

I put the incident out of my mind, pretended it never happened, denied the experience to myself as well as to any teaching colleague brash enough to mention it to my face. But it was never forgotten. Nothing is ever really forgotten. Yet denial was what I had learned all my life. The denial my parents modeled. The denial I was raised with. It was my main coping mechanism.

I sometimes wonder how well denial really works. Can people truly lock away painful memories, truths that cannot be faced? Or do those memories and truths simply find a place in the heart to grow and fester, to become deformed, warped from lack of attention, lack of sunlight and fresh air? I can't help but believe that it was those festering memories, that painful denial, that later proved too much for my father to bear. Denial got the better of him, and eventually deteriorated into death.

Mom's denial is still intact, but her memory is not. Her denial has worked its wicked ways, like a cancer slowly eating away at her memories until they are beyond recognition, beyond my memory of how things were. My siblings, too, have memories of shared life events quite different from my own. This may not be denial, but rather a different way of seeing an event as it happened, as well as a different way of remembering. What *is* denial is the fact that we seldom talk about it.

I know that my memories are based on feelings, on the emotions of the time, and perhaps my emotions overshadow the events themselves. Perhaps my siblings choose to remember the events because the emotions were not a strong part of their reality, or maybe the emotions were denied.

* * *

When Maureen turned thirteen, I was long gone. Doreen had left home for university by then, and besides Maureen, only Michael and Andrew still lived at home. But they had each other; their adventures didn't include a kid sister. Maureen was alone. She lived in a large, lonely house with exhausted, working parents who had no time or energy left for the last of nine kids. Her best friend and constant companion was her dog, Shugly. They were an inseparable duo. It was as difficult to imagine one without the other as Batman without Robin.

Yet they were separated, by the needless violence of a thoughtless neighbor. One afternoon, the neighbor's dog wandered down the driveway and into our yard. Shugly, a full-grown watchdog by then, decided he needed to defend to his territory. A dogfight ensued. Maureen ran out of the house screaming, trying to pull the dogs apart. The neighbor ran from his garage, a two-by-four in hand.

"Wait! Wait!" screamed Maureen. "Don't hit them. Just separate them. Don't hit them. Don't hit them."

But the neighbor pushed her out of the way and swung the two-by-four at the dogs, trying to stop the fight. He failed miserably. I don't know if he hit Shugly on purpose, but I do know that the board crashed down on Shugly's head. He died on the spot.

Maureen collapsed on the ground beside Shugly's body. "Look what you did! You killed him! You killed him! You killed him!"

"I'm sorry. I'm so sorry," the neighbor repeated, standing over them. "It was an accident. I didn't mean to hurt him."

"I told you not to hit them. How could you be so stupid? How could you be so cruel? Why didn't you stop?"

"I just didn't want you to get hurt."

"Why don't you just hit me over the head with that board, too? Why don't you crack my head open, too?" She sat on the gravel driveway, cuddling Shugly's body, sobbing and covered in blood. The neighbor had killed her best friend.

I wasn't there for her. Having been disowned, I didn't learn of Shugly's death until a few years later. I was jumping around in my undergraduate studies, moving from Seattle University to the University of Washington to the University of California at Santa Cruz. I drifted from Seattle to Santa Cruz to Caracas and back to California, with a few trips to Mexico thrown into the mix, but the emptiness within me continued to gnaw away at my soul. I couldn't settle, not on a school, not on a major, not on a place to live. I was lost in a search for something I couldn't identify.

It was summer 1978, and Dad and Mom still weren't talking to me. Although I was still living in California, I was no longer living with Eduardo, so I thought it was time to see if I could weasel my way back into their good graces. I drove for two days straight from Santa Cruz to Issaquah, pulled into their driveway, and walked in unannounced through the kitchen door.

In the three years I'd been disowned and gone, my father had built another house on a few acres of land that were adjacent to the original acreage my parents had bought years before. My parents and the Little Kids moved for the third time since the summer between my junior and senior years in high school. This house was huge, despite Mom telling me years before that they sold the house I grew up in because it was too big. As I drove up to the house, I knew I was entering new territory in more ways than one. I didn't even know the layout of my family home.

It was evening, dark. The flicker of television light shone into the kitchen from the living room. I stood for a moment, trembling. Had I made a mistake walking straight into the house? Should I have come home at all? Pushing these thoughts aside, I called out cheerfully, "Hello? Anybody home?"

"Marleen? Is that you?" Dad struggled out of his recliner, more asleep than awake.

"No, Dad. It's me. Arleen." I was terrified. Would he turn and walk out of the room? Would he tell me to leave? Where was Mom, anyway?

Dad straightened, stood for a moment, then walked toward me and wrapped me in a huge, warm hug. The kind of hug only a father can give.

The evening after my surprise arrival, we sat around the dining room table in an awkward silence that was very different from the large, rowdy family meals of my early childhood. Maureen sat at my side, a skinny fifteen year old with a row of braces reshaping her smile. She was shy, maybe we both were, and I had trouble finding things to say to her, or questions that prompted more than a simple yes/no response. Still, she was with me most of the time during that week in Issaquah, like a slender, timid shadow.

It was a short visit. I still had an apartment and a job in California. I didn't plan to stay in the Seattle area. I just wanted to know if I still had parents. I returned to Santa Cruz a week later, stronger, but still not whole.

* * *

Only three months after that trip home, Robert came to see me in Santa Cruz. I didn't know his reasons for being in California, but

I was overwhelmed with joy to see him again. Sometime earlier, Robert had re-entered my parents' life in much the same way I had. He merely showed up for a brief visit and acted as though he'd never been disowned. When he appeared at my door in Santa Cruz, it was much the same. I didn't ask any questions. I was just thrilled to see him.

I lived in a tiny, two-room guest cottage in the middle of the large, untamed backyard of an old Victorian mansion. That first afternoon, Robert and I were eating a picnic lunch in the garden under a cluster of tall fir trees when we began reminiscing about similar trees on our childhood farm in Issaquah.

"Remember how we used to climb those things, Arleen? God, it was like being on the top of the world."

"Yeah," I agreed. "But those days are long past."

"No way," he said, with a smirk on his face. The next thing I knew, he was climbing high into the tree beside my cottage.

"My god, you wouldn't believe the view of Monterey Bay from up here," he yelled down to me.

I was at the end of a Bachelor of Arts program and a dead-end relationship with Eduardo when Robert showed up. My big brother had a win-win solution: leave Santa Cruz and come to his Hawaiian paradise to work for him as a house sitter and a caretaker for his girlfriend's two children from a prior marriage, while the two of them and their baby went sailing.

He gave me a plane ticket, and I followed him to Hawaii. The North Shore of Oahu in the late seventies was a culture as strange to me as that of Caracas, Venezuela, or Mexico City. The language was the same, but that was all. Daily life seemed to revolve around the height of the waves crashing on Sunset Beach. Tourists and beach bums populated the North Shore. To me, it felt like everybody was on an endless vacation. In contrast, my life revolved around the kids' school schedule, the number of horseback-riding hours I could squeeze in before they came home, and the evenings when I could lose myself in the nightclubs. My younger brother Michael was on the island during part of my stay, and we often went out together. That was the best part of my time in Hawaii—hanging out with Michael.

When Robert returned from his adventures, he offered me help getting set up in my own apartment on the island, or a plane ticket anywhere I wanted to go. I wanted to leave; the North Shore of Oahu wasn't for me. I could too easily get lost in the drug and surf culture that permeated the place. I was weak. And I knew that for me, Robert was as powerful and overbearing as Dad, even when it wasn't intentional. Or maybe I just recognized my own vulnerabilities. I needed to get away from a drug culture that I didn't want to sink into, and I needed to get away from my brother, the same way I had needed to get away from home a half dozen years before. I had to figure out who I was, and I couldn't do it in the shadow of my older brother's strength. And besides, I knew where I had a friend. So I said, "Mexico City, please. I want to go back to Mexico City."

* * *

I arrived in Mexico City with two boxes, mostly books, and a few hundred dollars in my pocket, uncertain what the future held. I knew a grand total of one person there, a girl I'd met at UC Santa Cruz. I'd only been there a few months, barely time to settle into my first apartment, when Robert sent me another ticket, this time round-trip. He wanted me to come back to Hawaii for his wedding. No excuses; I was coming.

My biggest concern, my only concern as I recall, was what to wear. I had no appropriate clothing for a wedding and no money to waste on shopping. I scoured the local open-air markets and ended up buying a bright red, embroidered Mexican peasant dress. It was probably the most inappropriate thing I could have bought, but I wanted to wear something indigenous, to make some kind of socio-political statement. I saw myself as some sort of enlightened radical. I was interested in Mexican leftist politics and the class struggle, and I needed something cheap. So I packed my dress and clogs and headed back to the North Shore.

Only two people said anything to me about that bright red dress, a flaming aberration in the wedding party of subtle white and sea blue. One was my future sister-in-law's best friend who said, "You're not going to wear that thing, are you?" I heard Mom's voice in my head, "If you don't have anything good to say, don't say anything at all." I said nothing.

Maureen loved the dress. She thought it was the most beautiful, the most original thing she'd ever seen. She wasn't remembering the red and white checkered taffeta dress of our early childhood, the dress we both wore. The dress that made each of us a princess. Now, I felt out of place. It wasn't a new feeling, so I chose to deny it and focus on my little sister's admiration.

After the wedding, I folded up the dress and gave it to

Maureen. She still had it years later, when Mom and Doreen were packing her things to vacate her apartment after she disappeared. They found that Mexican dress among her meager belongings and packed it into the bottom of Maureen's cedar hope chest.

I wonder what hopes, what dreams, Maureen filled it with.

As we were growing up, Mom and Dad gave each of the sisters a hope chest—all but me, that is. For some reason, probably a tight family economy, I never received one of those beautiful cedar chests. When I moved back to Seattle five years later, after Maureen's disappearance, Mom gave me Maureen's hope chest with my red dress folded in the bottom. "It's right for you to have it," she said, as Dad loaded that receptacle of lost hopes and dreams into the back of my small truck.

There was a brief period of time many years later, when my daughter, Erin, also thought that the red dress was the most beautiful thing she'd ever seen. As a toddler, she loved to play dress-up, tripping around the house with the long, embroidered dress wrapping around her ankles. It broke my heart to watch her, remembering Maureen, still wondering what had happened to my beautiful little sister. But Erin loved that dress so much that I couldn't take it away from her. Like all things, that period passed. Dress-up became a baby's game; the red embroidered dress was washed, and again folded and placed in tissue at the bottom of Maureen's cedar hope chest. I'm not sure I'll ever be able to get rid of either the hope chest or the dress. I have too little of Maureen left.

* * *

Robert and his bride were married on March 17, 1979, another Saint Patrick's Day. Robert wanted us all in Hawaii for his wedding, and he was willing to help with plane tickets for any of us who needed financial support or encouragement.

Still, Mom and Dad didn't attend their eldest son's wedding. In their eyes, it was a shameful second marriage, for both Robert and his fiancée. To make matters worse, they were already living together and had a child. Also, my parents felt sadness and jealousy because, after several visits to the islands, Michael and Andrew had chosen to live in Hawaii and work for their older brother, instead of staying in Seattle and joining Dad's union. While a college degree was always expected of my sisters and me, my brothers were informal apprentices to my father from the time they could walk and talk. Dad was a strong union man and always assumed his sons would follow his path. With his help, his sons were assured admissions into competitive apprenticeship programs. When all three of his sons chose to turn their backs on the union and leave home to work in Hawaii, it cut Dad to the quick.

But most of all, I think Mom and Dad weren't at Robert's wedding because Laureen and her daughters were. Dad had refused to even hear mention of her name for over ten years. Laureen was divorced by this point, but still Dad would not, perhaps could not, forgive and forget. It simply was not in his nature. Given his strong feelings, it's a credit to him, or perhaps to Mom, that they allowed Maureen, their only child still in high school and living at home, to attend the wedding. In the pictures, she is a teenager with short, curly blonde hair and bright blue eyes, in a white sundress with straps tied in bows at the shoulders. A dress that made her look much younger than her fifteen years. In my favorite photo, she's on some kind of bus, maybe the Wiki Wiki bus at the Honolulu airport. She's glancing back over her shoulder with a look of annoyance in her eyes, like "Oh lord, is she gonna be taking pictures the whole time?"

The nine siblings converged on the North Shore of Oahu for a St. Patrick's Day wedding. It was in a beautiful tropical garden—a casual, relaxed exchanging of vows, a joining of lives. It was a Hawaiian wedding ceremony, complete with soft ukulele music whispering in the palm trees. The bride wore a simple white cotton lace dress; her long, strawberry-blonde curls pulled back, her neck encircled with several *pikake* strands. The groom wore a white safari suit, his neck encircled by a traditional Hawaiian *maile lei* of green leaves. A proud father, he held his baby daughter in his arms throughout the ceremony. The sweet fragrances of plumeria and ginger filled the air.

Together, my seven siblings and I smiled, sharing in the union as Robert, his bride, and their children became a family. After the ceremony and the dinner that followed, as evening began to fall with the gentleness of a tropical breeze, we heard the whirring of a helicopter. It landed in the same spot in the garden where, only a few hours before, vows were exchanged. Robert flew his bride off in this helicopter as the rest of us clapped and cheered in surprise and joy, then watched in silence. The eight of us stood together, our arms locked around each other. We rejoiced in being together but were saddened that Mom and Dad weren't with us.

"Too bad Mom and Dad aren't here," somebody ventured, as the helicopter rose above our heads.

"Dad would've gotten a kick out of that," somebody else said, nodding towards the helicopter disappearing in the distance.

"Mom would've loved taking charge of the baby," another sibling commented.

My sisters and I—Marleen, Laureen, Charleen, Doreen—went to a club at the tip of the North Shore to dance and drink. When the musicians struck up the old Pointer Sisters song, we sang along at the top of our lungs and danced together as only sisters can. But where was Maureen? Too young to be at the club, she had been left behind to babysit her nieces and nephews.

After that brief couple of days together, my brothers and Laureen stayed in Hawaii, my other sisters returned to the Seattle area, and I returned alone to Mexico City. Communication, contact, understanding, were never strong in my family. Truthfully, I never expected letters, and I thought a phone call would only mean seriously bad news. After the wedding, the subsequent lack of contact seemed normal.

Robert's wedding was the only time all nine siblings had been together since before the Big Kids left home in the sixties. We were strangers reaching out to each other, trying to be family. But for me, it was too little, too late.

Maybe for Maureen, too.

Chapter Eight: Mexico City

Mexico City is a place I never understood, despite my mastery of the Spanish language. It's a city of contrasts so pronounced that you couldn't ignore them. Wealth and poverty, beauty and filth, contentment and desperation, were side by side, hand in hand. Strong contrasts that made denial of stark reality impossible.

I walked the wide, tree-lined avenues of the wealthy areas of the city, marveling at the beauty of the cobblestone streets and walled gardens with their trailing bougainvillea. The streets were lined with boutiques, beauty salons and restaurants, for the small minority who could afford such luxuries. I also walked the streets of the less fortunate, the neighborhoods of the forgotten ones, where doorways opened directly from the sidewalks into dark, single-room dwellings. *Campesinos* from the countryside huddled on the street corners, lost and confused. They had come looking for work, for hope, and instead found indifference and despair.

Mexico City was, at the time, the largest city in the world. From the top of the tallest buildings, you saw city and smog that stretched to the horizon in all directions, as flat as the plateau the city was built on, an endless sea of squat buildings and no highways. Just surface streets jammed with chaotic traffic at all hours.

There was only one main north-south avenue, *La Avenida de Los Insurgentes*. But there were innumerable other streets going every which way. Some lines of the subway were already completed. New lines were under construction.

I felt like a rat in a maze, with no way out. No freeway to jump on and exit the city. Trapped. Several years after I settled into my new life in Mexico City, my parents came for their only visit. I was thrilled that they wanted to spend time with me, and did everything I could to make my tiny apartment comfortable for them. But there was nothing I could do about the air quality. It was thin and very polluted. Mom and Dad were appalled that I went running each morning, convinced that the pollution would kill me and that I was only speeding up the process by breathing so hard. They were probably right. The air was always dry, dusty and dirty. Actually, everything was dirty. Coming from the Pacific Northwest, I longed for rain-washed fresh air and greenery. Anything green. My apartment had a cement wall running the length of the building in front of the door. I covered the wall with hanging pots overflowing with green plants, and watered them daily.

At first, it was an exciting adventure, learning to negotiate life in such a strange and different place. But soon, too soon, the novelty wore thin. The dust, the smog, and the pungent smells of the markets with their raw meat and fish, overripe fruits and vegetables, and overflowing garbage receptacles, and the urine-soaked subway corners, all intermingled and saturated my soul, entering my body through every pore.

I always kept busy. Busy, busy, busy. I had to fill every waking moment with activity: subway into work in the morning; teach classes; subway home at night; read, read, read. Activity, lots of activity to keep me too busy to stop and wonder what I was running away from, what was missing in my life. Too busy to stop and wonder why I always lived alone, even though I was horribly lonely at times. But if I kept busy, I had less time to feel lonesome, or at least less time to be aware of my loneliness.

So I worked. Multiple jobs, all over the city, which meant I spent a good deal of time traveling from place to place, at first on public transportation—the subway, buses, *peseros*. Later, when I'd worked enough to afford that beat-up old VW bug, I drove. There's nothing like Mexico City traffic to keep a lonely person, a lost person, busy.

One day, I was driving south on *Avenida Insurgentes* towards the university when a policeman on foot tried to flag me down. I kept driving, confident that I had done nothing wrong. The next thing I knew, the officer had flagged down another car and was chasing after me. He was in the passenger seat of the car to my left, hanging out the window and waving for me to stop. I pulled to the side of the street and waited as the driver of the other car pulled in front of me, stopping only long enough for the policeman to hop out before taking off.

"You were speeding," the officer told me.

"I was going the same speed as everyone else," I responded, well aware that it was common practice for cops to stop drivers from whom they thought they could get the best bribes.

"I'm afraid I'll have to give you a ticket," he said.

"Okay, if you must," I told him.

"But I left my ticket book back there at my work station," he said, pointing north up the wide avenue. "You'll have to give me a ride back to get it."

"No, that's not something I'm going to do." I was absolutely not about to allow this man with a gun into my car. The doors were locked, the window only partially open.

"But I need my ticket book to write the ticket."

I could see the frustration in his face. "You go ahead and go back to get it. I'll wait right here. I promise."

He knew he was trapped, and he realized he wasn't going to get a bribe. Muttering a few unspeakable words under his breath, words he probably assumed I wouldn't understand, he waved me on. As I pulled away from the curb, relieved to get away from him, I watched in my rearview mirror as he began the slow trek back along the sidewalk. I almost felt sorry for him. After all, he hadn't created the corrupt system he worked under.

After a few years, even my busy work schedule wasn't enough. I still had too much time on my hands. I had friends, and we partied at night and made short weekend trips outside of the capital when we could afford it. But I still had time to fill, so I went back to school.

First, I enrolled in the national university, *la Universidad Nacional Autonoma de Mexico* (UNAM). The Mexican government had passed a new law requiring all public school foreign language teachers to be certified. In order to make that possible, they started a certification program at UNAM, offered through *El Centro de Ensenanza de Lenguas Extranjeros* (CELE). I applied and was accepted into the first class that would be awarded the new Mexican Foreign Language Teaching Certificate. It hangs on my office wall, a formal document embossed with a passport photograph of a young teacher with wild, curly hair, wearing a floral peasant dress.

But not the red one. Maureen had that.

At the same time, I needed to complete my BA for UCSC. I had left California with all my course work finished, but no thesis or comprehensive exams, and thus no diploma. Without a diploma, I'd never get into graduate school. So, I made the necessary arrangements and wrote my thesis in Spanish. It was accepted, and I had a diploma.

In my family, education was always an acceptable escape, so I used it as a tool to fill the void in my soul. But still I felt empty. I continued to push away those I loved most, unable to bridge the gaps that endless years of silence had created.

I was alone in Mexico City, alone with my empty mailbox, and no amount of activity changed that reality. Or rather, I was alone in Mexico City with no mailbox at all. I lived in one of four tiny apartments in a two-story cement block that was semi-attached to the main house. Incredible Mexican ingenuity. Who needed backyard space for a garden, anyway? You could always grow enough vegetables and flowers in old cans on the flat rooftops. In the late 1970s and early 1980s, Mexico City was one of the most densely populated cities in the world. Every square meter of land was used productively, particularly in working class neighborhoods like *la Colonia Vertiz Narvarte*. A student of mine located the vacancy. Like most things in Mexico City in the late 70s, just like in Caracas, finding an apartment depended on your contacts. Renting an apartment was impossible without a friend of a friend, without a connection. *Colonia Vertiz Narvate* was a good place to be a single, foreign woman, a safe place. I had a tiny one-bedroom apartment on the lower level, at the back of the property. Cement walls two stories high along the property line created a narrow walkway to the front door, the only door. Fire escape? There was none. No escape.

I was fortunate to have left Mexico before the big earthquakes of September 1985 devastated the city. Two quakes: the first, with a magnitude of 8.1, shook the city for three horrible minutes. Only thirty-six hours later, another with a magnitude of 7.5 rocked the city again.

This tiny space with its concrete floors and stucco walls was what I called home for most of the six years I lived in Mexico City, a space light years away from the high-rise condominium my friend, Judi, shared with her husband and son in Coyoacan. Her rooftop servants' quarters were almost as spacious as my apartment. I knew she wasn't happy, so how could I begrudge her a large two-bedroom luxury condo, with lanai, in one of the most exclusive neighborhoods in the city?

At first, my landlady, Adela, was hesitant to rent to a young *gringa*. Could she trust me? Would all the things she'd heard and seen about loose *gringa* women be true? Would I be a bad influence on her young children? But my friend was persistent, Adela relented, and the apartment was mine.

To reach my new home, I entered the walled property through a solid, corrugated metal front gate that opened to a sidewalk running between Adela's house and carport. I walked right past

Adela's front door and her kitchen door as I headed to and from my apartment each day. Through the open windows and doors, I saw the daily activities of the household. I greeted Adela. I joked with her children. I tried to time my entrances and exits to avoid Adela's husband, his lecherous eyes and his mean temper.

One day in late October, I heard excitement in Adela's greeting of *"Buenas tardes, Maestra,"* and I wondered if there was a letter. Would it be from home or from a friend? Would it be a late birthday card? Did someone remember that I'd had a birthday the week before? Birthdays and holidays and Sunday afternoons were always the hardest, but I'd adapted.

Adela leaned into her living room and reached towards the small table placed just inside the door. *"Aqui está, Maestra. Ojalá que sean buenas noticias."* ("Here you are, Teacher. May it be good news.") Her smile was like that of a shy, young girl as she handed me a square envelope. She was certain there was something enclosed, and hoped it wasn't broken. "We all know how bad the postal service is," she confided.

"Gracias, Señora." I thanked her and headed to my apartment. I never opened up to Adela, formed a friendship. I never tried. I could have opened my envelope there with her. I could have shared it with her. I could have given the United States stamps to her young children to collect. I could have told her about the gift I received. But I did none of those things. I shared nothing of myself. I went back to my tiny apartment, locked the door, and opened my envelope. I trembled with anticipation, hoping it was a birthday card, hoping it wasn't bad news.

As I opened the envelope, a tiny gold chain slid into my hand. I toyed with it, fascinated that something so precious had reached me. The small paper that wrapped the bracelet read, "With love from Doreen and Maureen."

I don't remember ever acknowledging the gift. My younger sisters had reached out to me. So many times, one of us would reach towards another with arms open wide, only to encircle air, emptiness. It worked both ways. Sometimes I was doing the reaching. Other times, I created the emptiness. I'm afraid I created emptiness for Doreen and Maureen. And I am sorry.

Chapter Nine: The Second Myth

If Dad was late from work when we were kids, if we didn't receive an expected phone call or letter, Mom's response was always the same. "No news is good news."

Maybe that's what kept her from calling or writing to me right after Maureen's disappearance. It was just a bad secret, and if we ignored it, it would go away. But I was writing letters to Maureen, and I was waiting for a letter telling me when she was coming for her second visit. Waiting for the details of her plans. No letter from Maureen ever came.

Mom knew she had to tell me eventually. After all, I was expecting to see Maureen in early November. I received Mom's letter on October 29, 1983. Maureen disappeared on September 28, 1983, one full month before I received the letter. Mom's letter arrived three days before the Day of the Dead.

The letter told me that my youngest sister wouldn't be coming for a second visit. It told me Maureen had disappeared.

My mother wrote a letter. She didn't call. Politeness dictated that my letters to Maureen had to be answered, so she wrote a letter to tell me that my little sister was missing.

MISSING! What the hell does that mean? Your keys can be missing, or even a favorite sweater, but not a whole sister.

Christmas that year didn't happen. It's all a blur. My mind stopped recording the daily events surrounding me.

I wanted to get on the next plane out of Mexico City, to go home and search for Maureen myself. But I couldn't, at least not legally. A few months earlier, I'd given my passport to the *Secretaria de Programmacion y Presupuesto* to process a work permit. I had no American driver's license or identification, and without my passport, I couldn't buy a plane ticket to fly home.

I called Marleen. As the oldest, she was the one I usually turned to for help. "Hi, Marleen, it's me, Arleen."

"Arleen? In Mexico? Are you okay?"

I could hear the fear in her voice. "Yeah, yeah, I'm fine," I quickly assured her. "But I got this letter from Mom saying that Maureen's missing. Has she come back?"

"No," my sister said, her voice heavy with exhaustion and grief. "We've done everything we can, but there's just no sign of her. The police haven't been much help at all, so Robert's flying in tomorrow to start his own search."

"I want to help. I want to come back and help find her."

"No," Marleen told me, her voice stern. "There's absolutely nothing you can do here. Just stay put. There's no reason for you to come home."

"But I could help somehow." I could hear the pleading in my voice. I needed my older sister's permission to act, just as I had when I was a young child and Marleen was the older sibling in charge.

"No, Arleen. It'd be better if you just stayed where you are. I'll call you when Maureen shows up."

I never got a call.

I let Marleen convince me that there was nothing I could do in Seattle. But what about just being together, offering love and support? These were notions as foreign to my family as the culture in which I was living. We had been taught to be stoic and silent, so I denied my fear and worry. I tried to bury them deep. I listened to my older sister's advice, and I stayed adrift with my hectic work schedule in Mexico City.

But I couldn't focus. Nothing seemed to make sense to me anymore. I tried to distract myself from the pain I was lost in by enrolling in classes that I'd always wanted to take: ballet and French. Somehow, I could never seem to find the time to attend them. I didn't even bother taking the final exam in French because I knew I'd learned nothing.

My husband, Arturo, supported me through those horrible months. He started running and insisted that I run with him every day. He pushed me to my physical limits, knowing that I needed to release the tension that was boiling up inside of me. But it didn't work.

Five and a half months later, I couldn't stand it anymore. The Mexican government had never returned my passport, I insisted when I reported it lost at the U.S. Embassy, so they issued me a new one. Still, I would need a visa in order to buy a round-trip plane ticket from Mexico City to Seattle. To obtain a Mexican visa through legal channels was a lengthy and costly process I wasn't willing to go through.

Instead, I took a bus up to the Texas border and walked across, as if I were just an American tourist returning home from a day of shopping. I wasn't even stopped by the U.S. officials. The following day, I reentered Mexico at a different border crossing and got a visa stamped in my new passport. At the time, an international ticket bought with pesos in Mexico was cheaper than flying from a southern Texas border town to Seattle, and I was on a very tight budget. Thus, I returned to Mexico City and bought a round-trip ticket to Seattle. I arrived home on April 12, 1984.

Later, when I was packing my belongings to return to Seattle permanently, I found that first passport, the one I had claimed the Mexican government had never returned to me. Lost in the pain and confusion of Maureen's disappearance, I hadn't remembered that I'd hidden it between some books in the bookcase. At that point, it no longer mattered.

Arturo stayed in Mexico, working on his thesis for UNAM. He was struggling to finish, and we were too broke to buy two plane tickets, so I went home alone. Then again, the thesis and our lack of money were only excuses. The truth of the matter was that I didn't know how to turn to Arturo, or to anyone, for that matter, for emotional support. Instead, I pulled inward and pushed him away. I didn't know it then, but our marriage was already beginning to fall apart.

I arrived in Seattle anxious to learn what little my family knew about Maureen's disappearance, but nobody seemed to want to talk about it. Instead, Marleen and Doreen convinced me to do a preliminary job search in the area. It was a distraction, something to keep us from thinking, worrying, or even talking much about the reason I'd come home: Maureen's disappearance. Besides, the attention felt good. It was the first time in my life that I felt as if my family really wanted me around.

Doreen helped me put together and mail out a résumé while Marleen gave me her copy of *Dress for Success* and dressed me for job interviews. Fortunately, we were the same size; I couldn't afford the high quality suit she insisted I wear.

I was just along for the ride, at first, but then I began to seriously consider returning to Seattle. I felt loved and needed. My parents and my siblings seemed overjoyed to see me, as though my return had somehow eased the pain of Maureen's loss. At the time, Andrew was back from Hawaii, living at home and working with Dad on another building project. I started teasing him about driving to Mexico City to move me. To my utter surprise, he agreed. "I'll be cruising into Mexico City in early July, so you better be ready, Sis!" It was no longer a joke or a dream. We all seemed to ignore the fact that I was married, with an apartment, a job, a life waiting for me in Mexico.

While I was in Seattle, I spent time alone with each of my siblings who still lived in the area: Marleen, Charleen, Doreen, and Andrew. I spent a day on the job with each of them, watching and listening. That was when I began to piece together the myths, the family stories that had begun to take shape in my absence. I began to realize how long I'd been gone. Twelve years had passed since I graduated from Issaquah High School and moved out of the house, and ten years since I left Seattle.

Maureen had been missing for seven months. I had known she was missing for six of those months. When I touched down at Sea-Tac, there was still no sign of her, and I spent the visit trying to piece together the stories about her disappearance. But no one seemed to want to talk about what had happened. Or maybe they thought I didn't want to talk about it. Or maybe I didn't ask the right questions. Or maybe I wasn't ready to listen.

One day, I was alone in the car with Mom. "Poor Maureen," she said, deep sadness in her voice. "I don't understand why she was so unhappy."

"Unhappy?" I asked.

"Self-destructive, really." I didn't know what to say, and in my silence, Mom continued. "I don't think she was ever right after that day in the garage."

"What day?"

"You know, the day she closed up the garage doors and turned the motors on. It was lucky I came home when I did."

I was stunned silent.

"It wasn't really a serious attempt," Mom said, her voice quiet, as if she were lost in memory. "We found her in the garage with the motors running."

I was still too shocked to say anything. Closing yourself in a garage with a station wagon and a Ford truck idling seemed pretty damned serious to me.

"She was just trying to get attention," Mom continued, her eyes focused on the traffic ahead of her. "As the baby of the family, I suppose it was hard on her when everybody moved away."

I didn't know what to say, or even what to think. Maureen had tried to kill herself when she was fifteen or sixteen years old. I don't even know when. Mom claimed she didn't remember. Maybe she didn't. We had all developed an incredible ability to block out what was too painful to face.

I was gone when Maureen had tried to take her own life. I left home without a thought for the well-being of my younger siblings. I left home, ignoring the buddy system for taking care of each other, ignoring the responsibility to my younger siblings that I had been taught. Tears of grief and guilt streamed down my cheeks.

Mom and Dad had used the buddy system because we were so many they couldn't keep track of us themselves. They taught us to be responsible for each other. The guilt of my failure cut like a knife. I had not protected Maureen years before, when she tried to take her own life, just as I had not protected her when she was a confused young woman moving into her first apartment in Seattle. A few years earlier, my sister had tried to kill herself, and now I was overwhelmed by the fear that someone had done it for her.

Mom looked panicked at the sight of my tears. "I'm sorry, Arleen. I thought you knew. I shouldn't have said anything. I didn't mean to make you cry. This is supposed to be a happy visit."

"It's okay, Mom. I needed to know," I assured her.

I wanted to say more. I wanted to tell her that this attempt that "wasn't serious" sounded to me like Maureen had been screaming for help—screaming at the top of her lungs, into a void where no one in the large, close-knit family of our first family myth was listening. I wanted to tell her that maybe Maureen needed some help, some saving. Mom's oft repeated words of wisdom surfaced in my mind, "A stitch in time saves nine." If only I—or someone—had taken that first stitch.

But I hadn't taken that stitch, and I now remained silent, afraid of causing more pain.

My mother talked about my little sister's attempted suicide because she thought I already knew about it. That happened a lot in our family. If Mom told one of us something, she assumed we all knew it. Other times, she just forgot who she'd told what. And, of course, because we were all lousy communicators, nobody ever knew anything.

Thus, it shouldn't have surprised me when Mom just began talking about Maureen's attempted suicide as though I was fully aware of what had happened, despite the fact that I had been away for years. During our visit and in our letters, Maureen had never told me about all the times when she was not happy. In fact, she was very unhappy, an unhappy teenager cradling her dying dog while craving to be cradled herself, unhappy enough to want to take her own life because no one was cradling her.

Poor communication still reigns today.

Case in point: since Dad's death in early 2002, Doreen and I have been alternating weekends going out to Grayland to visit Mom, unless another sibling is in town visiting. We want to be sure that no more than two weeks pass without one of us checking to see that she's well. About a year after Dad's death, I got a phone call from Doreen. "Guess where I am," she said.

"Grayland, right?" I knew it was her turn for a visit.

"Yeah. We're here, but Mom's not. And get this, her calendar says, 'Ellensburg with Charleen and Laureen.'"

Doreen and her husband had driven two and a half hours from their home in northwest Seattle, only to find that Charleen had come and taken Mom away for the weekend. Neither Charleen nor Mom had called either Doreen or me to let us know their plans. When I spoke to Charleen about it later, she said it was not a last-minute plan at all. However, Doreen had spoken to Mom on Wednesday about visiting on Saturday, and Mom hadn't mentioned anything. In Mom's view, one of her children knew, so all of them must. It was so ridiculous, it was almost funny. But it sure wasn't funny to Doreen. Lousy family communication had cost her a weekend, and weekends have become a valuable commodity since Dad's death.

Years before, during that horrible car ride with Mom when she told me of Maureen's attempted suicide, I remained silent. Mom wanted it to be a joyful visit. I suppose we all did. They were glad to see me, and they wanted me to move home to stay—to fill the hole left by their daughter, their sister, the one who was missing. But pain, fear, and shame overshadowed the visit, as well as the years that followed.

The pain and fear were the easiest emotions. The shame, the embarrassment, the condemnation associated with the Green River case was even harder for my family to bear. Because Maureen was listed as a Green River victim, the news media and popular culture automatically condemned her as a prostitute. With that label came shame and, my family being who they were, also absolute denial.

During that Easter visit, in Maureen's absence I learned the second family myth: Maureen was gang-raped, drugged, and forced into prostitution. She hadn't done it by choice, or because she had personal problems. No, she was the perfect girl, manipulated by the desires of others.

My sisters told me of the horrible fight in Maureen's apartment the night she disappeared. Tears in her eyes, Doreen choked over the words, telling me that the neighbors saw several large black men going into Maureen's apartment in the middle of the night, and then heard endless screaming and sounds of violence. "They didn't even bother to call 911," my sister cried, as if her frustration and pain were beyond control.

I carried the images of that night for nineteen years, horrible pictures of several big men strong-arming their way into Maureen's apartment, brutally beating her and gang-raping her. I saw them drug her and put her out, forced into prostitution. I believed it, too. For nineteen years, I told myself that my sister was a victim of two vicious, violent unsolved crimes within a period of only a few days.

This myth, like most, grew from a fragment of truth. My family created it to explain that despite what the media, the police, and just about every living soul in Seattle in the early 1980s seemed to be saying about the Green River victims, Maureen was not a prostitute. The family continued to believe their initial version of what happened in spite of what SPD—and later the Green River Task Force—put in their files.

As I've said, there were the conflicting stories from Maureen's neighbors about what they heard and saw the night Maureen disappeared. Was it one black man? Tobey, obviously. Or were there several men? Was it an argument, a lovers' spat? Or was it a prolonged physical fight, with screaming and banging noises that lasted for hours? The stories changed, depending on the teller and the audience.

In short, no one in the family wanted to believe that it was possible, so we grasped at any explanation. To believe that shy, innocent Maureen, the farm girl who loved her dog more than anything else in the world, the kid who loved working with children, the vegetarian who wouldn't kill a mosquito, had gotten involved in prostitution was absolutely impossible. If she were a prostitute, then obviously, somebody had forced her into it.

* * *

Three months later, on July 1, 1984, Andrew strode into the lobby of the Guadalajara Sheraton like some mythical hero. Heads turned to take in this tall, handsome American in his T-shirt, blue jeans and cowboy boots. His straight, dark hair contrasted sharply with his pale skin. His green eyes caught mine as I rose from the calfskin chair where I sat, waiting.

My youngest brother, still my "little" brother at twenty-two, towered over me as he wrapped me in a tight bear hug. "Hi, Sis. Been here long?"

"Wow, you made it!" A wave of relief washed over me.

"Yeah, we drove straight through. Think we could get a beer in this joint?"

It took me a moment for that to register: my brother and his friend had just driven nonstop almost three thousand miles, from Seattle to San Diego, across the Mexican border at Tijuana, and straight across the Sonora Desert to Guadalajara, in the heart of Mexico. My hero had arrived to take me back to the homeland I had abandoned. But he didn't ride into town on a spirited white stallion. His steed was a bright red 1983 F140 4-wheel-drive Ford truck, with a canopy on the back.

In April, when I'd gone home to Issaquah, I made the decision to move back to the States. I needed to be close to my family. Arturo agreed. That my car had been stolen while I was away in Seattle made it that much easier to leave. My love affair with Mexico had soured. I didn't realize at the time that I was also making the decision to leave my husband. For the time being, he was still part of my life.

Andrew and I had formulated a plan. Driving into Mexico City and trying to find my apartment seemed a bit too overwhelming for him, so we agreed to meet in Guadalajara. Mom and Dad had been there with me a few years earlier; they had stayed at the Sheraton. They assured Andrew that he'd be able to find it. I would wait in the lobby of the Sheraton from 11 a.m. to 1 p.m. for four days, July 1 to July 4, until we connected.

When Andrew walked into that hotel lobby on July 1, I felt safe. I felt loved and protected by this tall young man who'd come to take me home. I'll never understand why he risked driving his cherished new truck across miles of desert in a country where he didn't speak more than two words of the language. He claimed it was just a good adventure. Or maybe he figured that despite his and Robert's efforts to find Maureen, Mom and Dad had already lost one daughter, and that he could bring me back to them, back to safety. In any case, that's exactly what he decided to do.

But first he wanted to buy cowboy boots. "Hey, coming into town we saw some billboards for boots. Think we could find a good pair here?"

"Andrew, I don't know a damn thing about cowboy boots, but let's have a look around." At that point, I would have walked across hot coals for him, with or without my boots on.

After a few beers and some hours poking around tiny leather shops, we headed for Mexico City. By now, Andrew and his friend, Dave, were running on pure adrenalin and beer. But they still had the energy to drive another six or seven hours.

We were in Mexico City for less than a week. Andrew was a country boy at heart, with no desire to spend any unnecessary time in a huge, noisy, dirty city, so we only stayed long enough to load all of mine and Arturo's belongings into the back of the truck. Arturo and I had already sold most of our large furniture and boxed up everything we wanted to take with us. After Andrew and Dave had caught up on lost sleep, the four of us piled into the cab of the truck and headed north, with my brother at the wheel. Intense heat in the daylight and headlights at night. I don't remember stopping for fuel, food, rest or even bathrooms.

My strongest memory of the whole odyssey is also a regret. Andrew and Dave were in the front seat of the truck's double cab, Arturo and I on the bench seat behind them. They were reminiscing about high school and high school sports. I interrupted their conversation. "Oh lord, don't tell me you were a wrestler, Dave."

"Yeah, Arleen," Andrew said. "And he was really good. He went all the way to Regionals."

"I've never understood how anyone could enjoy that sport."

"Why? It takes a lot of strength and skill."

"Yeah, but think about it. Two sweaty guys with almost no clothes on rolling around on a mat together. I always figured all the wrestlers in high school were gay. How could a straight guy do it? It's really disgusting."

Andrew cracked up, reaching over to slap his friend on the shoulder. "Hey, did you hear that? My big sis just called us a couple of homosexuals!"

"Yeah, I heard." I couldn't see Dave's face from the backseat, but I could hear the anger in his voice.

It was evening then, and it was hot, and after that short conversation, there was tension in the cab of Andrew's truck as we sped northward across the Sonora desert. My brother laughed it off. After all, he'd been a wrestler, too. But his friend didn't laugh at all. In fact, he didn't speak to me for the remainder of the trip.

As I look back on that conversation, I'm embarrassed by my insensitivity. I admit, I still don't like any contact sports, but slamming wrestlers or homosexuals isn't something I typically do. But I did then, and I still don't know where it came from. It was as though Dad's black-and-white thinking had come out of my mouth.

* * *

On July 14, two weeks after I met Andrew in the Sheraton lobby, we rolled into Mom and Dad's yard in Issaquah. By the end of the month, Arturo had returned to Mexico. For the next three years, he traveled back and forth, trying to finish a research project and degree at the National University in Mexico City, and trying to keep our marriage together in Seattle.

His visits grew increasingly strained. I desperately needed him with me to cushion the pain, and I was angry and hurt that he couldn't seem to finish his degree and make the decision to move to Seattle. When he came for visits, I found that trying to express my feelings in Spanish, when I didn't understand them myself, was just too difficult. I started acting just the way my family had during my last visit before moving back. I tried to make each visit a "happy visit," but eventually the strain became unbearable.

In a forty-month period, we spent only fifteen months together. All along, we both knew we were growing apart. We were doomed. We tried to keep it together for a few more years, but by early summer 1988, our marriage was over. With no children or property to dispute, we signed and filed simple divorce papers that I photocopied from a library book and went our separate ways.

Chapter Ten: The Third Myth

Four days after we drove into Mom and Dad's driveway, exhausted and dirty from our non-stop drive north, I started teaching ESL classes at a language school in Seattle. I had hand-delivered résumés during my April visit, so when I called prospective employers on July 14, letting them know I was back in town to stay, it was a simple matter of being in the right place at the right time. ESL teachers are always in greater demand during the summer months, to meet the needs of intensive language schools that offer summer classes to students from around the world. I was hired by the school where I had worked as a resident assistant ten years earlier, when I was an undergraduate at Seattle University. The school where I'd fallen in love for the first time, with Eduardo, the Venezuelan physics student. The school where I'd decided to leave Seattle. I'd come full circle.

I jumped into my new job with both feet and started swimming as fast as I could. I had no time to readjust to life in America, no time to deal with culture shock, no time to get reacquainted with my family. Just long hours of teaching English every day, surrounded by a multitude of different languages and cultures. Although I rarely spoke of Maureen with anyone, she was always present, right under the surface.

I never told any of my co-workers or students about my missing sister. I found it impossible to confide in anyone, so I wore my horrible secret like a shroud. I tried to act normal, but I wasn't sure what that was anymore. I watched the other female teachers who were close to my age and did my best to mimic them in both dress and manner. But unlike them, I was silent. When I did speak, I came across as arrogant or short-tempered, to which many of my colleagues, naturally, took offense.

One day, the director called me into her office. I thought we were going to discuss an article I'd submitted for publication; I thought I'd earned her approval. Instead, I found myself flopping like a fish on the deck of a boat, unable to find escape and facing certain demise.

"Arleen, I've had some complaints about you," the director said as I stood in front of her desk. She gave no greeting, no lead-in, only those startling words. I collapsed into a nearby chair as though she'd slugged me in the stomach, but I said nothing. "Some of the other teachers find you abrasive," she continued. "You're going to have to try to fit in here." Her threat was implied, but as clear as day. My job was on the line.

"What about my students? My evaluations are good, aren't they?" I whispered, in the voice of a timid child being scolded by an overbearing parent.

"Stellar," the director admitted. "Your teaching is not the problem."

I knew she was right. I loved being in the classroom working with students. It was the only time I could completely and totally forget who I was, leaving my pain at the door. It was the teachers' room that was the problem. It was reminiscent of my high school cafeteria at lunchtime, and I just didn't fit in. Too consumed by my concern for my sister, I didn't even make a serious effort. The director's little talk only made matters worse, because now I felt as though all of my colleagues were talking about me behind my back. I was only able to keep my job because my teaching skills and experience were needed. With time, however, I was able to make a few friends.

Those first few months, I lived with Mom, Dad and Andrew, and commuted into downtown Seattle by bus every day. One of the three, depending on their respective work schedules, would drive me the seven miles into Issaquah in the early morning to catch my bus to Seattle. After about a forty-five minute ride, I'd walk a few blocks to another downtown bus stop to catch a transfer up one of Seattle's many steep inclines to the Capitol Hill neighborhood where the language school was located.

During the short walk between bus stops and the ten or fifteen minutes I waited for my transfer, and during the bus ride up James Street, I searched for Maureen. In my mind, the third family myth—that Maureen was still alive and trying to find her way home—was very real. Every morning, I sat on the bus and searched the faces of the women on the streets, the prostitutes, the runaways, the homeless, hoping against all logic that my sister's face would appear.

I suppose I knew, even as I searched for Maureen, that she

wouldn't just be sitting on a street corner somewhere. If so, why hadn't she come home? Shame, I rationalized. She'd be ashamed to come home and face judgment. Or, I told myself, she was so heavily drugged that she was lost to the world around her. If I could only find her, I could get her into counseling and rehab.

After a few months of commuting by bus (maybe it was only a few weeks, but it felt like years), Dad took pity on me. Just before my return to the States, he had bought a used, silver VW Rabbit pick-up truck that was too small and low to the ground for a former football player with high school knee injuries. He offered to sell it to me over time, in easily manageable installments. I had never imagined buying a truck, much less a diesel truck, but it was an offer I couldn't pass up. It turned out to be one of the best vehicles I've ever owned, even though it left me stranded on the freeway once, with black smoke billowing from under its hood. Apparently, you're not supposed to fill the crankcase to the top with oil. I thought it was like putting diesel in the tank.

Now, I had a job and a vehicle. Next, I needed an apartment in Seattle. I hated the commute, even in my own little truck. Living in Issaquah made for a very long day. I heard my parents' words echoing from childhood, "The early bird gets the worm," but I knew I was just wasting time in traffic. No worms were being caught by me then. Besides, I was starting to meet people and form friendships. I knew Arturo was coming soon, for a long visit, if not to stay, and I wanted a place of our own.

I didn't think about how hard it was for Mom and Dad to watch me move out again so soon after returning home. And not only was I moving out, I was moving into Seattle, the place where Maureen had disappeared, and was working within a few blocks of where she had lived. At least I wasn't so heartless as to rent a place on Capitol Hill.

I spent several weeks searching for an apartment. I didn't know the city well, but my sister, Doreen, was a big help. She would read the newspaper ads with me and drive around to look at the apartments that sounded promising. Unfortunately, I had little savings for the obligatory first and last months' rent, nor could I afford the rent in some of the nicer neighborhoods.

As I continued my search, Mom began to drop comments like, "You know, Arleen, this is a big house. There's plenty of room for you here." When I complained about the commute, one of my parents would point out that Dad had been doing it for over twenty years. Or when they caught me whining about not having any savings because I'd been earning pesos for the past six years, I'd hear, "You could stay here for a while and save your money."

In the end, one of my colleagues located a roomy one-bedroom apartment in an older, pinkish-red brick building with white trim on the corner of Beacon Avenue and South Spokane Street. I fell in love with the towering tulip trees standing on both sides of the front door, like sentries at their post. It was a great apartment, spacious, bright and airy with lots of windows and beautiful, old hardwood floors. There were only two problems.

The first had no solution. My apartment was on the third of three floors. When I took the place, I had thought that three floors up, the traffic noise of the busy intersection wouldn't bother me. I was wrong. You'd think that after almost six years in Mexico City, I'd have been immune to noise, but South Spokane Street was a major thoroughfare from Interstate 5 to the Rainier Valley. The traffic was heavy, but it wasn't continuous. It stopped and started with the traffic light changes, and there was the inevitable impatient driver who insisted on honking if the driver in front didn't gun the engine the second the light turned green. To make matters worse, the Jefferson Park Fire Station was right across the street from both my living room and bedroom windows. I suppose it all sounds petty, but the constant noise grating on my already shattered nerves became insufferable.

But when I found the apartment, I hadn't noticed the traffic or the fire station. What caught my eye was on the southwest corner of the intersection: the Jefferson Public Golf Course, with its beautiful, green rolling hills and ancient shade trees. Just south of the fire station, there was a reservoir and the Jefferson Park Community Center. The area felt open, green, peaceful.

The second problem with my new apartment was in the bathroom. It was a wonderful old bathroom, with black and white checkered tiles on the floor and doors at each side. One door opened into the front entrance hall. The other opened into the walk-in closet, which in turn opened into the bedroom. Both the bathroom and the closet were larger than any I'd enjoyed before or since. I loved both the size and the layout of the place, but there was a problem with my beautiful old bathroom and its luxurious, deep bathtub. There was no shower.

A few Saturdays after I moved in, Mom and Dad showed up, armed with soldering equipment, several long lengths of copper pipe and a showerhead. After a quick cup of weak coffee, made just the way Dad liked it, he set to work. Within a few hours, he had connected the copper pipe to the faucet, run it up the wall, and fastened a removable showerhead. I was thrilled. I've always loved baths for relaxation, but I can't wake up without a pulsating, hot shower in the morning. Thanks to my dad's ingenuity, I had the best of both worlds.

I settled into my new apartment, unpacking the boxes of household items and books I'd brought from Mexico. I scoured garage sales for used furniture and accepted cast-offs from family and friends. It certainly wouldn't have made the pages of any home decorating magazines, but it was a comfortable space, a space of my own. I was beginning a new life, full of colleagues and students, jogs along Lake Washington after work, and long bike rides on the weekends. And scanning each passing stranger to see if she was my sister.

In that apartment, with the traffic noise from the intersection below, I learned that the third myth, the myth that Maureen was still alive and that someday she'd find her way back to her family, was a lie. It happened on a clear, warm spring day, the sky a bright Seattle blue. The kind of day when it seemed like nothing could possibly go wrong.

May 3, 1986, precisely thirty-one months since Maureen had disappeared. Never long enough to forget, only long enough to allow moments, even days, of happiness. That day, I was cycling with a former student who would later tour the United States on his bike before returning to his native Switzerland. For him, the ride had been little more than a warm-up, but for me it was my longest ride ever, over thirty miles. I was sweaty and exhausted as we rode up Beacon Avenue in the late afternoon. I wanted to get home, off my bike, and into a cool shower, now that I had one.

There was a woman pacing outside my old brick apartment building. A professionally dressed, serious looking woman, who was obviously waiting for someone. I knew right away she was waiting for me. I knew it wasn't good news, and I knew I didn't want to hear it. I coasted to a stop, got off my bike and walked slowly towards her. I could feel the beat of my heart and see my hands trembling on the handlebars. I wanted to jump back on my bike and flee. If I didn't hear the truth, if I didn't face the horror, I could hold onto hope. Without hope, my world would shatter.

The moment I saw that woman, I knew I would never see my sister again. As she walked towards me, I froze.

"My name is Linda Barker. Are you Arleen?" I could only nod my head. "Your parents asked me to contact you. Can we go inside and talk?" She handed me her card, and I stared at the simple black lettering verifying her identity: "Washington Victim/Witness Services."

I turned to my biking partner and asked, "Can you ride home?" When we planned the ride, I'd offered to throw his bike in my truck and give him a lift home, so this change of plans came as a surprise.

"Sure," he said. "But is everything okay?"

"I'll tell you about it later," I lied. "Thanks for the ride. It was great." With that, I unlocked the door to my building and, in silence, shouldered my bike and carried it up the three flights of stairs with Linda Barker right behind me. I had already started to cry.

She waited quietly while I set my bike down in the corner of my bedroom, and we took seats in the living room. The apartment seemed unusually quiet. Bright rays of sunshine filtered through the windows. "As I said outside, your parents asked me to find you." She paused for a moment. Then, looking directly into my eyes, she said, "Your sister's remains have been found."

Not your sister has been found, but your sister's remains have been found. I felt the horror of a sharp, jagged object cutting into my soul.

Jumping to my feet, I screamed and sobbed, "No! No! No!" I kicked and punched the walls, tears streaming down my face. I felt alone in my misery, a dark hell closing in around me as I collapsed on the floor. Slowly, I became aware of Linda Barker's arms around me, rocking me, comforting me like she would a young child. We sat together on the bare hardwood floor. Time stood still.

While Maureen was merely missing, there had always been room for hope. No matter how many horrors she had endured, she could still be alive. I'd told myself that over and over again during the long months of waiting, like some kind of mantra. She could overcome whatever hell she'd been through. Those hopes kept me going, made me jump every time the phone rang, made me stare out of bus windows in the seediest areas of Seattle, made me feel guilty when there were days of pleasure, like that day had been. But at that moment, with those words—"your sister's remains have been found—" the myth shattered like one of Mom's Waterford crystal wine glasses, and I shattered with it.

Somehow, I got from my apartment on Beacon Hill to my parents' home in the Issaquah Valley. I think Linda Barker drove me. I don't remember anything until I was standing in my parents' front parlor, the special room reserved for guests. One of my sisters looped her arm through mine and spoke softly in my ear, "I'm glad you got here so quickly." I only nodded in response, as I watched my father, now a broken, crumbled man, trying to be strong, trying to protect Mom from pain that was totally beyond his control. And as always, Mom was standing by his side, supporting him, worrying about him, not allowing herself to mourn the loss of her youngest daughter.

Her mourning was done. She had known, she told us. She had known that her youngest was dead. Now she feared losing Dad.

Mom and Dad stood close together, holding hands like high school sweethearts, listening to more words they didn't want to hear from the other people who were in the room. Social workers, like Linda Barker. And police detectives—a black female officer and a white male officer.

There was no way the Green River Task Force could have known that they had made the worst possible choice in the officers they sent to my parents' home. In Dad's world, women shouldn't be cops. In Dad's mind, a black man, Tobey Hicks, was responsible for his baby's death, and he didn't want a black officer in his home, telling him about it. All he wanted was to be left alone with Mom. To be able to suffer alone in Mom's arms.

But when was anyone ever alone in a family of eleven? Marleen, Doreen, and Andrew must have been there. Charleen was also in the Seattle area. Robert, Laureen, and Michael were living in Hawaii, but Laureen was not allowed in Dad's home, anyway. When the police notified the next of kin before the news release, I wonder if Mom and Dad even gave them Laureen's name. More likely, they left it up to Robert to tell her.

My memories of that day remind me of how people talk about where they were and what they were doing when Kennedy was shot, when Martin Luther King Jr. was murdered, when terrorists flew passenger jets into the World Trade Center. But in my family, what's the likelihood that we'd communicate such details? I wonder where each of my siblings was, I wonder what each of them was doing when he or she received the news that Maureen's remains had been found.

We never talked about it. Not once. Our baby sister had been killed. A few scattered bones were found by Mom's co-worker at Echo Glen Children's Center thirty-one months after Maureen's disappearance. But we didn't talk about it.

Frankly, I don't foresee a time when my siblings and I will sit together over cups of tea, glasses of wine or something stronger, talking about our baby sister, about who she was and what went so very wrong in her short life. We certainly didn't do it that day. Nor did we stay up all night, reminiscing, as we collected piles of used tissues in our laps, and our eyes and noses grew puffy and red. I have no memory of talking to any of them about Maureen, or about their thoughts, feelings, or reactions to her life and to her death on that day, or in the years that followed. If they talked, and I doubt that they did, I wasn't part of those special moments of sharing.

What happened next? Does it matter whether I spent the night there in Issaquah, or returned to my empty apartment on Beacon Hill? The memories are gone, lost in a fog of silence and pain. Only the excessively numerous newspaper articles printed at the time, and the Green River Task Force files, remain to fill in the spaces void of memory.

* * *

Maureen was the news of the day on every television station and newspaper in the Seattle area, perhaps even in areas far beyond our beautiful corner of the world. Among the local headlines on Monday, May 5, 1986:

"Seattle woman No. 35 on Green River killer list." *(Seattle Post Intelligencer)*

"19-YEAR-OLD ADDED TO GREEN RIVER VICTIMS LIST." *(The Seattle Times)*

The coverage focused on the prostitution angle of the Green River story, and my family was mortified. One of Dad's favorite maxims was "Fools' names and fools' faces are always found in public places." Now we were the fools, and my father's world was crumbling around him. There is no greater loss of control than the murder of your own child.

Linda Barker, the victim advocate the Green River Task Force had assigned to our family, dealt with the relentless media for us. Through her, we provided the following press release in hopes of quelling speculation about Maureen's morality:

> The family of Maureen [deleted] is hurt and angry
> at the implications by some of the press that because her
> case is being investigated by the Green River Task Force
> that she was therefore involved in running away,

prostitution, or drugs. None of this behavior was part of Maureen's background.

To avoid any further misstatement by the media, the [deleted] family is providing these facts:

Maureen was born at Overlake Hospital in Bellevue on October 5, 1963. She was raised in a rural setting on the eastside. After graduating from high school, she attended Bellevue Community College, studying early childhood education. While attending B.C.C. she worked at a church affiliated daycare/preschool untill she disappeared. She had been living with her parents until she was nineteen. With the intention of changing jobs and working in a Seattle Headstart program, she had moved into an apartment on Capitol Hill only one month before her disappearance.

She always kept close contact with her family, spending weekends at home even after she moved to Seattle. She talked to her mother the day before she disappeared. Maureen was a quiet, shy, gentle girl who loved animals, children, hiking in the woods and the ocean beach.

Contrary to some media broadcasts, Maureen was missing not four years, but two and a half years. The Medical Examiner places her death at approximately two and a half years. Her parents reported her missing within twenty-four hours, although Seattle Police took no action for three days. There was no unaccounted time from her family and job for her to have a background of prostitution or drugs. These insinuations by some of the media are unfair and hurtful to the family.

The family would appreciate if the news media would contact Linda Barker of the Washington Victim/Witness Services for factual information.

I don't recall who suggested issuing a press release, or even who wrote it. Was it Dad, one of my siblings, or maybe Linda Barker? I remember thinking at the time that releasing a statement of any kind seemed rather futile, and possibly even a bit disingenuous. How could we continue to insist that Maureen was uninvolved in prostitution when one of our own family myths acknowledged the possibility of white slavery?

The following morning, Tuesday, May 6, 1986, *The Seattle*

Times ran an article entitled "SLAIN TEEN'S FAMILY SLAMS PROSTITUTION IMPLICATION." While quoting from the family statement in a seemingly unbiased fashion, the writer also included the following reminder for readers: "Many of the Green River victims were prostitutes." Other papers ran similar articles, and my family tragedy continued as water cooler fodder for another few days.

On May 8, 1986, five days after Linda Barker stood waiting at the door to my Beacon Avenue apartment building, I was sitting with my family—some of my family, anyway—on a hard wooden pew at Saint Joseph's Catholic Church. White chrysanthemums adorned the altar. Father George O'Connor officiated, but I have no memory of his words of comfort. For many years, I had no knowledge of the location of Maureen's ashes. My parents did not include me in their plans; I don't think they included any of us in their decision to release our sister's ashes into the winds over the Pacific Ocean. It was a decision I honored with all my heart, but it was a ceremony, a ritual, I would have liked to have been a part of, to have shared with my parents and with my siblings. I wish they had given me a choice.

Chapter Eleven: A Birth and a Death

By 1986, you'd think everyone in my family, Dad included, would be used to people vanishing. First my older siblings, next me, and then the ultimate disappearance—Maureen in 1983. Maureen's disappearance was followed by an even greater sense of loss when her remains were discovered in 1986.

You might think Ridgway's arrest in 2001 should have provided some kind of closure, along with his confession and sentencing in 2003. But stress works in funny ways. It doesn't necessarily let go when you think it should. It clings, and it suffocates.

In 2003, a Green River Task Force detective offered to send me information on dealing with the stress related to violent death. A few days later, a small booklet arrived in the mail: *Coping with Traumatic Death: Homicide* by Bob Baugher, Ph.D. and Lew Cox, Victim Advocate. I paged through the table of contents and cried bitter tears. These are the chapter headings: The First Few Days, The First Few Weeks, The First Few Months, The First Year.

What about twenty years later? My heart screamed in frustration. Did they truly believe that the pain would be gone, that I could come to terms with my sister's unsolved murder in only one year? I turned to the last two sections of the final chapter: Life After Homicide and The Journey. Despite the reference to the first year, I found a gem I could use; I found validation:

> Challenge yourself to figure out ways of getting you and your family through this maze of grief. You must believe that you also can survive even when you think you are sinking. Do not avoid your grief. Talk about your grief until you are on top of it *(Baugher and Cox, 2000).*

I suppose I was *under* the grief for over twenty years. Not just the grief of Maureen's disappearance, but also that of my older siblings' departure from my life when I was young. I still hold my stress in my gut, but I'm on top of it now, and I can move forward with my eyes wide open. I don't believe my father ever could.

On August 12, 1986, only three months after Maureen's quiet memorial service at Saint Joseph's Catholic Church, three months after Mom and Dad released Maureen's meager ashes to the winds over the Pacific Ocean from the stern of their small fishing boat just off the coast from their Grayland beach house, Dad suffered a massive heart attack.

He and Andrew were working on the roof of the third Issaquah house when Dad collapsed, pain ripping through his chest. Andrew helped him off the roof of that tall two-story house, supporting his large body as together, they climbed down the steep ladder and stumbled into the living room. Once there, Dad refused to go to the hospital. At least, he refused until Mom got home and wouldn't take "No" for an answer. Two days later, Dad had triple by-pass surgery at Providence Hospital in Seattle.

After Dad's heart attack, my Beacon Hill apartment proved to be in a convenient location. Mom stayed with me while Dad was hospitalized, so she could be close to him. I'd like to think I was of some comfort to Mom at that time. I can only imagine the hell she endured. Endured with strength and stoicism. Every evening she returned to my apartment, exhausted after hours of worry at Dad's bedside. I'd make us each a cup of tea, and we'd drink it in silence. There was nothing to say. The fear of losing Dad permeated the air of my apartment. But he pulled through, and after that horrible surgery, Mom nursed him back to health and kept him alive for another sixteen and a half years.

My parents sold their home in the Issaquah Valley and made a final move into their beach house. After finishing the first house in Grayland, Dad had built two more, each a few blocks closer to the beach. As Mom often says, "He left us before he reached beachfront."

There are only a few stretches of long, flat shoreline on the West Coast of the United States where cars are allowed to drive on the beach. Over twenty years ago, my parents bought land and built their first house in a tiny community between Grayland and Westport, Washington, where cars are still permitted on the beach. As a staunch environmentalist and avid beachcomber, the cars racing across the sand drive me nuts. And yet as the daughter of aging parents (now only my mother), my will to fight diminishes.

For many elderly people, cars offer the only way to enjoy the beach, or to even get to the beach. When the arthritis in Dad's knees became unbearable, walking the beach, a passion of many decades, was no longer an option, but with his car, getting close to the water was still possible. He could get close enough to hear the roar and crash of the waves, to watch the seabirds rise, as if on command, and swarm in unison like monster bees, and to drive along the shoreline at sunrise to see what the last incoming tide had washed up onto the beach.

During those sunrise drives, Mom collected her glass balls. These are hand-blown, semi-opaque glass balls in ocean hues of green and blue. They are heavy and scratched, bearing the telltale signs of age and hard work, of spending years knotted into heavy commercial fishing nets to keep them afloat, and of even more years tangled in those same broken fishing nets, lost in the depths of the ocean. Scratched and dinged, each with a story to tell.

Dad was a man of very few words. He was not a storyteller, but he loved to tell the story of the largest ball in Mom's collection. For all his jeering ridicule, you could hear the pride in his voice as he spoke. "I was driving along, and all the sudden, she starts screaming at me to stop the truck. And before I could even bring it to a full stop, the door was open and she was up to her waist in the surf."

Mom had seen a prize in the surf that she wasn't about to lose, even if it meant fighting the precarious Pacific undertow and the frigid temperature. Dad hollered at her to get back, to get out of the water, but ended up out in the surf with her. He dragged her to shore, a tiny woman clinging to a huge glass ball, holding it close to her belly, her arms locked around it. It was a treasure larger than any of her nine children, even during their ninth month in her womb. Dad dragged her and her treasure back to dry sand, where they collapsed together in laughter.

Mom's days of beach walking are rapidly coming to an end, but her collection of glass balls on the hearth of the third and final beach house are a constant reminder of the youth and energy, the strength and determination, of the woman she used to be.

* * *

Beyond all hope or denial, the discovery of Maureen's remains in May of 1986 shattered the myth that my little sister was still alive—the third myth. But the second myth, that she was gang raped and forced into prostitution, lived on as strong and terrible as ever, a cancer eating away at my soul. After all, Maureen was classified as a Green River victim, so by all accounts, she was a prostitute. But I could not come to terms with the notion that she had chosen to prostitute herself, and I had the story of the fight in her apartment the night she disappeared to back me up. Still, I found no cure for the cancerous pain that permeated every cell of my body. I lived with the disease, searching for meaning.

The continued media coverage didn't help. In September 1987 *The Seattle Times* began a six-part special report written by Carlton Smith and Tomas Guillen entitled "GREEN RIVER—WHAT WENT WRONG?–POLICE AT FIRST FAILED TO NOTICE PATTERN." Maureen's picture was again on the cover of the Sunday paper, along with those of forty-two other victims and three black silhouettes representing unidentified remains.

The Green River story stayed in the media for another handful of years, until the number of bodies turning up tapered off, the cases became cold, and task force funding was cut. Within a few years, the search for my sister's killer was at a standstill.

*   *   *

In February 1989, I remarried. Tom is a creative, understanding man with the patience of a saint. My parents refused to attend our wedding. It was a second marriage for both of us, and I was six months pregnant at the time. My parents would have nothing to do with us.

In May I gave birth to a beautiful baby girl. We named her Erin. She brought me joy so intense that at times I couldn't breathe. But there was deep, profound sadness there as well, for despite my mother's intense love for infants, she remained totally uninvolved in my life. No calls, no cards, nothing. Silence. My daughter was born at Providence Hospital in Seattle, the same hospital where Dad had endured triple bypass surgery only three years earlier. My parents never saw her, never held her as a newborn, never shared in the joy of her birth.

For three months, the pain of their silence bore down on me. My pain was greater than my anger. To be more specific, my desire for family, for my daughter to know her grandparents, was greater than the anger. I accepted the idea that she might never have much more than a superficial relationship with them, but I was determined that she would meet them. So I braved the trip to Grayland, knowing my odds of success were pretty good. If I showed up on their doorstep with my baby in my arms, I was fairly certain they wouldn't be able to resist her, even if I wasn't their favorite person.

I packed an overnight bag, unsure whether I would need it, put Erin in her car seat, and fretted through the two hour drive to Grayland. As I pulled up to the front gate of their large fenced yard, I broke into a nervous sweat. I got out of the car, pulled the gate open, and drove up to the house. At the sound of the car engine, Mom walked out of the house into the August sunshine. I heard her surprised voice call out, "Arleen's here."

I parked the car and climbed out. Circling to the other side, I opened the door to the back seat. Still, neither Mom nor Dad approached. I lifted my daughter from her infant seat and walked up to my mother. "Here's your granddaughter," I said, putting my baby into her arms. "Her name's Erin."

My father embraced me. He acted as though we visited every weekend, as though they'd been at the hospital the day Erin entered the world. Had I not danced this dance before, I would not have believed it possible.

Soon, Mom was sitting in a rocker in the sunroom, a wall of windows behind her, bathed in golden sunshine and holding baby Erin on her lap. She grasped Erin's tiny hands in her own as she sang nursery rhymes. Not much later, my father was sitting in his recliner. It was his turn to hold baby Erin. She rested in the crook of his right arm. One large hand cradled her back, the other covered her entire tummy and chest. His gnarled hands encased her tiny body like giant clamshells. She looked up into his face with the innocence and curiosity of new life, and laughed.

With that short visit, I was once again able to bridge the gap that had grown between my parents and me. I was overjoyed. But under my joy was the nagging cancer of worry over the second myth. As Erin grew, I began to confuse names. In my mind, I'd catch myself calling her "Maureen." Every so often, the wrong name escaped my lips.

On every visit to Mom's house, I study the faded family photographs on the hallway walls. I stare at our family portrait. We were raised to believe that as a family, a collective unit, we were in some way unique. Our special clan.

Lately, that family portrait has haunted me. Not because it is the only complete family picture that will ever exist, or even because 1966, the year the picture was taken, also signaled the beginning of our unraveling. It's the eyes that haunt me, the eyes and the expressions on our eleven faces. From the eldest to the youngest we are deadly serious. No smiles, not even in our eyes.

There I am, at the end of the sofa, my arm wrapped around my baby sister, wrapped around Maureen. All of us with blank stares for the camera, stares of worry or maybe of wonder. Something is written in our eyes that I cannot comprehend. A mystery, a secret, is hidden there.

* * *

It was a bright, sunny day in the summer of 1989. My parents, my sisters, and I were at a rehab center in Aberdeen to learn how to support Michael, who was in treatment after coming too close to the dark abyss of self-destruction, too close to a precipice that would allow no return. We were attending an informational meeting for families to learn about addiction and the factors that can lead to it. I sat with my family and listened as the therapist spoke of the different types of abuse: sexual abuse, physical abuse, verbal abuse, neglect. As he went on, I could see the lines on my father's face contract. I could feel his temperature rise. Through the years, I learned to read my father, and I knew he could not, would not accept those words. He would not allow himself to even consider the possibility that his behavior was or had ever been abusive in any way.

"How dare he accuse me, ME, of child abuse? I never laid a finger on any of my kids," Dad said, smoldering. At the first break, he pushed his way out of the crowded room without speaking a word, letting loose his anger only as we reached the parking lot, only when we were far enough away to avoid making a scene in public. Then he stormed towards the car with Mom and the rest of us trailing behind. I knew Dad would be upset by the therapist's words, but I was too stunned by his rage to say a word. I followed him in silence. A woman in my mid-thirties, once again I felt like a pre-teen.

I remember thinking, "But Dad, there are many forms of abuse. Even silence can be abusive." I thought the therapist had hit the nail on the head, but Dad was incapable of even hearing the "A" word. Instead, he left during a ten-minute break and never returned. All of us left with him. None of us said, "Wait Dad, I want to hear the rest of this." As usual, we followed his lead, like cattle to the slaughter.

Dad took that presentation of information as though it were a personal insult directed at him, alone in the room full of people. He had so much emotion bottled up inside of him that I was amazed he didn't just explode. It was as though he compartmentalized his memories, his pains, into little boxes in his brain, with little doors with little locks, like rows of safety deposit boxes in a bank vault. The pains were locked away and all was well until someone pried open one of the compartments. If a painful memory escaped, he couldn't bear it. After each flare-up, Mom would slowly, gently, patiently massage his soul until the pain was safely locked away again. This pattern repeated itself through fifty years of marriage.

As a child, I had learned to behave in certain ways in order to be accepted, to be loved, to avoid unlocking the wrong compartments. When Dad no longer had the energy to keep all the compartments locked up tight, when he still couldn't communicate his feelings, he let go of life.

Not long after that day in Aberdeen, I was sitting in the office of a mental health therapist trying to put together the pieces of me, the shattered shards of a middle child. For although my father never accepted counseling, I knew I wouldn't survive without it. The therapist asked me if there had been any sexual abuse in my family. She felt I displayed some of the symptoms or characteristics of an abused child. My reaction—vehement defense of my father—made her back away, as any good therapist knows to do when she touches a core that the client isn't ready to deal with.

But with time, I grew to consider the possibility of abuse, to consider that perhaps the therapist in the rehab center in Aberdeen had touched on a truth that needed to be faced head-on, needed to be tackled the way Dad had tackled his opponents in high school football games. But Mom and Dad didn't, couldn't, wouldn't, and the "A" word became yet another family taboo. But I faced it. I thought about it, I acknowledged the emotional distance and the silence with which I had been raised. Yet I was never strong enough, then or now, to talk to my parents about what was missing in my childhood. I guess I figured that if Maureen's death and Michael's despair hadn't been enough to get them to consider that our family, like most, had its fault lines, and if a professional therapist couldn't do it, I sure as hell couldn't break through the ice encasing them. And I was afraid to try.

My father's words at the rehab center were true. He never physically or sexually abused me, or any of his children, in any way. He never raised a hand to us, using only his stern gaze as a disciplinary tool. He never touched me enough, either. As a child, as a teenager, he never caressed my body or soul with hand or voice, to show me that he loved me the way I needed to be loved. Human touch, human contact, human communication assure us that we are valued, that we are loved. That's what was missing for me. That's probably what was missing for all of us.

Once, when I was still in elementary school, I remember picking up an acquaintance at her house for some church event. She kissed her mother good-bye. A simple kiss of love between mother and daughter, and I was flabbergasted. This was something I didn't know. I didn't know that parents kissed their children, gathered their children in hugs and gave them kisses to say hello and good-bye, to say they loved them and hoped they were well, to say they were glad to have them in their life. I felt like I'd stumbled onto some rare kind of unearthly beings.

Years later, when I returned from my life in Mexico, something had changed in my family. Something more than Maureen's disappearance. Mom and Dad both greeted me with a hug and kiss every time they saw me. The first few times, I held back in surprise or turned to offer my cheek, Mexican-style. But I watched, and I saw that their quick little kisses on the lips had become common practice with all my sisters. My adult self was thrilled by this physical expression of their love, but the child in me missed all of the kisses I didn't get back then, when I desperately needed them.

The abuse in my family was that of silence. Without a doubt, Dad was a good provider. He worked harder than any man I will ever know to provide for his large family. So did Mom. But with all that work, there was no time left for love, and neither of them provided what I needed most: love, touch, communication—a relationship between parent and child. There was always food on the table, but where was the nourishment for the heart and soul? When Marleen, Robert, and Laureen all disappeared, I needed explanations to quell my fears. None were given.

Mom and Dad had each other. They nourished each other with an intensity I always envied, but they did not include their children in that circle of adoring love. There were too many of us. We stood on the outside, looking in, like penniless children at an old-time candy counter. And as Johnny Lee lamented on the old *Urban Cowboy* soundtrack, I grew up, left home, and went in search of love. I went to California, I went to Venezuela, I went to Hawaii and I went to Mexico, searching for the love that was missing from my life. But none of them were the right place to find it.

I fled home at seventeen without a single look back because, by the time I reached seventeen, the house felt like a stifling prison cell and the silence could be cut with a knife. I wanted to scream and yell. I wanted explanations. I wanted to ask what had happened to my vanished siblings, but the wall of silence was more impenetrable than the Berlin Wall had ever been. Unlike the Berlin Wall, our wall never toppled. I accepted the silence. I held in the screams, and I matched my behavior to their expectations until I began to crumble, shattering like Humpty Dumpty, fallen from the top of that other wall in fairyland. I knew I had to escape to survive, so I fled, using education as my escape route, knowing it was a route Mom and Dad honored. I left with no concern for my younger siblings, for the Little Kids. As the years passed, each of them also left, until only Maureen remained at home with Mom and Dad. Then she, too, was old enough to leave.

Maybe the lack of communication, the distance, the silence would not have been such a problem if there hadn't been so many of us. In the nursery rhyme, the old woman in the shoe "fed them and smacked them and put them to bed." At our house, they fed us, ignored us, and we put ourselves to bed.

And yet Mom and Dad did the best job of parenting that they were capable of doing, the best they knew how to do. They were drowning, weighed down under the burden of the enormous responsibility they had created for themselves. We, the kids, were the stones weighing them down—like the stones weighing down those first victims pulled from the Green River.

Years later, after Maureen's disappearance, after I returned home from Mexico, after the discovery of Maureen's remains, after my failed first marriage, I tried to reconnect with my siblings. I figured that I already lost one sister I hardly knew, I didn't want to lose any more of my family.

Michael was back in Hawaii and doing well. One day I called to say hello and give him a bad time about never writing to me, lamenting the distance, both physical and emotional, between us. "You know, Michael, I really miss all the good times we had in Hawaii. Remember when we used to go dancing at that club up on the North Shore?"

"Everybody thought I was your bodyguard or something. And you sure needed one, Arnie! You were a wild one! God, those were some fun times!" Arnie, his special nickname for me. The only nickname I've ever had.

"Yeah, I miss them too. How did we let so much time and distance come between us, between all of us?"

"I don't know. Just too busy working, I guess. I'm going to try to be better about calling and birthdays and shit like that. You know what I need? I need a list, a family list, something that's got all the birthdays, phone numbers, addresses, the whole thing."

"Come on. You're telling me you don't have all that stuff?" I was genuinely surprised, having kept fairly accurate information on everybody throughout my adult years, despite my physical distance. But then, I was an avid letter writer, and my brother wasn't, so I understood what he needed.

I put together a complete family list: names, addresses, telephone numbers, spouses, children, birth dates, even anniversaries. It was two pages long when I finished, and that was only the immediate family.

Christmas was only a few months away, and Erin was less than six months old. Maybe being a new mother heightened my need for family. Maybe I just wanted to connect with everyone in my large family over the holidays. In any case, I wrote a short note and mailed a copy of the family list off to everyone, including Mom and Dad. Within the week, I got a response from my dad. The envelope carried no return address. Only my mother's handwriting and the postmark told me it was from my parents. I stared at the envelope, a feeling of foreboding creeping into every cell of my body. My father did not write letters. He didn't even talk on the phone, unless he had to. For Dad to write a letter, something had to be very wrong.

In the truest sense of the word, it was not a letter. Only an angry, scrawled note on the bottom of my own typed letter.

Arleen, I see no purpose in this, other than more heartach. The... family is extinct. Mother and I know very well when each child was born, who lived and who died, who is white and who is black. Most of my offspring respect enough to let sleeping dogs lie. You don't, so get out of my life – R.F.

Extinct? How can a family be extinct? But in Dad's mind, in his dreams of what his family should be, we had failed him miserably.

With that list, I had cracked open one of those little doors in Dad's mind, where all the shut down feelings and memories he couldn't deal with were locked away. On that list, I had committed the heresy of including Laureen's name and the names of her two daughters, granddaughters Mom and Dad had never acknowledged. I had also included Maureen's date of death. Those were two realities Dad couldn't face. Couldn't see in black print on white paper. The family he remembered, that he wanted to remember, was that family in the 1966 family portrait that still hangs on Mom's wall: the large, happy, close-knit family of our first family myth.

My mother also scribbled a note on that letter I sent them. A note that reminds me still of the profound power of denial as a coping mechanism when life doesn't turn out the way we plan.

> This was a sad reminder at Christmas. Sometimes we happily can go months without thinking about the shame of it.   Mom

A year passed in silence. Despite my repeated invitations, my parents refused to come to Erin's first birthday party in May 1990. In autumn, my brother Andrew's wife gave birth to their first son. A visit home was planned for December, and a large holiday dinner was arranged at my eldest sister's home. Several of my siblings and their families were coming together to celebrate. It was a dinner I had no intention of missing. Despite my fear of rejection, I was determined that my daughter would have some kind of relationship with her grandparents. Or maybe I was just too stubborn to let Dad get the last word. In any case, I knew there would be comfort in numbers, and that the distraction of a new grandson would make it easier for my parents and me to pretend that no letters had ever been sent, and to turn the clock back to that day over a year before, when I showed up at their doorstep with a three-month-old infant in my arms. And I was right.

Once again my parents and I danced the dance of denial. In a holiday whirl of greetings and smiles, we pretended that I had not been told to get out of my father's life. In fact, we never spoke of Dad's note at all. When I sent the family list out again with updates, I did not send my parents a copy. We'd reached an unspoken truce, a truce we maintained for the rest of Dad's life.

* * *

Doreen and I pulled off a surprise eightieth birthday party for Dad on November 30, 2001. It surprised us almost as much as it did him. Seven of the eight living siblings showed up—all but Laureen. She was working overseas at the time, but Dad wouldn't have let her through the front door anyway. The three brothers flew in from Hawaii, and Marleen and her son flew up from California. We met at the Chateau Westport, a local beachfront hotel, where we all booked rooms for the night. Then we caravanned over to Mom and Dad's house and knocked on the front door.

For a second, I feared that Dad's heart couldn't bear the shock. He stumbled out of his armchair and his face turned bright red. He struggled to hold in his tears. He was stunned speechless.

It was noisy and crowded in my parents' tiny living room with nine adults and a number of grandchildren all talking at the same time. There wasn't enough room for everybody, so despite the winter cold, we gradually moved out into the front yard. After a short visit, we chauffeured Mom and Dad to a nearby restaurant decorated for the party, and celebrated with all the typical birthday trappings.

Saturday morning, we each made our way from our hotel rooms to the breakfast area. There was nobody there when I walked in. Tom and Erin were still in our room getting dressed, but I needed coffee before I could even begin to function. I filled a cup with weak institutional swill and made my way to a table. There were copies of Westport and Seattle newspapers scattered on the tabletops around the room. The headlines caught my eye, and I almost dropped my coffee. "GREEN RIVER ARREST" was in bold, one-inch headlines across the front of *The Seattle Times*.

I stumbled into a chair, numb. My stomach contracted and my hands began to shake. I was alone in a sterile breakfast room full of empty Formica tables, on the second floor of a large, almost-vacant hotel, situated on a gray, barren beach, reading newspaper headlines that claimed my sister's killer had been arrested on the day of my father's eightieth birthday. I felt as though I'd been transported into some kind of third-rate horror movie.

I watched as each of my siblings entered the room. Their reactions varied little from my own. We were all too stunned to say much. Gary Ridgway had been arrested the day before.

At 3:00 p.m. on the day we were toasting our father's longevity, Detectives Jim Doyon and Randy Mullinax were arresting his youngest daughter's killer. Gary Ridgway was charged with four of the Green River murders, the four for which the Green River Task Force had indisputable DNA evidence.

A Seattle-area man was arrested yesterday after DNA in saliva samples taken nearly 15 years ago linked him to several of the Green River killings, the notorious slayings of dozens of women that remain the nation's largest unsolved serial murder case.

Authorities apprehended Gary Leon Ridgway, 52, as he left his painting job yesterday afternoon at Kenworth Truck

Co. in Renton. Last night, investigators were searching his house in the Auburn area near Lake Geneva.

King County Sheriff Dave Reichert was careful not to call Ridgway the "Green River Killer," so named because the first victims were found in the South King County river in 1982. But Reichert, the original lead investigator in the case, was ebullient.

"I cannot say with certainty that Gary Ridgway is responsible for all of those deaths...but boy, have we made one giant step forward," said Reichert, who always believed Ridgway was one of the top five suspects. "This has got to be one of the most exciting days of my entire career."
(Seattle Post Intelligencer, December 1, 2001)

Sheriff Reichert was proud of this arrest, proud that he had finally solved the worst case of serial murder in American history. He even went on to write a book about it a few years later, to boost his bid for a seat in the U.S. House of Representatives. The cover reads, "My twenty-year quest to capture the Green River Killer."

I came across an advertisement for the book in *The Seattle Times* on August 30, 2004 that stated, "It took him twenty years to capture America's most notorious serial killer." Frankly, I don't think I'd be so proud of twenty years of failure. I also don't think Reichert should get the credit, if there's any to be had, for finally putting Ridgway behind bars. The release of Reichert's book just before the November 2004 election and his manipulation of the Green River tragedies to build his political career are an affront to my sister's memory and those of all the victims, and also to their families and friends.

Earlier in 2001, the only remaining detective assigned to the Green River murder cases, Detective Tom Jensen, determined that new developments in DNA typing might provide the concrete evidence needed to solve these long-open cases. The Green River Task Force had biological evidence that had been taken from the bodies of the earliest victims, which had been recovered shortly after death. Biological evidence that they were able to harvest before it was destroyed by decomposition. Detective Jensen sent the evidence to the Washington State Patrol Crime Laboratory. The DNA profile that was developed matched that taken from Gary Ridgway's fifteen-year-old saliva.

My family was unaware of Detective Tom Jensen's existence. We were not notified in advance of the arrest. We were caught off guard.

We all headed back to the house. Dad didn't, wouldn't talk about the arrest. None of us would. We tried to pretend that nothing had happened, but the silence was heavy. The silence of what wasn't spoken, what needed to be spoken, was thick and suffocating.

The party was over.

For the next two months, Dad sat in his armchair, watching the news and stewing in his own thoughts. Was he facing his own demons, or just brooding?

Tom, Erin, and I were visiting in early December. A single child, my daughter loves any excuse for a big family meal, so Christmas seemed like a logical choice. "Boppa," she asked, "will you come have Christmas dinner at our house?"

"No," my father responded, in a gruff monosyllable.

"But why? It would be so much fun." Unlike me at twelve, my daughter was fearless. She wasn't satisfied with his answer and she pushed for more.

"Because I said so," was my father's childish response. At that, I intervened and cautioned Erin against pushing any further. She knew about the Ridgway arrest and understood that her Boppa was in a bad mood. She just wanted to cheer him up. But I knew that Dad was no longer comfortable driving into the city. Mom had told me so in private. Dad was too proud to admit it, though, and wouldn't let one of us give them a ride.

Throughout the month of January, both Doreen and I called on a regular basis, trying to set dates for visits, but Mom kept telling us not to come. "Your father isn't feeling well. It's nothing serious, but it'd be better if you didn't visit right now."

We learned she took him to the doctor. We learned he was on antibiotics. We learned he had pneumonia. We learned he refused to be hospitalized. But still, we were told not to come.

Despite this prohibition, by early February, we had to see him. Doreen, her husband and I decided to drive to Grayland on Saturday. We wanted to find out how serious Dad's condition was, and we wanted to give Mom a little break. Maybe lunch out with one of us, while the other two stayed with Dad. She sounded more exhausted with every phone call.

While Doreen was getting ready to go that Saturday morning, Mom phoned. "I just called 911. Meet us at the hospital in Aberdeen."

Packed into the back seat of Doreen's Jeep, uneasiness in my heart, the two-hour drive seemed to take forever. I pulled out my cell phone and called directory assistance. "Grays Harbor Community Hospital, Aberdeen, Washington, please." The operator placed the call, and I asked to speak to someone in the Emergency Room. A nurse answered, and I told her who I was. A solemn voice asked me to hold while she found my mother.

"Hello?" A timid, frightened question.

"Mom, it's Arleen. We're on our way. How's Dad?"

"He's gone." So simple. It was all she could force from her body.

Doreen turned around in her front seat, looked at my face, and started to cry.

The nurse came back on the line. "Is there anyone we can call? A friend, maybe? She's so alone here."

How could I tell this kind nurse that Mom had just lost her only friend? "No. There's no one. We're on the road from Seattle. We'll be there within the hour."

I hung up and spent the remainder of that endless drive punching numbers into my cell phone, calling my siblings, telling them the horrible news. I had to do something. At least I had a list of their numbers.

* * *

I've heard and read that some people learn to say that final good-bye. They express their love, they say they're sorry, they make amends. My father was not one of those people. I wonder if he knew he was dying, if he wanted to die, if he was tired of the scars around his heart.

When I walked into the hospital room to say good-bye to Dad's body, he had already left it several hours before. The room was small and dimly lit, with metallic cabinets and counters along the walls. It was cold, and so was I. There was a stretcher in the middle of the room, the kind of stretcher emergency workers use; the kind that they had, in fact, used to carry my father from his home at 7:00 a.m. that morning, so they could try to resuscitate him.

Beside Dad's now-cold body sat Mom, holding his hand and waiting for us to arrive. When I leaned over to kiss my father good-bye, his face was as white as the sheet he lay on. His skin was as cold as stone.

He had died at home with Mom at his side. He died as he had chosen to die. And then they brought him here.

The ER doctor said Dad died of pneumonia. Dad's death certificate states that he died of pneumonia complicated by asbestosis of the lungs.

In my soul, I knew differently. I knew my father had died of a broken heart. Pain, sadness, guilt, release overwhelmed me.

* * *

A memory intrudes: I feel Dad's large, calloused, arthritic hand close over mine, and I am a little girl again. Yet I have no memory of him holding my hand as a little girl. And in this memory, I am no longer little. I am an adult. I hold the power. I can walk firmly and rapidly, with confidence and strength. But I must hold myself back, slow myself down, because Dad can no longer keep up with me.

We were walking the small mall in Aberdeen, about half an hour from their Grayland home, a year before Dad's death. He was suffering. Pain stabbed through his legs with each step. Still, he tried to walk. He walked the mall year-round. The smooth, level linoleum was predictable and safe. The beach sand had become too unpredictable, the road too rough, and there were no sidewalks in the community where they lived. The weather in the mall was always the same, the route unvaried, the goal pre-established.

I had arranged to meet Mom and Dad at the Aberdeen mall on my way to Grayland for a weekend visit. Mom was having her hair permed, so I kept Dad company. We walked slowly, hand-in-hand. Dad couldn't do the whole mall. His body, worn down by too many years of hard work, had given out on him. Not only were his knees no longer able to support him, but his hearing was also failing. Conversation with Dad had always been hard for me. Now there was a physical complication.

Returning to Seattle after Maureen's disappearance, I longed to establish a deeper relationship with Dad and Mom. But I failed. And after fifteen years, I still struggled with the discomfort of not knowing how to talk to my father, what to say, how to connect. On this day, though, we connected through touch. His rough, gnarled hand holding mine in his still-strong grasp. A hand so large that mine was hidden inside his.

That was Dad's way. He never felt words were important. He never found words to communicate. As he would say, "actions speak louder than words."

Not for me. Never for me. I've always wanted to find words to express my thoughts, my ideas, my emotions. And I've always needed others to use words to communicate with me. In this, Dad and I were total opposites.

At best, some of my father's actions were confusing. Without words of explanation and understanding, at times they became downright abusive. Still, he was my father. And that alone meant a lot to me. Because we shared the same blood, the same moody personality, and the same need to control our personal destinies, I have always loved him. And always will.

After saying good-bye to my father's body in the Aberdeen hospital, I took time off work and stayed in Grayland with my mother. While making the funeral arrangements, I spoke with her about Laureen and her daughters. I asked her permission to invite them to the funeral and to the house afterwards. Mom had no objections.

Laureen was teaching overseas and could not return in time, but her two adult daughters attended their grandfather's funeral—the funeral of a man they'd never been given the opportunity to meet. They approached their grandmother with caution, unsure of their reception. As my siblings and I stood by and watched, tears filling our eyes, my mother opened her arms and embraced her granddaughters for the first time,

Sitting in the chapel listening to the eulogy my siblings and I had written in praise of my father and the life he led, Mom was as stoic as she had been during fifty years of marriage. Tears lingered at the corners of her eyes, now red from days of dry-eyed sorrow and minimal sleep. Perhaps she had endured sleeplessness for longer than I'd realized, throughout the last weeks, even months, of the illness that ended Dad's life. Her face was shadowed. She tried hard to hold herself together, to be the tough woman she'd always been. I realized then how old she'd become, and how very lonely she would be.

*　*　*

On one of my regular visits with my mom in Grayland after Dad's death, I found a tiny piece of paper tucked into the pocket calendar by her kitchen phone. On this paper, in Doreen's handwriting, I discovered the address of my father's first home, the house where he was born and had lived in his early childhood, just off Delridge Way in West Seattle. I teach at a community college that is off Delridge, and have for over twenty years. Had I been driving past the ghost of my father's childhood all these years without knowing it, like a workhorse with blinders, focusing only on the present, on what was in my immediate line of vision?

I have a whisper of a memory of driving with Dad, just after I moved home from Mexico. We were in the Delridge area of West Seattle.

Dad pointed. "I was born in a house just a few blocks over there."

"Really? I thought you were born in that house up on Genesee Hill next to Schmitz Park. Grandma's old house."

"No, we moved there later. I was born down here."

"Where? Can you find the house?"

"Not today."

And that was it. Now, years later, my father was gone, but I had the address. I sat on this information for several months, allowing it to settle into the bruised crevices of my heart, to soak into my pores. With Dad's death, Mom's loneliness, and Ridgway's arrest, I was dealing with more than I could handle: a volcanic eruption of repressed pain and memory. I needed to see my father's roots, the place where he began his journey through life.

So I went in search of the house, not at all sure it still stood. But the house had outlived my father. As it turned out, I had not been driving past my father's childhood home each day on my way to and from work. The house was two short blocks from the street I take.

I parked in front of a small, blue-gray house that had fresh white trim and a new front porch. It stood on a small knoll just above street level. Behind the house flows Longfellow Creek. Across the creek and through the trees, the rolling green hills of the West Seattle Public Golf Course are barely visible.

I pictured my father, a young boy in knee pants and suspenders, his thick, black curls damp from boyish exertion, his mischievous blue eyes twinkling. The voice of my paternal grandmother calls him from his adventures in the creek bottom, telling him to come wash up for dinner. I see this little boy who was my father covered in mud, and I wish I had known him.

When Tom and I bought our own West Seattle home in the early nineties, an acquaintance made an off-hand comment about how we were moving from a rental at the top of Genesee Hill, with its sweeping view of Puget Sound, down into what was once referred to as Poverty Gulch. Yet since that comment was made, our elderly neighbors have assured us that this narrow valley between Genesee Hill and the West Seattle Junction was not, in fact, known as Poverty Gulch. The Delridge Valley, where my father spent his early childhood, had earned that dubious label.

I sat in my car for a long time, in front of Dad's childhood home, watching the ghost of my father tossing a football with his friends in the quiet neighborhood street. Too long for a young man bending under the hood of a bright orange and yellow sedan, apparently. His inquisitive stare turned darker, and then darker still, the longer I sat. But I couldn't pull myself away. I was lost in a world of tears. Sadness, pity and love engulfed me as I thought of the life my father had led, beginning from his earliest roots in the humble house atop the knoll in front of me. I thought about how much I loved him for his energy, creativity and determination, and how much I hated so many of the decisions he made throughout his lifetime, and his inability to admit when he was wrong. I wondered about the illogical contradiction of intense emotions my father was able to evoke in me, even after his death.

* * *

My father's final home on the Pacific coast is just south from the fishing town of Westport. There are two state parks along the coast, within the city limits. In 1993, a concrete walking path was completed, connecting Lighthouse State Park and Westhaven State Park. The hilly path follows the rise and fall of the coastal dunes. Dotted along the 1.4-mile length of the path are benches, where walkers can stop to rest and absorb the immense beauty of the Pacific waves crashing on the sands. They are memorial benches placed there by grieving families in memory of lost loved ones.

When Dad died in February 2002, plans were already underway to extend the walkway another mile or so from Westhaven State Park, along the coast of Half Moon Bay and into downtown Westport. My family put our name on the list for a bench site and waited. Almost two years later, Dad's bench was set in place along the new section of walkway. It was in easy walking distance from the parking lot and had a sweeping view of the bay.

Unfortunately, severe winter storms washed away the beach at Half Moon Bay that year, along with a seventy-foot long section of the new dune trail. By the time the U.S. Army Corps of Engineers finished the first phase of their reclamation project, a hill of sand the size of a two-story house covered the new concrete walkway that led to Dad's bench. The bench had to be moved several hundred yards down the path.

It is not Dad's final resting place, of course. The urn holding his ashes sits on a bookshelf in Mom's living room. Still, this bench is the closest thing I have to a gravesite, a place to visit, a place to remember, a place to be with my father. But when I go there now, my vision is blocked by that immense sand dune, which conceals any view of the bay. I can see no farther than a double arm's length in front of my face, and all I can think about is the irony of it all. In death, as in life, Dad's point of view cannot see the gray. Not even the gray of the Pacific coast horizon.

* * *

After my father's death, Doreen and I began alternating visits to check on Mom. We never let a fortnight pass without making sure one of us makes the trip. Though she never complains, the only company my mother has now is her old dog, and he doesn't hold up his end of their conversations very well. Still, she refuses to leave the last home she shared with my father. When I go, I usually take Mom out to dinner to get her out of the house.

One visit, about a year after Dad's death, we were eating dinner at the pizza place in Westport, the one with the name that neither of us can ever remember, when I asked her a question that had been bothering me for years.

"Mom," I began, "what in the world possessed you to have so many kids?"

Mom shrugged and became very busy with her salad. I heard Dad's voice telling me to close my big mouth, but I ignored it.

"I mean really, nine kids is a lot."

"You'll have to ask your father that," she said, a sly smile on her face.

"It's a bit late for that. I can't get much of an answer from his ashes, Mom. And even if I'd asked when he was still here, he wouldn't have answered me." There was another long pause, and I tried another angle. "Did Dad really want such a huge family? Did you?"

"That's just how it happened. It was nature's way."

"But you were, you are, an RN. You could've interfered a little with Mother Nature."

"Oh, no," she said, shaking her head.

Unwilling to give up, I tried again. "It must've been really difficult with so many of us. I have trouble just trying to keep up with everybody, even now."

"Now is the best time. I have all of you to take care of me."

"But you won't let us take care of you."

"Not yet," she said. "I don't need it yet."

After another long pause, she continued to speak, a dreamy tone in her voice and a faraway look in her eyes. "There were no regrets. Your father and I loved all of you very much."

I wish I had been able to feel that love as a child, I wanted to tell her, but I remained silent.

As long as Dad was alive, I rarely allowed myself the luxury of deep emotion. Some part of me knew that if I let down my guard to feel love or joy, I would also feel pain and anger. I was terrified of anger, be it Dad's or my own. His denial became mine, and it overpowered me. I suppose that's why I couldn't face Maureen's death, or truly mourn the loss of my baby sister, until after my father was also gone.

Chapter Twelve: A Reality Check

"Do you want a cup of tea?" Mom asked as she filled the stained old teakettle for the third or fourth time that day. Mom has always been a tea drinker, never fond of coffee, but since Dad's death, she seems to have a cup in her hand continuously. Perhaps the warm tonic offers solace to her lonely heart.

"Sure, Mom. It'll help pass the time until he shows up."

I sat at her tiny kitchen table and watched as she found cups and tea bags—generic, for it's the warmth, not the taste, that matters to my mother. The kitchen blinds were half closed. They are always half closed. She says it's so the neighbors can't see in the windows. She doesn't have any neighbors living close enough to see in through the windows, but the blinds remain half closed.

It was late September, 2002. The week before, Doreen had called me with the news. A detective from the newly resurrected Green River Task Force had called Mom and wanted to take a DNA sample from her. Doreen was worried about how Mom would handle it. After all, Dad had died only eight months before.

I called my mother. "I heard you got a phone call, Mom."

"Yes, a nice detective called. He's going to drive all the way down from Seattle to visit me next Tuesday."

I wanted to remind her that I'd been making the two-hour drive every other weekend since Dad's death, but I didn't. "Mom, I'd like to be with you when he visits. Would that be okay with you?"

"Oh, that would be really nice." I heard relief in her voice, and realized again how hard she was trying. Trying to be strong and sure, under the stress of so much loss.

I asked her if it would be all right for me to call the detective and ask him to reschedule his visit to a Saturday, so I wouldn't have to miss work. By the time I got off the phone with Mom, it was too late to make the call, so I waited until the next morning. It gave me time to think, to wonder. For many years, I'd considered trying to do a bit of investigating on my own, to see the Green River files on my sister. Perhaps I was ready now. I wanted to know what had happened to Maureen.

In the morning, following another sleepless night, I called. "May I speak with Detective Pavlovich?"

"Speaking," was the brief reply. It was the voice of a busy man, buried in work that my call had interrupted.

"My name's Arleen Williams. I'm Maureen's sister. You called my mother for a DNA sample."

I felt this unknown man lean into the phone, more attentive, listening to my words. "I don't know if my mother told you, but my father died recently and I'm concerned about her well-being."

"Yes, she mentioned it," Detective Pavlovich said, his voice quiet and comforting. "I'm sorry for your loss."

"Because of this," I continued quickly, wanting to brush off his sympathy and the possibility of my tears, "I'd like to be with my mother during your visit. Would it be possible to schedule it on a Saturday, rather than midweek?"

He agreed. His gentleness, his willingness to drive to the ocean on a weekend, pleased me. My first impression was positive, and we set a date, but I wasn't done yet. "The accusation of prostitution has always been hard to face. My parents never wanted to talk about it. Please don't bring it up. In fact, please don't ask my mother anything."

"Okay, agreed. But I'll be happy to answer any questions either of you have." He showed neither surprise nor a desire to do anything that would trouble either my mother or me. I don't know what I expected, but Detective Pavlovich sounded genuinely kind, and I was relieved.

I thanked him, hung up the phone, and began to shake. When my sister's remains were found, and she was identified as a confirmed Green River victim, the press had been merciless, like hungry *piranha*, and my parents were the prey. Despite Mom and Dad's isolation in the Issaquah Valley, reporters called and showed up on their doorstep at all hours. Issuing the press release that directed inquiries to Linda Barker and spending as much time as possible at their remote beach house in Grayland had been my parents' only escape. They were intensely private people, and never wanted to talk about "family business" with anyone outside the immediate family. Or with anyone inside the family, for that matter. They certainly weren't going to talk about their youngest daughter's murder, or morality, with strangers who would then write or talk about it publicly. Now, almost twenty years later, it was going to start all over again. Or was it?

As my mother loved to say, "Don't make a mountain out of a molehill."

On the day of the appointment, Mom and I sat and drank tea in the kitchen behind the half-closed blinds waiting for Detective Pavlovich. I could feel my mother's tension as she stood every few minutes to look out the front window checking for his arrival. Just as a car pulled up to the gate and stopped, I realized what day it was: October 5, 2002. Maureen's thirty-ninth birthday.

Detective Pavlovich drove an unmarked car, one that looked like any other. I was glad. A police car in her front yard was not something Mom would be comfortable with under any circumstances. She was already worried enough about what the neighbors would think when they saw a strange man visiting.

We watched as a tall, athletic man got out of the car and took a large case from the trunk. He wasn't wearing a uniform, and I breathed another sigh of relief. I went to open the front door and introduce myself to him, this detective who was my hope for answers to the questions that had plagued me for so many years.

"I'm happy to answer any questions you may have," Detective Pavlovich told my mother as we settled into our seats in the living room. His tone was gentle and inviting, his manner relaxed. I could almost see the tightness in my mother's face and shoulders relax in his presence.

"Oh, no," she said, dismissing the very idea that there were any questions she would ever ask. A dreamy look crossed her face, and she added, "Maureen was such a good girl."

Detective Pavlovich and I remained silent. Mom stood and randomly selected a few of the many family snapshots that seemed to have appeared from nowhere since Dad's death. It started during the first six months after his funeral, when I found more photographs stuck up around the house with every visit. They were wedged into the corners of framed pictures that had been in the house for years, they leaned against lamp bases, vases and knick-knacks, and were stacked in piles on every available surface. There were photographs of Dad, of Maureen, and even of Laureen and her daughters—photographs that would never have been allowed in the house while Dad was still alive. I didn't even know she had so many. Where had she hidden them?

Picking up a couple of photographs of Maureen, Mom handed them to Detective Pavlovich. "That was Maureen. She was such a good, sweet girl."

Detective Pavlovich took the photographs and smiled. "Did she like to go hiking a lot?" he asked, holding up a shot of Maureen sitting on a rock, a pack on her back, feeding a wild bird from her bare hand.

"Oh, yes," Mom said. "She loved animals and nature. And she was going to school, too. She was renting an apartment in Bellevue, near the college, when that horrible man grabbed her."

Detective Pavlovich glanced in my direction, and I gave him a tiny shake of my head. We both knew Maureen had not been living in Bellevue when she disappeared, nor had she been randomly "grabbed" off the street as my mother preferred to believe. I still didn't know exactly what had happened to Maureen, but I knew my mother's fading memory was altering the truth. Still, I remained quiet. I saw no reason to contradict her in front of this stranger, and I could see in his eyes that he recognized her confusion.

"I'm so glad you caught that horrible man," she said. Then, turning to me, on the sofa beside her, she added, "I worry about Erin. You have to be really careful nobody gets her, too."

"My daughter," I said, in response to the question in Detective Pavlovich's eyes.

"I'm just so happy you got him off the streets, so he can't hurt any more girls," my mother repeated.

"Well, that's why I'm here," Detective Pavlovich said. "We want to get as many DNA matches as possible, so we can bring more charges against him. Right now, he has not been charged with your daughter's murder."

"Oh, it's him," my mom assured him.

I have no idea where that certainty came from. Was it the same intuition that had told her years before that her youngest was dead? Or had she simply chosen to convince herself that this confident man of authority had done a good job? Detective Pavlovich smiled, also unwilling to contradict her.

Mom was more talkative than I had expected. After all, she'd been silent for nineteen years. But her memory was distorted, and her facts were false, so I was glad when Detective Pavlovich glanced at the clock chiming above the rollback desk in the corner of the crowded living room.

"If you're ready, let's go ahead and take those samples." He slowly unfolded himself from the loveseat and began to open the large case he'd set on the floor next to the ottoman.

"Okay, I'm ready." Mom sounded as childish and innocent as a schoolgirl. "What do I need to do?"

"We use these swabs. I'll need you to gently rub each one along the inside of your cheek or gum line. Then it goes into one of these vials." He pulled on surgical gloves and prepared a swab, using a thin wooden stick similar to the cooking skewers I use to make shish kabobs and a piece of what looked like an ordinary cotton ball. He wrapped the ends of two sticks with the cotton and held them between his fingers with great care, in order to prevent contamination. In his other hand, he held a vial. "All right, let's do the first one."

"Like this?" Mom's voice was timid and uncertain.

"Perfect. Okay, that should do it." He took the swab from her, put it in the vial, and slipped it into a large manila envelope. The envelope was labeled and looked official. "One more time, now. Just in case the lab wants a second one."

The Green River Task Force hoped to match Mom's DNA against any trace evidence they might find that could tie Maureen to Gary Ridgway. They needed a close relative, since so little of Maureen remained. Not even her DNA. A mother's DNA is the closest match, Detective Pavlovich explained. Having DNA from both father and mother would have been even better, but it was too late for that.

Soon after taking the samples, Detective Pavlovich said his good-byes. As I walked him to the door and out of Mom's earshot, I asked if we could meet again. Without asking for a reason or explanation, he nodded. A little over three weeks later, I met with him in the offices of the Green River Task Force.

* * *

The office was in an industrial area of Seattle, just south of Boeing field, on a wide street with frequent stoplights and no trees. The air was dusty, and everything seemed gray. For years, I'd toyed with the idea of trying to gain access to Maureen's case files so that I could find out what had happened to her, or at least what the Green River Task Force thought had happened to her. Now, I finally had a chance. It was a good gray, a hopeful gray.

I drove slowly, staying in the right lane, trying to read the numbers on the buildings. I doubted that there would be a big, neon "Green River Task Force" sign glowing on the side of the road, so I looked for the number. I pulled into the parking lot of a squat, non-descript building, then sat for a few minutes trying to catch my breath and relax. I had a list of questions that I was still hoping to memorize.

Inside the building, there was no directory and no signs. The foyer was empty. To one side, there was a glass door with blinds that blocked any attempt to see through the windows. Intuition led me in that direction, and I reached for the door knob. The door didn't budge. I noticed an intercom button on the wall next to the door and pushed it.

"Hello, can I help you?"

"Yes. My name's Arleen Williams. I have an appointment with Detective Pavlovich. Am I in the right place?"

"Yes, you are. He's expecting you. Come on in."

I heard the lock click open, and I pushed myself inside.

A young woman walked towards me. No uniform. "Have a seat right here. Detective Pavlovich will be out in just a minute." She motioned to a couple of gray office chairs lined up along the wall, just inside the door. As I sat and waited, I saw rows and rows of harsh fluorescent lights overhead, and gray cubicle walls that divided the large room into a maze of tiny workspaces. And I saw boxes and boxes, large piles of boxes. Later, I learned that the Task Force was just moving into this building, and there were still many more boxes in storage. With the arrest of Ridgway and the reopening of all the cases, they needed more space to work.

But then, I wasn't thinking about the magnitude of what I was seeing. I wasn't thinking about the bureaucracy of grief surrounding me. I was only trying to stop my hands from shaking and focus on the questions I had come prepared to ask. A few moments later, Detective Pavlovich walked towards me, hand extended, welcoming me into this cold, impersonal space with a warm, friendly smile.

"Let's go back to my desk." He led me through the maze until we stopped at his cubicle. One wall was covered with a chart that showed all the known victims of the Green River Killer. It looked like some type of record-keeping or data-collection system.

Noticing my stare, Detective Pavlovich explained. "Those are all the families I'm collecting samples from. See, here's Maureen's name. This indicates that we have her DNA sample. These other families are the ones I'm still working on. Here, why don't you sit right there?" He pointed to the chair across the desk from his own. "Can I get you a Coke or anything?"

The last thing I needed was caffeine, to make me even more jittery than I already felt. "No, thanks."

"What would you like to know? I'll tell you as much as I can."

I took a deep breath and began. "I want to know what you

think, what the Task Force thinks, happened to my sister. I have a few specific questions."

"Okay, what's the first one?"

"Is there any undeniable evidence that my sister was working as a prostitute?"

"Undeniable? No. There's circumstantial evidence, but not undeniable. We know she was involved with Tobey Hicks."

"Yes. I think she was in love, or at least she thought she was in love with him. And I know about his police record."

He nodded. "And then there were the two Kris Ponds pedestrian tickets with Maureen's address and phone number."

"But someone could have been using Maureen's information. Tobey Hicks could have given it to anyone." I could hear a pleading note in my voice. I didn't want it to be true. I didn't want to have to admit that my sister and Kris Ponds were one and the same person.

"You're right. And the handwriting expert we called in couldn't confirm a match, and the ticketing officer couldn't identify Maureen as Kris Ponds from a photograph. So, there's no confirmed identification."

He stressed the word "confirmed," and I knew he was holding back. He believed that Kris Ponds was, in fact, Maureen. "Okay, let's say Kris Ponds was a name Maureen used," I said. "Is there any way of knowing if she made a voluntary decision to prostitute herself, or if she was forced?" At this point, I was reading my questions off the notepad I brought in with me, having given up all attempts to memorize my questions. Or his responses, for that matter.

"Force is an interesting word. There are a lot of different kinds of force." He spoke slowly, measuring each word.

"What do you mean?" I demanded, interrupting his train of thought with my own impatience. "There was that fight in her apartment the night before she disappeared. Was she raped, drugged, forced into prostitution?"

Detective Pavlovich thought for a moment. "Like I said before, there are a lot of forms of force. I don't think Maureen was forced in the way you describe. She was probably coerced. Tobey was a pro. First, he convinced her that he loved her, then he got all her money from her, and then he put the pressure on her to get more. Fast."

"For how long?" My voice was little more than a whisper. "How long do you think she was on the streets?"

"Two weeks. A week. A couple of days. The twenty-sixth could have been the first time."

"The day of the Kris Ponds tickets?" I said, hopefully. Somehow, in an odd and disturbing way, it was comforting to learn that my sister might have been killed only two days after her first day on the street.

"Sure. Maybe Tobey was mad because she'd been ticketed. Maybe she didn't bring him any money. Maybe she refused to do what he wanted. There was a fight. There's no way of knowing what happened."

"Tobey knows."

"True. But there's no way we can make him talk."

I wasn't at all sure I believed that, and I was very tempted to let loose a verbal attack on the Task Force and the Seattle Police Department for not having done more at the time of Maureen's disappearance, and again when her remains were discovered. But that wasn't the reason I was there. Refocusing, I pressed on with the questions I'd come to ask. "Okay. How do you know she was a Green River victim? What's that based on?"

"Again, circumstantial, but logical. We're looking at two factors: the location where her remains were found, the fact that they were in a cluster with several other known victims, and her connection to prostitution through her relationship with Hicks."

"Where's Tobey Hicks now?"

Detective Pavlovich turned to his computer and did a brief search. "He's still in Seattle. He's been in and out of jail a few times."

I felt my stomach turn with disgust and grief. "But he's free," I managed to say. "He's out on the streets coercing other young, naïve, confused kids, like Maureen. Ruining other lives."

"I'm afraid so. And he's not alone out there." Detective Pavlovich was solemn, and a trace of sadness washed over his kind face.

I took a deep breath and pushed forward. "Okay. Let's say Ridgway was Maureen's killer." Seeing Detective Pavlovich shift in his chair, I knew I was edging too close. He wouldn't be able to talk about the Ridgway case. "Or let's just say she was a Green River victim. How was she killed?"

"Probably strangulation," he said, relaxing into his chair again. "Probably right away, in his vehicle."

"How much did she suffer? Was there any evidence of sadistic torture, or anything like that?" I could no longer hold back my tears. This was the toughest question I had to ask, but I needed to hear the answer. No matter how horrible the truth might be, I knew it couldn't stand up to my nightmares.

Detective Pavlovich handed me a box of tissues. "No sign of torture on any of the victims. We think he killed his victims shortly after picking them up."

I closed my eyes for a moment and filled my lungs with the air my sister could no longer breathe. I felt an immense sense of relief: at least she hadn't been tortured. Pulling myself together, I pointed towards the large notebook on his desk, the one he had paged through when checking the Kris Ponds date.

"May I look through that?"

"Sure," he responded, not seeming at all surprised by my request. "Just a minute, though. There are a few more of these." He pushed the four-inch-thick notebook towards me, turning it in my direction, and then left his cubicle. He returned a few minutes later with two more large notebooks. "If you'd like, I'll leave you alone with these. Holler if you need me," he said, and left.

I sank deep into the pages of those notebooks. I lost all track of time. I read my sister's letter to me, telling me that she wouldn't be able to come for a second visit to Mexico, "due to an unfortunate mistake." I saw her bankbook with its notation, "withdrawal for T." I saw a photograph of Tobey Hicks, and I could almost understand her attraction—dark eyes and a bright, cocky smile. I read the King County Medical Examiner's autopsy report. With an unsteady hand, I copied these words onto my notepad: "In view of the circumstances and site of discovery, the cause of death is attributed to homicidal violence of undetermined origin."

My hands shook as I continued to turn the pages. Detective Pavlovich checked in on me several times. Slowly, finally, reluctantly, I realized it was time for me to go. He undoubtedly needed his desk back.

"I'm sorry I've taken so much of your time."

"No problem. You're welcome to call or come back anytime you have more questions. Maureen's case hasn't been reopened yet, but it won't be long now. I don't know who it will be assigned to, but feel free to call me if I can help in any way."

I thanked him, and he walked me out the door into the bright autumn sunshine. We made small talk. I was dazed. He asked if I was okay, and I assured him I was. I lied. I said good-bye, got in my car and drove off. A block away, I pulled into the parking lot of another nondescript office building, and sat in my car and sobbed.

The second myth, the horrible myth that my sister was forced into white slavery, was just that: a myth. I knew in my heart that

Maureen was coerced, a victim of her own vulnerability, an easy target for an experienced pimp and con man like Tobey Hicks. An equally easy target for a murderer like Gary Ridgway, who preyed on vulnerable young girls in the streets of Seattle.

For nineteen years, I had told myself that Maureen was a victim of two violent crimes. Detective Pavlovich had helped me understand a little about force, and about how a pimp like Tobey Hicks works. Tobey had zeroed in on my naïve little sister the afternoon they met at the 7-Eleven. He wooed Maureen, and fooled her into believing he was crazy about her. When Doreen and Marleen questioned him about his relationship with Maureen, Tobey made a revealing comment. Later, he repeated it to Robert: "I couldn't believe how little she knew about the area. I was like a tour guide or something."

Tobey Hicks had seduced Maureen, and in her innocence, she became convinced that he was in love with her and she with him. She gave him her money because he had told her he was making travel arrangements for a trip together. Then he told her they needed more money, and there was a quick and easy way to get it. If she really loved him, she'd do it just this once for him. For them.

She was coerced, or she was in love, or both. Let's assume she made the decision to try prostitution for Tobey because that was what he wanted, because she'd do anything for him, because she was in love. Let's assume she tried it once, the day Kris Ponds was given the jaywalking tickets. Monday, September 26, 1983. Maybe she brought some money home to Tobey. Or maybe she came home empty-handed, except for two tickets that needed to be paid. Tobey was angry.

The next evening, Tuesday night, there was a fight in her apartment. Neighbors identified the man as Tobey. Was there a second man or even more? According to family myth, yes. According to police interviews with the apartment manager and neighbors, no.

The following day, Wednesday, September 28, Mom talked to Maureen at 10:00 a.m. She was never heard from again. She was out on the street that day or night. She was inexperienced, young, and naïve. A perfect target. She was picked up by the Green River Killer. He could have been the first, and the only, john who picked her up. In fact, Ridgway may have been only the second man with whom my sister had sex, assuming she was sexually involved with Tobey Hicks.

She was strangled during or after sex. According to Detective

Pavlovich, all of the victims were killed almost immediately: no prolonged contact, no torture. Then the killer drove out and dumped Maureen's body in a site he'd already selected and used for two other victims, at the Highway 18 and Interstate 90 intersection.

Does that let Tobey off the hook? Hell, no. He didn't kill her, but he tricked her, lied to her, and coerced her. There is enough evidence, both factual and circumstantial, to convince me of that. But, given time, she could have changed her mind. She could have gotten away from him. She could have made the decision that the lifestyle he was offering was not for her.

But she didn't have the time. Gary Ridgway killed her before she could reconsider.

Whenever things get just a little too crazy at the college where I teach, I always ask my friend and colleague, Dorrienne, for a reality check. Is this or that what just happened? This is how I see it, how do you see it? That's what Detective Pavlovich was for me: a reality check. For nineteen years, I believed that my sister had been brutally victimized twice within a forty-eight hour period. For nineteen years, I believed this second family myth.

But I was wrong.

Chapter Thirteen: The Fourth Myth

The fourth family myth goes something like this: Maureen was killed when she thought she was getting help. She was trying to escape from Tobey, from the life into which he was pushing her. She was trying to reach Mom at Echo Glen Children's Center. Or she was trying to get home to Issaquah. This myth is an attempt to explain why her remains were found so close to my mother's workplace, so close to our family home in Issaquah.

The false logic behind this myth was as follows: Maureen could not have possibly chosen prostitution, therefore she was doing it under duress. So when she had the opportunity to ask a stranger for help, for a ride out of Seattle to Issaquah, she took it. Since she wasn't really a prostitute, she had to be trying to escape, right? Maybe she was hitchhiking, something Mom and Dad knew she sometimes did, despite their admonitions.

Maureen's remains—her skull, her jawbone, and a few other scattered bones—were found at the intersection of Interstate 90 and Highway 18. Our family home on Tiger Mountain was only a mile or two from the on-ramp to Highway 18, off the Issaquah-Hobart Road. From there, it's only eight miles to the Interstate 90 intersection, which is an easy horseback ride, or a longish walk. Echo Glen Children's Center, where Mom worked as the evening infirmary nurse, is near the intersection of Interstate 90 and Highway 18

Maureen's remains were found by an Echo Glen employee. By then, they could only be identified by dental records. But she was not alone. For twenty years, it was only due to the clustering of Maureen's remains with those of two other victims, as well as her relationship with Tobey Hicks, that Maureen was considered a victim of the Green River Killer. She didn't seem to fit the profile, otherwise. Evidence from other Green River victims indicated strangulation, that they were killed shortly after they were picked up, and that they were killed in his vehicle.

If this was all true, Maureen was dead before her body left Seattle. Had Maureen actually asked her killer for help, and knowing this, had he left her body close to Mom's workplace, not far from the family doorstep? Probably not. More likely, the killer had already chosen his dumpsite before he even began his hunt that night. Was the site where Maureen's young body was left to decay just a cruel coincidence, an ironic twist of fate?

My family was not the only group of people speculating. On May 6, 1986, *The Seattle Times* reported that Maureen "was last seen leaving her apartment on East Madison Street." On August 19, 2003, the same newspaper printed that she was last seen at a "Seattle bus stop." In *The Search for the Green River Killer*, Smith and Guillen *(Penguin Books, 1991)* wrote that Maureen "had been hitchhiking to a job interview in Seattle" when she disappeared.

The discrepancies in these stories don't allow them to give me much confidence or comfort. Last seen by whom? Who was providing this information? Were they reliable sources?

Even now, even after Ridgway's confession, the Prosecutor's Summary of Evidence only states that she was picked up in Seattle. Even Gary Ridgway says he doesn't remember the details of Maureen's final hour. "I killed so many women, I have a hard time keeping them straight."

Where truth cannot be found, imagination creates myth. In my mind, I don't see Maureen getting off a bus, nor do I see her hitchhiking. I see Tobey dropping her off, armed with nothing but the clothes on her back, her pockets empty. I see her in the International District, the same area where a police officer had given someone using the name Kris Ponds two jaywalking tickets, two days earlier. In my mind, Tobey says, "I'll be back at midnight. You make sure you got something for me by then, you hear me?" And he drives off.

I want to believe that after the fight in her apartment the night before, Maureen was frightened. She was beginning to realize that this was not love. That Tobey was not the man she thought he was. She was scared, she was sad, and her sense of self-worth had hit rock bottom.

"I need to get away," Maureen thought. "I want to go home." And home, the home the baby voice inside of her cried out for, was not her new apartment on Capitol Hill, not the apartment Tobey had moved his clothes into and made his own. The home she wanted was the house in Issaquah, with Mom and Dad. But how could she get there? She felt desperately lost and helpless.

In the dreams that have haunted my days and nights for over twenty years now, I see a truck pull up to the curb beside her, to the curb where Tobey told her to stay until the first john came along. A man motioned for her to climb in. He was a young workingman, white, with straight brown hair flopping down into his eyes. Not so different from her own older brothers. Two thoughts surfaced in Maureen's mind at the same instant: he looks safe, and maybe he'll help me. She climbed in.

But the man was not interested in being a Good Samaritan. "You want to show me some fun, honey?"

"I'm not what you think. I need help."

"Sure, honey. Whatever you want."

"Look, I need to get out of here. I want to go home. Can you give me a ride?"

"Where to, honey?"

"Issaquah. My family lives in Issaquah. Or can you just take me away from here and give me a dime to call my parents? I'm sure they'll come and get me." She couldn't go back to her apartment because Tobey might be there, and she was afraid that if she waited where he'd dropped her off, Tobey or one of his friends would be watching her.

"Well, I don't know. That's a bit farther than I want to go right now. We'll have to see if you're worth it, honey."

In my nightmares, I see him pull away from the curb and drive into an area Maureen was unfamiliar with. New to Seattle and without a car, without even a driver's license, she knew very little of the city. As she looked out the window, the fear in her stomach rose to her heart. With the man's last words, she knew she was in trouble.

"No, you don't get it. I'm not a prostitute."

"Sure you're not, honey. None of them are."

"I'm not. Just stop this damn truck and let me out."

"Not quite yet, honey."

I see my sister reach for the door handle. She was ready to jump, ready to do anything to get away, but there was no door handle. She was trapped. She started screaming at him to stop the truck, to let her out. What she didn't realize, or notice, was that he'd pulled into a dark, isolated, deserted area.

"I'll stop, honey, and I'll leave you alone for a long, long time. But not till I'm done with you. Issaquah, huh? Yeah, honey, I think I'll take you to Issaquah. But first, you need to be quiet. And first, we need to have a little fun."

These words did not come slowly, calmly, or gently. I hear them spoken with measured violence, coming in the pauses between Maureen's screams and scratches and slaps as she tried to fight him off. But he was larger and stronger. And it wasn't the first time he'd done this.

After he gagged her, after he tore off her jeans, after he forced himself inside her and brutally, viciously, violently raped her, Maureen thought the worst was over. She was wrong. As she saw him slowly, deliberately pull a cord from his pocket, her innocent blue eyes filled with terror. My baby sister knew her end was near.

I imagine it as a thin piece of braided Cordova leather, as fine as heavy string. I feel the smooth, soft leather of the used cord, rolled into a ball inside his jacket pocket. He was fondling this soft piece of leather while he drove to this dark, isolated spot. I see the bloodstains soaked into it, the blood of how many women?

With the practiced skill of a seasoned killer, he wrapped the cord around my sister's neck. I see her struggle. I see the cord tighten around her neck. Tight, tighter, cutting into soft white skin, drawing blood, stealing life. Suffocation. As Maureen's young body relaxes in death, I see the soft, cruel cord loosen. Its job done, it is returned to the pocket. I see this cord in countless nightmares.

I know the killer had a number of different dumpsites. Dumpsites—what an awful expression. It's an expression to which I've slowly become hardened, just as I have grown accustomed to reading about decomposition of the human body and forensic science. They were remote sites, in wooded areas that unscrupulous people often used for the illegal dumping of household items or garbage. The killer had a dumpsite near Issaquah, straight out Interstate 90, less than thirty minutes from Seattle on a night without traffic. He had already left two other victims there. I see him start his truck engine and head east, relaxed and confident after his new kill.

"Sure, honey," he murmurs to Maureen's lifeless body, pushed onto the floor of the passenger's seat. "I'll give you a ride to Issaquah."

I awaken from my nightmares, but reality offers little in the way of comfort. For years, these horrors were fueled by our family myths, which denied that my sister chose to prostitute herself. The reality check with Detective Pavlovich helped me come to understand how Maureen could have been coerced into doing exactly what Tobey wanted her to do. I only hope that when she found herself facing death, she was so high on Tobey Hicks's drugs that she did not suffer as intensely as she does in my endless nightmares.

Chapter Fourteen: Closure?

From November 20 to 26, 2002, Carlton Smith published the serialized version of an extensive, detailed article entitled "TRUTH OR DEATH" in *Seattle Weekly*. He examined the possibility of there being more than one Green River Killer and the dangers inherent in the King County Prosecutor's highly publicized refusal to consider a plea bargain for Gary Ridgway.

"We will not plea bargain with the death penalty," King County Prosecuting Attorney Norm Maleng said last December. Maleng might have thought he was seizing the moral high ground. But the consequences of that posture are profound: Without a confession in exchange for a life sentence instead of death, the community might never know what really happened in the worst serial-murder case in American history, because a cogent case can be made that Ridgway might not be the only person responsible for the murders. While putting Ridgway to death would satisfy some narrow—in some cases political—ends, it would leave unresolved the question of whether someone else is still out there, still killing.

By early August, the papers were reporting that Prosecutor Maleng might reverse his decision. When I learned that he was considering the possibility of offering a plea bargain that would allow Gary Ridgway to cooperate in an ongoing Green River investigation, in exchange for his life, I sent an e-mail message to the King County Prosecutor's office. I expressed my hope that, through a plea bargain, the full extent of Ridgway's gruesome activities would become known, whereas if he were convicted and executed for the deaths of only a small number of the victims, my family would never know with certainty if he had, indeed, killed Maureen.

The following morning I received an e-mail response from Detective Karen Larson, offering to discuss any questions or concerns I had regarding my sister's case. Because I had already given my opinion on Maleng's decision, and because I knew I could call Detective Pavlovich if I had further questions about my sister's case, I did not respond to Detective Larson.

Sixteen days later, I found another e-mail in my inbox, this one from someone by the name of Mary Kirchner. She identified herself as "the Victim Advocate working with the surviving family members on the Gary Ridgway case for the Prosecutor's Office." She invited me to send her my contact information so that she could include me on her list of family members to whom she would pass on information about the developing case against Gary Ridgway, as it became available. I responded immediately, providing her with the information she requested.

For several months, I heard nothing. In fact, I never received any informational updates from the Prosecutor's Office at all.

* * *

Every morning, rain or shine, Tom walks barefoot into the front yard to bring in *The Seattle Times*. He reads while I'm showering and rushing through breakfast. Usually, I'm yelling at Erin to hurry and at Tom to stop giving me a verbal run-down of the day's headlines because I can't listen, eat, and get out of the house on time for my first class without going nuts.

We have finally returned to our crazy, comforting morning routine, but for many months after the Ridgway arrest, it took on a slightly new twist. As Tom read through the morning paper, he would pull out sections he knew I'd want to read, the ones with the latest Green River news. He'd set those sections at my place at the kitchen table. Some mornings, if I managed to move quickly, I took the time, or I made the time, to read the latest article. Other mornings, I only had time to read the headlines or look at the photos.

October 17, 2003 was one of the days I made time. Tom set out two articles for me to read, both about the far-reaching ramifications of the twenty-year-old murder mystery and the possible plea bargain. My attention was drawn first to the article about one of the victims' fathers, who was speaking out. He'd been assured by King County Prosecutor Norm Maleng that his daughter's murderer would get the death penalty. Now all the evidence pointed to a plea bargain. Ridgeway would get life imprisonment in exchange for information. And this dad was mad.

Tom and I talked about this during our morning rush. The crux of the matter lies in one's beliefs about the death penalty. Since I do not believe in institutionalized killing, in "an eye for an eye," since I do not believe that we can justify taking another human life, except perhaps in self-defense or the defense of those we feel compelled to protect, I do not see any justification for killing Ridgway or anyone else on Death Row. Because Tom and I share this fundamental ethical belief, our brief discussion centered around the issue of appropriate punishment for a mass murderer. I opted for re-establishment of the chain gang, but Tom felt that total, permanent isolation would be more appropriate. He was probably right. The worst punishment you can give a social animal is separation from all human contact. That would be much harder than being allowed to work, to converse, to share with other inmates.

Unfortunately, we would have no say in Ridgway's ultimate punishment. We knew that the warden of the correctional facility he was assigned to would determine the conditions of his incarceration. The only thing certain was that Gary Ridgway would be behind bars for the remainder of his life. For that, I was grateful. I was relieved. At least he was off the streets. He would kill no more.

The other article dealt with the inequity of a plea bargain in the Ridgway case, arguing that Ridgway, accused of seven murders and suspected of at least fifty, should not be offered a plea bargain that would save his life while other prisoners were on Death Row for a single murder. I agreed with this view, yet my solution would not be to deny Ridgway the plea bargain, but to abolish capital punishment altogether.

Without a plea bargain, Marie Malvar's remains, as well as those of a host of other victims, would never have been found. There are over fifty more victims, missing and murdered girls, above and beyond the original fifty identified Green River victims. What are we, as a society, willing to do to find the answers?

* * *

By early November, I had still heard nothing from the Prosecutor's Office about any progress being made on the Ridgway case. Tom was out of town, so I'd put a hold on newspaper delivery and wasn't getting my morning updates. Sunday night, November 2, 2003, I happened to turn on the television news, and I heard a fragment of a report about the possibility that the Prosecutor's Office would be entering guilty pleas on a large number of cases at a hearing the following Wednesday. I also heard that meetings involving representatives from the Prosecutor's office and victims' families had been taking place.

We hadn't been invited.

I went to school the next morning, trusting that I'd hear something from Mary Kirchner, or the Task Force, but by evening, I still hadn't heard a word. I was feeling very uneasy.

At 9:20 p.m. that evening, I got a phone call from a friend who works for KOMO television. She told me that the Ridgway hearing, scheduled for Wednesday, November 5, 2003, would be televised, and she confirmed that he was expected to confess to the murders of forty-eight women, Maureen's included.

I was frustrated and angry that no one from the Task Force had contacted me. And I was worried about Mom. If KOMO was pre-empting all their morning programming to televise the entire hearing live, this was big. Mom couldn't be alone; someone had to go to Grayland. I wanted to be in the courtroom, but Mom came first. I called Doreen to see if she was available, but she had to work. I could live with that. She'd been through all she could handle twenty years before, when Maureen first disappeared. I knew it fell on me to be with Mom. The rest of my siblings were too far away.

I hung up the phone, went back to my computer, and sent the following e-mail to Mary Kirchner:

> Please let me know what is currently happening. Is there some kind of hearing or meeting of victims' families this week? I've heard nothing. Please advise.

Between classes on Tuesday, even during classes when I could, I made phone calls and left messages. I called Detective Kathleen Larson. Her machine gave me another name and number, that of Detective John Earhart. I spoke with him, but he couldn't answer my questions. I wanted to confirm that the hearing was going to be televised, that the judge was allowing cameras in the courtroom. I wanted to know when and for how long, and whether it could be prevented. I wanted to know why nobody had notified me or anyone in my family.

Why had the Green River Task Force left us out of the loop?

I called Mary Kirchner, but she wasn't in. I dialed, but then hung up on, Liz Rocca, the news reporter whose number my friend at KOMO had given me. I didn't want to talk with the press. Not yet. I was still distrustful of them, still angry about the coverage that victimized my family in the weeks following Maureen's disappearance and the discovery of her remains. I was still angry about the seemingly endless display of her young, smiling face in the news. And I still had a few other options.

In retrospect, I know my anger and distrust of the press was unjustified. They were doing their job, reporting on a newsworthy story that the public, naturally, wanted to know more about. But it was hard to cope with the constant pain caused by the news coverage.

After dialing and disconnecting from Liz Rocca's number, I tried Detective Pavlovich and got another machine. Then I turned over the business card that he had given me when we met the year before. On the back, I found the general office number for the Green River Task Force. I dialed that number and got a real person, a receptionist. I identified myself and told her I needed to know what was going on, that I was very concerned about my elderly mother. She left me on hold for several long periods as she tried to get answers for me. As we were talking, Detective Kathleen Larson arrived at the office and took my call.

While she was very apologetic, she wasn't really very helpful. But then, what did I want? There was no way to stop the telecast. She said it would be "a media frenzy" and that my mother should not be alone. She was kind. She told me to call her "Katie." She gave me a new direct phone number because, after the hearing, all the old numbers would be changed or disconnected for a while, if not permanently, in order to avoid crank calls and excessive hounding by the press. I wanted to ask if she expected my mother to change her phone number as well, but I remained silent.

After talking with her, I knew I had to call Mom. But before I got a chance, I received a call from someone by the name of Sergeant Gates, who told me that a person from her office had called my mother the day before to set up a phone meeting with her. It was scheduled for 5:00 p.m. that afternoon. "Didn't your mother tell you?" Sergeant Gates asked.

I wasn't clear on who was going to be speaking with my mother that afternoon, but I knew that was irrelevant. I explained to Sergeant Gates that I had spoken with my mother the night before, and she hadn't mentioned any phone meeting. I told her that I doubted my mother would remember the appointment, and I asked her not to make the 5:00 p.m. call because it wouldn't give me enough time to get to Grayland. I didn't want Mom to be alone. Sergeant Gates agreed to postpone it. In fact, the phone meeting was never rescheduled. It simply never happened.

I hung up and called Mom. I told her that Ridgway was expected to confess to Maureen's murder. I explained that the hearing would be televised, and that the media might try to find her. I told her that I wanted to be with her, and asked if she'd like to come and stay at our house for a few days, which is something she's usually reluctant to do. I assured her that her stinky old golden retriever was also welcome to come, and that I'd drive down to pick them up that evening. After letting her know I'd be later than usual, I asked her if she'd gotten any calls from the Green River Task Force, or from the nice detective we had met last summer. I knew it wasn't Detective Pavlovich who called her the day before, but I wanted her to remember, to make connections.

"Yes," she said, "I think Ridgway called me."

I realized how confused she was.

The television was her constant companion, but I had no idea how much of the news she was grasping. I felt a deep, profound sadness. I hadn't lost my mother yet, not as I had lost my sister and father, but she was no longer the strong woman who had raised me. Now, it was my turn to take care of her.

I left Seattle as early as I could, after making overnight childcare arrangements for my daughter and arranging class coverage for the following day. Traffic was horrible, and I didn't reach Grayland until 8:30 p.m. What struck me first was that Mom was totally packed and ready to leave. No argument. No persuasion. She wanted to leave. She probably would have left that night, had I been willing and able to drive home. Bags of groceries, another bag of dog food and dog toys, all set by the front door. A packed suitcase lay open on her bed. She just needed to toss in a toothbrush, and she was ready to leave. Or maybe she needed me to tell her it was time to go. In any case, she was ready.

My mother and I sat and talked, drinking cups of warm tea, for about an hour on that abnormally cold autumn night. But even though the temperature dropped below freezing, once again the tea was more to comfort our souls than to warm our bodies.

I passed on to Mom what I knew about the latest developments in the Green River case: that the hearing would begin at 9:00 a.m. the next morning, and that the prosecutors would go through each victim by name. Ridgway was expected to enter forty-eight guilty pleas. If he did plead guilty, a sentencing date would be set in two weeks, and a time established for victims' families to address the court and give input to the sentencing process.

"The death penalty," Mom interrupted, setting her cup down so abruptly that she sloshed tea onto the table.

Getting up to grab a sponge, I explained that the death penalty was no longer an option, because a plea bargain had been made. And I repeated what Detective Larson had told me when I reached her by phone earlier that day—if the death penalty had been sought, the case would have been in litigation for at least another twenty years, and in the end, they'd be putting an eighty-year-old man to death. What was the point? Better to lock him up in solitary confinement for the rest of his life.

"Besides," I told her, "I don't believe in the death penalty, even in these circumstances, even after what he did to Maureen."

"That's not right," my mother argued. "He deserves to die." But it was a gentle, quiet comment, spoken more from pain and sadness than from any desire for revenge.

We didn't get into a lengthy philosophical discussion of the death penalty that night. Instead, I listened quietly as Mom talked about working at Echo Glen, about the kids she took care of there, and about not being able to get up the hill one snowy winter night and the nice guard who came to help her. She seemed tiny and fragile. The Ridgway arrest was taking a toll on her, both physically and mentally. "Sometimes, it makes me physically sick to think I was driving right by the place where he was leaving bodies," she whispered.

We kissed, or rather avoided kissing because we both had colds, and went to bed. We needed our sleep if we were going to get up and watch the telecast of the hearing at 9:00 a.m.

On Wednesday morning, Mom was up before me, something that very rarely happens when I'm visiting. I got out of bed at 8:30 a.m., made coffee, and turned on the television. I had no intention of leaving the house without seeing the telecast of the Ridgway confession. Mom ate a bit of cereal and toast. All I could handle was toast and coffee. From 9:00 a.m. to 11:00 a.m., we sat transfixed, watching Gary Ridgway confess to the murder of forty-eight young women, including Maureen.

Forty-eight times, he admitted his guilt. Mom was stoic, getting up only a few times for tissues to wipe her eyes. She sat in Dad's old leather chair. I couldn't move. I couldn't offer her comfort.

Then we heard the words we were waiting for, the words we didn't want to hear, the words we knew we needed to hear: "How do you plea to the charge of aggregated murder in the first degree as charged in count thirty-nine?"

"Guilty."

How can I describe the horror of watching someone admit to having picked up my sister with the intent of killing her, and then strangling her until she was dead? It was a visceral reaction. I felt my whole body tighten. My heart, lungs, stomach, all contracted. Bile accumulated in my throat. I found myself swallowing hard, repeatedly, hiding my desire to vomit from my mother. I tried to be strong, like her. I would have preferred to have wrapped her in my arms, or been wrapped in hers, and cried together, openly and honestly, rocking in each other's embrace. But that didn't happen. We kept our distance, each of us struggling to hide our emotions. Why was it so impossible for us to let down our guards? Was there really anything more fearful, more horrific than what we'd already endured?

The two hours had passed quickly, like a perfectly choreographed dance, and then it was over. I felt empty.

I feel empty.

Nothing can fill the void. I was once a middle child. Now I am not.

I loaded my mom's suitcase and grocery bags into the trunk of my car, and we left Grayland. I found myself driving in circles, trying to find Duffy's Restaurant in Aberdeen, for lunch. Both of us were too stunned to say much. Neither of us knew how to comfort the other. After picking at our lunch, we drove to Seattle.

* * *

Mom stayed with us in Seattle for the better part of the week. As expected, the news was flooded with stories of the Ridgway confession, told from every possible angle. Fortunately, Detective Larson's warnings that the press might hound family members for interviews did not materialize, at least not for our family.

The Seattle Times, Seattle Post Intelligencer and *USA Today* all had bold, front-page coverage that listed the victims' names and the Gary Ridgway quote, "I killed so many women I have a hard time keeping them straight."

On Friday, November 7, 2003, my daughter came home from school and handed me the front page of the *Seattle Post Intelligencer* from the day before, plastered with the same sad photographs of the Ridgway victims. Photographs cut so tight around each girl's face, they resembled police mug shots, even those that were not. "GUILTY – 48 TIMES" it read.

"Here, this is for you," she said, knowing that I was reading everything I could find on the case, knowing that her dad set articles out for me to read almost every morning. "My teacher said it was trash and threw it in the garbage, but I dug it out. Which one is Maureen?"

I put my arm around her slender waist and pulled her close to me as I pointed to Maureen's picture. "This is your aunt Maureen." The photographs in the paper were so numerous, and so distorted, my daughter could not even recognize her aunt.

I do not know what Erin's teacher meant by calling the newspaper trash. Was he referring to Ridgway, to his victims, or to the way the article was presented? "I don't know," was Erin's response when I asked her about it. And then she added, "but it was just plain rude the way he threw it away."

"Did he know about Maureen?" I asked her, not knowing how many of her teachers she'd told.

"I didn't tell him. But it doesn't matter," she insisted. "It just wasn't right to be so rude." In her own way, my daughter was defending her aunt's honor and that of the other victims paraded across the front page that day, by digging a discarded newspaper out of a classroom garbage can.

On the same day, *The Seattle Times* carried an opinion piece entitled, "Ridgway's plea agreement brings healing and truth" that was written by Norm Maleng. In it he states, "Our Green River nightmare is over. We have seen the face of justice: It brings truth for our community and for the families of the victims. Now the healing can begin... This is a historic day for King County, one that will allow us to close this terrible chapter in our history."

I stared in disbelief.

Close?

My nightmare was not over, and I was furious at him for his lack of understanding and sensitivity. "Whose nightmare?" I wanted to scream in anger, but I knew the answer to my own voiceless scream. I understood that his nightmare, and that of Sheriff Reichert and the Green River Task Force, was over. Their nightmare was over because finally, after twenty years of ineptitude, the Green River Killer was behind bars and they could pat themselves on the back for putting him there.

For me, there are still times when I cannot breathe, I cannot sleep. I try to take a deep breath, and air does not fill my lungs. I think of Maureen, and I feel Ridgway's arm around my neck. I feel his breathing in my ears. And I am filled with hatred so intense it prevents the air from entering my body.

Anger is an odd emotion. Once you let go of the reins, it runs rampant, out of control, like a runaway horse. Only now am I beginning to understand how angry I have been and how unsuccessfully I have controlled that anger over the years. I have been angry at the whole world. At the police for failing to stop Ridgway sooner, at the press for writing about it, at the public for reading about it, at King County Prosecuting Attorney Norm Maleng for saying it was all over, at Sheriff Dave Reichert of the Green River Task Force for building a political career on it.

Most of all, I have been angry at Ridgway for killing my sister, at Tobey for forcing her into Ridgway's path, at my parents for raising us in silence, and if I'm honest, maybe even at Maureen for making that final, fateful decision that led to her death. My anger has been illogical, and at times, unreasonable. It has lashed out at one and all, indiscriminately, as anger often does.

* * *

During the next few days after the Ridgway confession, I continued reading the newspaper, watching the news, and trying to make Mom as comfortable as I could in our little house. By Sunday, November 9, 2003, the confession was no longer front-page news, and Mom wanted to go home. I drove her back to Grayland and started another week of trying to work, trying to act normal while a nightmare nobody knew about was still eating me up inside. Through the years, I rarely told co-workers much about my family, or about Maureen's murder. Work was a refuge for me, where I could bury my pain and focus on something totally outside of myself.

At the time of Ridgeway's arrest, only one of my fellow instructors knew of my sister's murder, knew of the hell I was enduring. In her quiet, gentle manner, Dorrienne was watching out for me. When she asked me how I was doing each morning, I knew it was more than a casual comment. Without her support, teaching would have been impossible. With it, each fifty-minute class became a refuge where I could focus on the moment and put aside the horror that engulfed me.

On Tuesday morning, November 11, I was rushing through breakfast and trying to get Erin off to school and myself off to work when Tom read another news headline from *The Seattle Times*: "Ridgway merchandise hits eBay." I left the house with tears in my eyes. It made no sense to me. Somebody was actually trying to sell a red T-shirt that had Ridgway's face and the words "I was good at choking" on it before it was pulled from eBay. Another person paid $29 for a Green River Task Force business card. The article closed with a quote from Andy Kahan, a Houston-based victim advocate, who stated, "If I was one of a victim's family members, I'd be absolutely disgusted."

The horror and the memories are everywhere. A few months later, I saw a young woman on my drive to work. It was a clear morning, and she was out walking a toddler, going up the Oregon Street hill in West Seattle. She was slender and attractive, a young mother in her twenties with short, tousled, light brown hair. She glanced in my direction as she looked first towards the street, then towards her daughter, and then back towards the street. A watchful mother. A good mother. Our eyes met, and we smiled.

Her daughter was a beautiful toddler of three or four, with pale skin, a round tummy, and a full head of fluffy blonde ringlets. Maureen as a toddler, I thought. Maureen as a mother, the mother she will never be. That toddler will grow to be an adult and a wife and a mother, if she chooses. Maureen's choices were stolen from her. Ridgway stole her choices when he stole her life. Maureen will never be that mother strolling with her toddler, feeling a love so intense it hurts.

Maureen feels nothing.

Maureen is dead.

Later that same day, I was in the Costco wholesale warehouse. I always browse the book tables. Ridgway's face stared up at me, bold green lettering over his red prison clothes. Again, my stomach contracted. I picked up the book and dropped it into my shopping cart without even leafing through it. As I checked out, the cashier and courtesy clerk started joking about Ridgway, about all the time he had on his hands now that he was behind bars.

I took the book home, where Erin and I looked through it and talked about it. It was published by the staff of the *King County Journal*, a summary of their stories and photographs. Without my knowledge, Erin used information from that book for a speech in debate class. She told the Marie Malvar story, and she explained why she didn't think the police should be quite as self-congratulatory as was depicted in the media. She came home ecstatic. "Mom, I gave my speech today, and I left them speechless."

What could her classmates or teacher say upon hearing that Erin's aunt had been killed by the worst serial killer in American history? I knew that response well: the silence, the look of shock and disbelief, and then, on some faces, the judgment. Had I known Erin was planning a speech about the case, I might have cautioned her, warned her about the possible responses she would receive. But she gave her speech, and it went very well for her. I breathed a sigh of relief and congratulated her on her success.

On one hand, I'm glad that my daughter knows her aunt's story. In fact, it was mostly for her that I knew I needed to put this story on paper. I needed to break the cycle of silence that controlled the world I had grown up in. On the other hand, it saddens me that such a tragedy has become a part of her personal history.

Still, I am the lucky one. I was the woman walking up Oregon Street with the toddler. Maureen was not. I know the joy of motherhood, and I know survivor's guilt. It's a guilt I share with veterans and with immigrants fleeing war-torn countries. My students do not understand how similar we are.

* * *

The King County Prosecutor's Office posted the *Summary of Evidence* on their website within hours of the confession. It took several days for me to summon the nerve to download all the posted documents. I was obsessed with learning all I could about Maureen's final hours, and unlike those people whose vicarious fascination with murder and serial killers leads to the "murderabilia" sold on eBay, this was my family story I was trying to understand, and it was inconceivable to me to deliberately ignore available information. I knew that part of my healing involved facing the truth. I knew I had to read the evidence that the prosecutor would have used had the case gone to trial. I had to know this beast who killed my sister. I had to know what he remembered about Maureen's last moments of life on earth.

So I stuffed the printed pages of the *Summary of Evidence* into a large folder and stashed them in a book bag, where they stayed for another week. Finally, one Friday night, I was home alone. Both Tom and Erin were out with friends. I poured myself a Scotch and pulled the folder from my book bag. I slowly turned the pages, fearful, trembling. Despite having watched Ridgway's televised confession, the documents I held in my hands seemed much more real to me, perhaps, because they were legal documents, or perhaps merely because I needed to read the black words on white paper.

Maureen was count thirty-nine. I read counts one to thirty-eight, forcing myself to notice similarities between the cases, to read the gruesome details of each murder.

Ridgway chose prostitutes because it was easy, it said; he preferred to kill his victims either in his house or in his truck. His truck had a canopy on the back, and he always killed in the back of the truck, not in the cab. I stopped reading and remembered the nightmare that I'd had so many times since Maureen disappeared. I was wrong about the cab, among other things.

He strangled his victims from behind, after having sex with them. Usually with his arm, sometimes with an article of clothing, but never with the braided Cordova leather strap of my imagination. He had sex with the dead bodies of his victims, too, and would go back to a dumpsite to "visit" a victim days after the murder.

Ridgway claimed he was a murderer, but not a rapist, and I suppose, legally, he was right. Rape is technically defined as a sexual act that is perpetrated against the victim's will. Because Ridgway's victims were dead, they were unable to withhold their consent. To me, the sexual violation of a dead woman is still rape.

By that point in the document, in my heart, I had already put together enough pieces to realize that Maureen was not hitching a ride or asking for help the night she was murdered. If that were the case, it is unlikely Ridgway would have gotten her into the back of his truck where he killed his victims. Or into his house, for that matter. No, I feared that Maureen moved into the camper at some point, to sell her sex to Ridgway. A move that would cost her, and us, her life.

I learned many more things about Gary Ridgway than I ever wanted to know, but I needed to know the truth, to face the pain and horror of Maureen's final hours in order to bury my nightmares. I kept telling myself that.

And then I reached "Count XXXIX" on page 104 of that horrible court document.

I saw my sister's name in black and white on the page, and I was sick to my stomach. I ran to the bathroom and vomited. My head was spinning, and I knew it wasn't from the glass of Scotch. I'd hardly touched it. I forced myself to read on.

Around midnight on September 28, 1983, Gary Ridgway took Maureen's body up to his cluster site at the intersection of Highway 18 and Interstate 90. So, although my brothers spent two weeks searching for her, she was already dead by the time they started looking. Ridgway also raped my sister's lifeless body before he left it to decay.

I no longer believe that my sister was trying to get help when she was killed. I believe Maureen was coerced into prostitution, if only for a few weeks, if only for a single day. Fate, or just plain bad luck, put her and Gary Ridgway in the same place at the same time. She was young and vulnerable. He was an experienced hunter, and she was easy prey.

Now she is "Count XXXIX" in the prosecutor's *Summary of the Evidence* in Case No. 01-1-10270-9 SEA, State of Washington vs. Gary Leon Ridgway.

And I am still haunted by the jade ring she wore on the night she was killed.

In the late seventies, fashionable young women in Venezuela and Mexico wore gold or silver rings combined with bands of jade, onyx, and coral. The stone rings were inexpensive, the gold or silver beyond my budget. On one of my visits home, I gave Maureen a jade band. She wore it on the ring finger of her right hand. It was the only piece of jewelry I ever remember her wearing.

According to the *Summary of Evidence*, Ridgway habitually removed all identifying evidence from his victim's bodies, including their jewelry. He liked to take his victims' jewelry to Kenworth Truck Company, where he worked, and leave it in a women's restroom for his female co-workers to find. If he was lucky, he would see them wearing it in the office.

I picture him looking both ways in the hallway to be sure no one was around, then sneaking into the restroom and leaving Maureen's jade band next to the water faucet on one of the sinks. As if someone had removed it and set it to one side before washing her hands. Did anyone pick it up? I wonder if Ridgway enjoyed the satisfaction of seeing a co-worker wearing Maureen's jade band.

One of Erin's teachers told me that she had worked at Kenworth with Ridgway in the early 1980s. I had to stop myself from asking if she'd ever seen anyone wearing a jade band.

Like Maureen, her ring, I am certain, no longer exists. It will never be recovered.

* * *

On Friday, November 21, 2003, I got a phone call from Mary Kirchner of the King County Prosecutor's Office, informing me that the Gary Ridgway sentencing was set for December 18, 2003. Family members had the right to address the court, in writing or in person. Letters had to be sent by December 5, 2003, along with a completed form indicating the names of family members planning to attend and/or address the court.

I called Doreen to tell her. We decided together not to mention anything to Mom, in a feeble attempt to protect her from more pain. We'd been watching her growing confusion over the past year, and we believed that silence was best. We also agreed that none of the other siblings were likely to have any interest in attending, and neither of us felt inclined to spend the time, energy, or money to contact them. I suppose at that point, I was just plain angry. Their silence, their distance and lack of involvement or support, were all bearing down on me. Doreen and I figured that since we hadn't heard a word from any of them after the Ridgway confession, why should we bother to contact them about the sentencing?

Thanksgiving passed. Dad's birthday passed. "Write letter" was still scrawled on my daily to-do list, but I kept procrastinating. I was writing the letter mentally, but I couldn't seem to sit down and put my thoughts on paper. Finally, on the second of December, three days before the deadline, I sat down with my laptop and started typing a letter to Judge Richard Jones.

The ripple effect is often spoken of in terms of acts of kindness, but the ripples of pain and devastation caused by an act of violence are equally as wide-spreading and long-lasting. I think of my sister's murder as a pebble tossed into a large lake, and I see the ripple effects of that act of violence as it has spread through my family history and the many characters in my family story. A day does not go by, a day has not gone by in the past twenty years that I have not thought of my sister, Maureen. I look into the eyes of my beautiful daughter and I see Maureen's eyes. I fear that the ripples of the violence that I have lived with for the past twenty years are influencing my ability to be a healthy mother and a strong role model. It was a bit easier when my daughter was younger, but as she gets older, as she approaches Maureen's age, the age of Maureen's death, my fears intensify. I know there is no basis, no logic to my fears. But fear has no more logic than the logic of those ripples that form when I throw a pebble into Lake Washington on a placid summer day. And I know that the pain and devastation that my family and I have suffered for the past twenty years can be multiplied by forty-eight. Families and extended families and friends of forty-eight women have endured unspeakable pain for twenty long years...

When I finished my letter, several pages later, I e-mailed a copy to Doreen and gave copies to Tom and Erin for their input. Two days later, I mailed the letter to the King County Prosecutor's Office, just barely meeting their submission deadline. Along with the letter, I enclosed the completed form stating my intention to attend the sentencing with Erin, indicating that I did not want to read the letter in court. I knew that I would be unable to read it without crying—I couldn't even get it written without tears—and I didn't want to make a scene in the courtroom. I am, after all, my father's daughter.

December 18, 2003. Erin and I arrived at the King County Courthouse on Third and James in downtown Seattle right on time, at 7:00 a.m. We entered the building through security checks and were directed to a designated elevator. Then, more security. My tiny Swiss army knife (more scissors and nail clipper than an actual knife) and my nail file were taken from me. We were met by a detective who introduced himself as Rafael Crenshaw, the detective handling Maureen's case. The one who had never called me, in fact.

"Are you planning to speak in court?" he asked.

I told him I'd sent a letter, and turning to Erin, I asked her, "Do you really want to read the letter, honey?" That morning, during the drive to the courthouse, she'd mentioned that she might want to read it in court. She was a debate student and comfortable with public speaking.

She thought for a second and asked, "Could I see it again?"

"I didn't bring a copy," I told her. Turning back to Detective Crenshaw, I asked, "Could we see the letter I sent?"

"Sure," he said. "Just wait here while I track it down." He disappeared into the crowd of people that was beginning to fill the hallway, as Erin and I sat on a wooden bench against a cool marble wall.

Detectives were swarming everywhere. After a moment of hesitation and then recognition, Detective Pavlovich extended a warm, friendly hand. "How's your mother?"

Detective Larson and Mary Kirchner both introduced themselves as they moved through the crowd. Detective Crenshaw returned with another victim advocate from the Prosecutor's Office, and together they thumbed through a large notebook, looking for the letter I had sent. Surrounded by detectives, my daughter reread the letter, trying to decide if she wanted to read it in the courtroom, a setting neither of us could visualize. Before she could reach a decision, Mary Kirchner approached again, telling us that Erin would not be allowed to read in court. The judge had already established the procedures for the day. I knew that if I pushed, if I insisted on being allowed to speak, or on Erin being allowed to read, I could've made it happen. But I didn't want to speak and Erin was ambivalent, so I let it drop.

We waited with a large group of detectives and other victims' families in a courtroom designated as a waiting area. We listened as Mary Kirchner explained the carefully planned choreography for the proceedings. She told us we'd be sitting in a special section of the courtroom behind the defendant's table. We'd be separated from, protected from, any contact with the media. We had been assigned different elevators, waiting areas and restrooms. Then, we were ushered up a flight of stairs into another courtroom.

When we entered the courtroom, I chose a bench four rows behind the defendant's table. The row in front of us was empty, except for one woman sitting right in front of me. I whispered to Erin, "She's a reporter."

"How do you know?" my skeptical daughter demanded.

"I just know," I whispered back. Maybe I was developing Mom's intuition, but I was certain this woman was on assignment.

She started talking to us. She invited us to move forward to share her bench, and we did. She asked, "Who are you here for?"

"You're with the media, aren't you?" I said, keeping all emotion from my voice.

"Yes, Kimberly Osias with CNN."

I told her I didn't want to speak with the media. I never mentioned Maureen's name. I told her she was sitting in the wrong place. But it was all good-natured, friendly, a shallow attempt at light-heartedness in a very deadly environment.

I saw Tomas Guillen, co-author of *The Search for the Green River Killer*, sitting in the same row, across the aisle in the media section. I was pleased to see his friendly face in the courtroom, and I walked over to say hello. He wrapped me in a comforting hug.

At that moment, Mary Kirchner approached and reprimanded Tomas. "Media cannot speak to victims' families." She was harsh and rude.

"He's a friend," I said.

"She approached me. I didn't approach her," he said, with his hands in the air, as if she held him at gunpoint.

As I made my way back to my seat next to the CNN reporter, I wanted to laugh and scream at the same time. Even now, even twenty years later, the Green River Task Force and the Prosecutor's Office continued to misdirect their energies. There were cracks in their perfect plan, and I was sitting right next to at least one. I wondered, I still wonder, how many other cracks there were. It's no surprise that it took twenty years to arrest Gary Ridgway.

At 8:35 a.m., Ridgway was led into the courtroom, surrounded by King County Jail officers and defense attorneys. A short, balding man with oversized, thick glasses, he wore a white, short-sleeved V-neck smock over a long-sleeved blood-red shirt and white pants. The back of his smock read "KCJ Ultra Security Inmate" in large block letters. He and his many attorneys (I counted eight) sat directly in front of Erin and me. Two hard wooden court benches separated me from my sister's killer. The back of his neck was clean-shaven, maybe too closely. Red razor burns spotted a white area just below his hairline that attested to a shorter than normal haircut.

This was the man who had strangled my sister to death, the pervert who had raped my sister's lifeless body. "He looks so normal," my daughter whispered to me, echoing my own thoughts. He was so average looking, he could have been anyone—our neighbor, the man who rang up our groceries, or the one who fixed our car. Fear crawled up my spine and put a chokehold around my neck. It was unreasonable, irrational fear for my daughter, based on the realization that she, like all of us, had to learn the lesson that my sister never learned: not all that is evil wears the face of evil.

At 8:40 a.m., Judge Richard Jones entered the courtroom. "We are here today for the sentencing of Gary Leon Ridgway..." For over two hours, we listened to the pain and anger of other family members. Erin sat to my left; we shared a package of tissue. At times, I reached out and touched her, tried to comfort her. She seemed to pull inward, not wanting to shed tears in public, but not being able to stop them, either. At one point, I whispered, "Do you need a break? We can go out for a few minutes." She shook her head.

I worried that it was too much for her. After all, she was only fourteen. A few weeks earlier, after she read the letter I wrote to Judge Jones, she asked if I was going to the sentencing and told me that she wanted to go with me. At first I was hesitant, but as always when she feels strongly about something, she was forceful and determined. Trying to understand, I pushed her for answers. "But why, honey? Why do you want to go?"

"I don't know," she said. "I just want to see him."

Sitting in that courtroom with Erin beside me, surrounded by the intense suffering of so many people, I felt a bit like we were all playing roles in a soap opera. I felt like a distant observer, watching my daughter and myself, watching the other family members, the detectives, the lawyers, the media, watching Maureen's killer, watching Judge Jones. The sentencing moved slowly through the same words, forty-eight times for forty-eight victims.

At 12:08 p.m., I heard my sister's name and the words, "life imprisonment without the possibility of early release or parole, and a fine of $10,000."

That was it. Gary Ridgway's sentence for taking my sister's life.

It would never be enough, but then, nothing could be enough, not even his life. His execution would not give me back my sister.

I stopped breathing during Judge Jones's forty-eight seconds of silence and respect for the victims. At 12:20 p.m., he ended the proceedings with the words, "This brings this matter to a close."

"To a close?" I asked myself silently.

Again, Erin verbalized my thoughts, whispering, "Is that it?" It felt unfinished, like something was missing, like turning off the DVD player five minutes before the end of a movie. There was no drum roll, no proclamation, no dropping of the guillotine. For a second, the room was still. It was as if nobody knew what to do next. Then Ridgway was handcuffed and escorted out the side door.

The press was instructed to leave next. The CNN reporter sitting beside me had already left, halfway through the proceedings. Sadness, anger and frustration lingered in the courtroom. Erin and I made our way out, receiving hugs from strangers as we walked down the aisle. I didn't feel any sense of relief or closure for myself or for anyone else, only exhaustion and overbearing sadness.

The Prosecutor's Office provided box lunches for all the families, but neither Erin nor I felt like staying. We wanted out, away from the other angry, grieving families. Away from the media. Away from Sheriff Reichert and the Green River Task Force detectives.

As I stopped to pick up my personal items, I asked how we could get out of the building without encountering the press. We were escorted to a stairway and then went down several flights of stairs. From there, we took an elevator to the lobby and walked out the front door into the mild December day.

The press filled the sidewalk in front of the courthouse. Because we were the first to leave the building, and perhaps because we were alone and kept our heads down, we weren't noticed at first. But as we made our way quietly through the clusters of waiting reporters, I heard a voice say, "Hey, weren't you at the Ridgway sentencing?" I looped my arm through Erin's, and we kept walking. At that moment, a large, noisy group of people emerged from the building, distracting the reporter who had recognized us. Erin and I were grateful to be left alone.

*　*　*

Fast forward to October 2005. I'm watching television alone on another Friday night, almost two years after Erin and I sat in the courtroom and watched the sentencing of Gary Ridgway. Sheriff Dave Reichert's face flashes before me on the screen: serious, stern, the police officer turned politician. The starched uniform and badge replaced by a starched white shirt and a tie. Every gray hair perfectly in place. A Colgate smile. Now a Republican representative to Congress, elected the year before, Congressman Reichert is again on the television screen. I don't hear what he's promoting, only the reference to his twenty years in pursuit of the Green River Killer. And again, I ask: how can twenty years of failure be a good thing? It took twenty years and over fifty murders to make Reichert a hero.

*　*　*

In May of 2004, I visited the office of the Green River Task Force a second time. The Task Force office had been dismantled and relocated to the King County Major Crime Unit facility in the city of Kent, just southeast of Seattle. I had called Detective Rafael Crenshaw, asking to see Maureen's file again. Could I retrieve some of her personal belongings still held there? I knew they had her Washington State Instruction Permit, her bankbook and her calendar, as well as assorted family photographs from her wallet. Most of all, though, I wanted to have the letter addressed to my apartment in Mexico City.

I remember little about the visit itself, the building, the office, or the people with whom I spoke. Frankly, none of it matters much.

What matters to me are the feelings of love, pain, frustration and anger that still blind me each time I pull that fragile, folded piece of peach-colored stationery from its matching square envelope, the anger I feel when I see the official white sticker with the number R 2015729 on the front, and another white sticker with the number R 2015730 on the back. Evidence numbers. Cataloging numbers. Tiny numbers handwritten in red ink. What matters to me is the pain of my sister's words, written in her childish longhand: "...an unfortunate mistake... I am sorry, for you and for me."

The letter is undated. It is short and it is thick with pain and regret. I wonder when she wrote it, where she wrote it, how far down the road to the abyss she had already traveled when she wrote it. Was Tobey looking over her shoulder? I wish it were dated. I wish she had found a stamp and dropped it into a mailbox, instead of leaving it on her desk where my sisters found it when they went searching for her.

But why? What would I have done if that pitiful little letter had actually landed in Mexico City? If my landlady, Adela, had delivered it into my hands? I might have felt disappointment, anger, even heartbreak, yes. But would I have known my little sister was in trouble? Probably not. Would I have been able to intercede, to change the course of history, to prevent her from crossing paths with Gary Ridgway? Probably not. So I endure the pain as I hold her final words to me in my trembling hands, twenty years after she wrote them at her tiny table in her tiny Capitol Hill apartment.

Epilogue: Still A Secret

I wrote these words while telling myself yet another myth: that I was facing the truth. Yet I kept these pages hidden. No one in my first family knew I was writing about us. No one even knew when I completed a yearlong memoir-writing program at the University of Washington. Only my husband and daughter watched me walk through the graduation ceremony in June of 2003.

Our house is small, and my office is the guest bedroom. When guests came to stay—my mother, out-of-town siblings, nieces—I hid all evidence. I locked the beautiful antique oak desk that my husband and I found on one of our afternoons of haunting the antique shops of Seattle. There are two cabinets, each with a storybook-shaped brass-lined keyhole. The key is also made of ornate brass. In today's world, they're too beautiful to be practical. I used this beautiful key to lock away my secrets, to lock away my truths.

The decision to seek publication for this story was very difficult. I have long questioned the ethics, the morality, of writing about my family, of breaking the code of silence. Whether I like it or not, whether my siblings like it or not, our stories are intertwined. I believe that my father would have disowned me again, disowned me as permanently as he did Laureen, for writing this memoir. I hope that my mother and my siblings will not follow in his footsteps.

One beautiful summer day in late July 2003, almost a year into the project, I was visiting my mother in Grayland. During dinner at a local restaurant, Mom said something about how I was more comfortable talking about Maureen and Dad than anyone else in the family. She said it was easy talking with me, because I was so open.

When she touched on openness, on honesty, I felt like a fraud. "I haven't really been totally open with you this past year. I have a secret that I need to tell you."

I saw a shadow cross her beautifully wrinkled face. "Is it okay here? Should we go out to the car?"

"No, no, it's okay. It's not that big of a deal, and you're a tough cookie."

We were already teary-eyed from talking about Dad and Maureen. She didn't want to make a scene in a public place, and she was truly afraid of what I might tell her.

"I've been writing a memoir about Maureen and myself and what I remember. Let me back up. For the past year..." I paused, hesitated, not sure how to tell her. Then I just plunged forward. "Last September, I signed up for a writing program through the University of Washington Extension because I wanted to write, but I wasn't sure what. Within a month, I knew I needed to write about Maureen. So I'm trying to write."

Mom was very quiet, but she looked relieved. It wasn't a horrible secret. It wasn't terrible, bad news. Not like the bad news she'd had to bear in the past.

"I know we're a big family, and everybody's story is different. But I had a unique vantage point as the middle kid. So all I can do is write my story, and Maureen's story as I know it, as I remember it. All I can do is be as honest as I can be."

"Okay, that's good." She paused. "She came to see you in Mexico."

"Yes. Those are the pieces I'm trying to put together, Mom. The little pieces of memory. But I'm afraid to tell anyone. I was afraid to tell you. Please don't tell anyone yet."

She put her finger to her lips and whispered, "I won't tell your secret to anyone."

Maureen and Arleen, Mexico City Airport (August, 1982)

About the Author

Arleen Williams has been recording her life in journals since she left home in her late teens. Her wanderings took her to Mexico City, where she completed a bachelor's degree through the University of California while earning a teaching certificate from the National University of Mexico. Arleen has been teaching the English language for over thirty years. She taught international students living in dorms in Seattle, and migratory workers in her living room in Santa Cruz, California. In Caracas, Venezuela, she faked an Irish accent in order to land a position at the British Embassy School, and in Mexico City, her high school students encircled her for her protection during an anti-American protest. In 1984, the disappearance of her youngest sister brought her back to Seattle. Later, she completed a master's degree in education at the University of Washington and accepted the teaching position she currently holds at South Seattle Community College. For the past fifteen years, she and her husband have been remodeling a small 1941 home in West Seattle, where they have raised their only daughter.

The Thirty-Ninth Victim is her first book.

Printed in the United States
125101LV00004B/25-120/P